Domestic Violence and the Politics of Privacy

Domestic Violence and the Politics of Privacy

KRISTIN A. KELLY

CORNELL UNIVERSITY PRESS

Ithaca and London

First published 2003 by Cornell University Press
First printing, Cornell Paperbacks, 2003

Printed in the United States of America

Library of Congress Cataloging-in-Publication Data

Kelly, Kristin A. (Kristin Anne)
   Domestic violence and the politics of privacy / Kristin A. Kelly.
      p. cm.
Includes bibliographical references (p.   ) and index.
   ISBN 0-8014-3908-6 (cloth) — ISBN 0-8014-8829-X (pbk.)
   1. Family violence—United States.   2. Privacy, Right of—United
States.   I. Title.
   HV6626.2 .K45 2003
   362.82'0973—dc   2002008358

Cornell University Press strives to use environmentally responsible suppliers and materials to the fullest extent possible in the publishing of its books. Such materials include vegetable-based, low-VOC inks and acid-free papers that are recycled, totally chlorine-free, or partly composed of nonwood fibers. For further information, visit our website at www.cornellpress.cornell.edu.

Cloth printing   10 9 8 7 6 5 4 3 2 1
Paperback printing   10 9 8 7 6 5 4 3 2 1

For my parents, Peter and Linda

Contents

Acknowledgments

ALTHOUGH THE ACT OF PUTTING WORDS DOWN on paper is a solitary endeavor, this book is in no way the result of my efforts alone. First and foremost I want to acknowledge the individuals who generously agreed to take time from their busy schedules to talk to me about the work that they were doing on domestic violence. This book would simply not have been possible without their help. By sharing their extensive experience, offering their insights, and putting me in touch with colleagues who might have more to add, the individuals whom I interviewed provided me with a unique and exciting opportunity—the chance to connect my theoretical knowledge of the public/private dichotomy to the practical dilemmas and challenges that this division can generate in the context of a specific social problem. I can only hope that the resulting book will be of some value to those individuals who continue to do the important and hard work of fighting domestic violence.

At the University of Wisconsin–Madison, where this research first began, I benefited enormously from the intellectual examples of both the faculty with whom I worked and my fellow graduate students, who continue to astonish me with their talent and energy. I am especially grateful to Bert Kritzer, Marion Smiley, and Donald Downs, who each provided invaluable feedback on the manuscript. Special thanks go to Bert Kritzer, who cheerfully endured what now seem like endless "first drafts" and who provided continuous advice and encouragement over the phone during the years that I worked on this project in northern California. Larry Berman at the University of California–Davis was instrumental in helping me to secure the library resources and writing space that I needed to continue making progress during this period, and the staff at the UC Davis

Women's Center have my enduring gratitude for always helping to make me feel that my work was important—even when my own self-doubts suggested otherwise.

At the University of Connecticut, I have been extremely fortunate to be surrounded by colleagues who have offered me a tremendous amount of intellectual and personal support. I especially want to thank Larry Bowman and David Yalof for the wonderful combination of mentoring and friendship that they have provided. Richard Hiskes and Ernie Zirakzadeh provided encouragement and helpful comments on portions of the manuscript. John Rourke, head of the Department of Political Science during my first years at Connecticut, deserves credit for his commitment to fostering an environment where junior faculty members could succeed. Thanks also to the members of my writing group—Cameron MacDonald, Jane Paulson, Eleanore Lyon, and Kathy Wright—who read and commented on multiple chapters. At Cornell University Press, I want to thank my acquisitions editor, Catherine Rice, whose enthusiasm and commitment to the book was a constant source of encouragement as I carried out the revisions. I am also grateful to the two anonymous reviewers, who provided unusually substantive and detailed comments on the manuscript. Finally, Betty Seavers and Bruce Acker deserve special thanks for their skillful copyediting assistance and for teaching me some important new lessons about writing.

Throughout the course of this project, I have been fortunate to receive financial support in variety of forms. A fellowship from the Marie Kohler Foundation helped me to finish writing the first draft of the manuscript. A faculty research grant from the University of Connecticut Research Foundation provided me with the resources that I needed to do additional field work in California, and funding from the Center for Interdisciplinary Research on Women's Health at the University of Connecticut (National Institutes of Health, grant number 5 K12 Hd01409) provided me with a semester of leave from teaching that enabled me to concentrate my energy during the final stages of revising the manuscript.

During the many years that it has taken to write this book, I have also been supported by many friends who have shared in the trials and tribulations that are inevitable with a project such as this. Although it is not possible to name all of the people who have helped in this way, I want to express my heartfelt appreciation to Mark Hesters, Daniel Hall, Nick Moore, Craig Turner, Lorraine Turner, Jeanne Schueller, Jon Graubert, Karin Niilson, Lisa Sharlach, John Baxter, Hassan Melehy, Carmen Wesson, Ben Liu, and Kathi Rees.

Last but certainly not least, I want to thank members of my family, Rose Gudbrandson, P. J. Kelly, Carrie Matthews, and Connor Kelly. You are my closest friends and the source of my greatest strength. But my greatest debt by far is to my parents, Peter and Linda Kelly, who have never once wavered from providing me with everything that I needed not only to pursue my intellectual interests but to live a happy life. I cannot imagine being blessed with more loving or supportive parents. It is to them that this book is dedicated.

Domestic Violence and the Politics of Privacy

One

Privacy and Domestic Violence

EVERY YEAR, MILLIONS OF WOMEN ARE BATTERED by their male partners.[1] Although exact numbers are difficult to establish because domestic violence usually occurs in the relative privacy of the home, statistical estimates range from 1.8 million to 3–4 million.[2] In 1998 the FBI reported that of the 3,419 woman murdered in that year, 32 percent had been killed by a man with whom they were, or had been, intimate.[3] Although these statistics suggest a crisis in American homes, it is important to understand that domestic violence is by no means a new phenomenon.[4] However, what *is* new about domestic violence is that Americans are now much more aware of both the frequency of battering and the scope of its brutality.[5]

As domestic violence becomes more visible, the enormous price it exacts from all members of society is increasingly clear. The annual monetary cost of battering, including medical coverage, workdays missed, and consumption of valuable legal and social resources, is estimated to be in the billions.[6] But perhaps even more noteworthy are the costs incurred when a generation of children who witness and are often the recipients of brutal treatment learn to view violence as normal.[7] Greater awareness of both the frequency of domestic violence and the breadth of its impact has contributed to a growing public consensus around the need to devise an effective policy response to the problem.[8] Although great strides have been made in various areas, such as protection orders and shelter provision, domestic violence has proved to be extremely resistant to countermeasures.

Domestic Violence and the Public/Private Dichotomy

Many of the difficulties facing those who seek to stop domestic violence have their origins in the confusion around whether this type of violence should be treated as a public or a private issue. A major source of confusion is in long-established custom. Throughout most of Western history, it has been widely accepted that men have the right, even the obligation, to discipline their families.[9] Although limitations of one kind or another on the right have always existed, the severity of the "discipline" was largely left to the discretion of the individual patriarch.

Elizabeth Pleck, an American social historian, locates the first public objection to family violence in the mid-1600s, when the "Puritans of colonial Massachusetts enacted the first laws anywhere in the world against wife beating and 'unnatural severity' to children."[10] Such early disapproval would seem to indicate a peaceful future for American families, but Pleck finds that the imposition of legal sanctions to punish violent acts committed against family members has been highly episodic. She identifies three periods of social interest in family violence and notes that each has been characterized by intense struggles between those who believed state involvement in the family was essential and those who maintained that "family relationships require or deserve special immunity."[11]

Today, domestic assault is illegal in every state. However, confusion about whether this is a public or a private problem has not disappeared. Instead, the debate has shifted ground. On the one hand, the criminalization of domestic violence transforms what authorities might have previously dismissed as a husband's prerogative into a problem warranting intervention and even sanctions. On the other hand, very low reporting levels, police and judicial indifference, and a pattern of blaming the victim all suggest that many people, including some victims, continue to see domestic violence as a private matter that should not be subject to public scrutiny or intervention.[12]

A commitment to maintaining the family as a private realm creates a dynamic whereby any state intervention, even when clearly needed to protect the physical safety of a family member, becomes inappropriate.[13] It is likely that the cultural message that domestic violence should be kept private has its most profound effect on the primary recipients of this type of abuse. Isolated, ashamed, and extremely vulnerable, the victims are hardly in a position to challenge powerful social norms that tell them that they should be able to restore peace in their families without bringing the force of the law into their homes.[14]

Although it is very difficult to measure the actual impact of cultural messages regarding the importance of preserving the home as a private space, the statistics on reporting rates are highly suggestive. According to the National Crime Survey of Victimization, at the reporting stage, privacy concerns play a key role in ensuring that the vast majority of domestic violence incidents never come to the attention of criminal justice authorities. The survey estimates that victims report only 14.5 percent of serious domestic assaults to the police.[15] Further, a primary reason that people fail to report incidents of domestic violence is a belief that what happened is a *private* matter: 70.9 percent of those who did not report an incident specifically cited privacy as a reason.[16] These figures have very serious implications for any effort to improve how we respond to domestic violence. After all, even assuming the development of foolproof methods of response and treatment, the advances would mean little as long as the majority of the individuals they are designed to help remain hidden from view.

Moreover, in instances where a domestic assault *is* reported to public authorities, the belief that it is a private matter continues to play a significant role. The refusal of the police to arrest offenders and the reluctance of judges to sentence them has been widely documented.[17] As Lisa Lerman notes, "Throughout the legal system, the family is treated as a sacred entity, as a stable social unit which must be preserved or at least left undisturbed. Viewed through this preconception, violence within families is minimized, treated as a minor disruption, a normal part of life."[18] Anne Jones reinforces Lerman's point with the observation that the failure of a public official or a medical doctor to take a battered woman's situation seriously can be psychologically devastating, sending a powerful confirmation that she is alone with her problem.[19]

Even individuals within the system who are committed to developing aggressive and innovative laws and policies to assist victims of domestic violence are not free from the tensions and contradictions that exist between public and private boundaries. A daunting dilemma that all persons who serve the victims of domestic violence confront (regardless of whether they are pro-victim or not) is balancing the desire for privacy within the home with the need for outside intervention and assistance in cases of abuse.[20] If, for example, law enforcement officers, judges, or victims perceive a particular solution as infringing on privacy to an unacceptable degree, the consequence is often poor enforcement, lenient sentences, and low reporting rates. If the principle of protecting privacy goes too far, it is likely that the plight of many battered women will go unnoticed and unaddressed. This balancing act is complicated even further by the presence of various interest groups who are battling to redefine *public* and *private* in a way that best serves their particular political agendas.[21] The result is a great deal of confusion and disagreement regarding not only the boundaries of public and private in the case of domestic violence but also the very meaning of the concepts of "public" and "private" themselves.

The dilemmas arising from the meaning of *public* and *private* in the context of domestic violence operate at both a practical and conceptual level. From a practical perspective, they negatively interfere with efforts to alleviate battering. Understandably, it is at this level that people who have made a commitment to respond to violence in the home have focused their energy. Some examples of contemporary strategies to counteract the persistent notion that domestic violence is really a private matter include public information campaigns designed to convince people that "domestic violence is everyone's business"; programs to train law enforcement officers, judges, social workers, and medical practitioners to recognize domestic violence and then take it seriously; and legal reforms structured to ensure that domestic violence is treated as a crime. During the past two decades, such efforts have had a profound impact on how domestic violence is viewed and on the types and range of public services available to victims. Still, even these efforts deal only with the immediate symptoms of the attitude that domestic violence is a private matter. What goes untouched are the deep-seated conceptual assumptions about public and private boundaries in our society that give rise to such attitudes in the first place.

One major cause of the lack of attention given to the distinctions that are drawn between public and private is the notion that such theoretical concerns are not relevant to the "real world."[22] This position reflects the mistaken assumption that individuals who live and work outside academia do not utilize theoretically based understandings in their daily activities. It is a premise of this book that all people, regardless of educational background, rely on conceptual frameworks to make sense of and act upon the events within the context of their lives.[23] The relationship between privacy and domestic violence is a case in point. As the above discussion shows, privacy concerns play an important role in determining what happens (or does not happen) when a woman is beaten by a man with whom she is (or has been) intimately involved.

It is important to understand that privacy concerns do not exist in isolation but are instead part of a larger system of expectations about the nature of political society. Within the liberal democratic tradition, these expectations have historically included a strong commitment to individual autonomy and freedom from government intervention. Defined as a nonpolitical unit, the family has evolved as a space where governmental involvement and legal regulation are expected to be kept to an absolute minimum. Over the years, these assumptions have contributed to the development of a dichotomous model of society wherein the "private" family is contrasted with the "public" realm of politics, law, and government. The "public/private split" (as it has commonly come to be known), in addition to shielding citizens from an overzealous government, has also played a role in preventing victims of abuse from getting the help that they need. In light of this fact, a systematic examination of the relationship between the conceptual split of public and private and the problem of domestic violence is long overdue.

In this book, I seek to fulfill this need by critically examining two different models used over time to structure the relationship between public and private in American society. I begin with a discussion of the distinction, most forcefully articulated by John Locke, between the domestic realm of the family and the political realm of government. Locke's model contrasts domestic relations (identified as nonpolitical and therefore private) with economic and political relationships. Within this framework, governmental activities are most commonly identified as "public" in terms of both their inherent nature and their operation. My emphasis on the family as the embodiment of the private half of the public/private split distinguishes my approach from the majority of the theoretical discussions of this topic, which typically contrast the public activities of government with the private, economically based actions of citizens in civil society.[24] Although the latter conceptual division provides an important perspective on the relationship between economic and state relations, the domestic realm is missing.[25] As Carole Pateman points out, "Because liberalism conceptualizes civil society in abstraction from ascriptive domestic life, the latter remains 'forgotten' in theoretical discussion."[26] In addition to the numerous critiques of feminists suggesting that this structure serves to erase many of the concerns most central to women,[27] the absence of the realm of domestic relations significantly diminishes the applicability of this particular model for those who are specifically interested in analyzing the problem of domestic violence.

The second model of public and private examined in this book is one that is premised on the separation of the state and the individual. The distinction, which initially served as an underlying motivation of Locke's separation of the family from politics, has subsequently been employed to establish a wide range of limits on government power. Its theoretical basis can be located in the political theory of John Stuart Mill, who devoted a great deal of intellectual energy to identifying the requirements for the cultivation and the preservation of individual liberty. Mill's conclusions on this matter eventually served to lend support to the idea of establishing and maintaining a private sphere in which the government would not be permitted to intrude without first obtaining explicit authority to do so through proper legal channels. This idea, and the division between public and private that grew out of it, have since become a central component of the American constitutional system. In the United States, the separation between government authority and private liberties is largely negotiated through legal rights and the enactment of laws that are the primary means not only for establishing government authority but also for protecting individual citizens from its abuse.

So we have, on one hand, a model of public and private that is primarily directed at distinguishing familial relationships from political interactions and, on the other, a model that is designed to protect individual citizens from unwarranted state intrusions. Central to my analysis of these two distinct but interdependent models is a consideration of whether they are able to account effectively for and respond to domestic violence. Battering within the home presents a profound challenge to both models because of their shared reliance on the private realm as a space that is relatively free of a state presence. As a result, when the state seeks to intervene in cases of domestic violence, serious tensions are generated. One of the primary objectives of this study is to explore the nature of these tensions through an analysis of a variety of theoretical and legal frameworks that have been used to understand the relationship between public and private in U.S. society. The underlying assumptions and historical manifestation of each framework are discussed; in addition, each is evaluated according to its capacity to illuminate a number of specific dilemmas that repeatedly arise when agents of the state become involved in domestic violence.

These discussions and evaluations provide the foundation for an analysis of a series of practical perspectives reflected in forty-five interviews that I conducted between 1997 and 1999 with individuals working on domestic violence. Utilizing the themes that emerged from these interviews, I develop an alternative model of public and private that I believe is better equipped to account for the complexities and policy dilemmas that surround the meaning and operation of privacy in cases of domestic violence.

The posited model, although seeking to preserve the liberal distinction between public and private, replaces the traditional dichotomization of these spheres with a triangular relationship. The state, the family, and the community are the three corners. The model's distinguishing feature is the presence of three separate boundaries that structure the meaning of public and private in our society. Each boundary is distinct, varying in terms of general characteristics and degree of permeability. The variations arise from the fact that, rather than being predetermined, the boundaries of the model are defined by the relationship between the two corners of the triangle that they bridge. In keeping with this feature, I argue that one of the major advantages of the model is that it makes room for an understanding of the public/private distinction as part of an ongoing, evolving relationship. Also central to the model is a strong emphasis on the role of democratic institutions and community participation in determining the shape that the relationship will take.

Outline of Chapters

I begin the book with an examination of the fundamental role that Locke's theory of politics has played in structuring the way contemporary liberal thinkers understand the relationship between public and private. Because Locke was one of the first liberal theorists to develop an explicit analysis of why the family should be viewed as distinct from politics, his writings provide many important insights into the continuing tendency to characterize the family as a strictly private association. Further, his ideas on the social contract and his emphasis on the natural rights of individuals furnish the foundation for later arguments about why a private sphere is essential for the development of individual liberty. In chapter 2 I consider the implications of Locke's theoretical framework for efforts to address the problem of domestic violence.

Chapter 3 extends the discussion by examining a range of feminist critiques that have been proposed as alternatives to the liberal model of the public/private split. Because the content of the critiques is wide-ranging, separate analyses of radical, liberal, and conservative feminist theories structure the chapter. The critiques yield many valuable insights into the limitations of the liberal model. Nonetheless, I conclude that viewing the alternative frameworks within the context of the particular issues raised by domestic violence undermines their promise as real alternatives to the liberal model. The fatal weakness inherent in the three approaches is a tendency to construct an *ideal* relationship between public and private boundaries that is dependent on an unrealistically narrow conception about what is required for women to achieve freedom and equality in this society. Thus, although each of the three approaches provides new perspectives on the relationship between women's private and public identities, they all fail to account for the fact that most women spend their lives negotiating some or all of these identities simultaneously. In the final portion of chapter 3, I bring the limitations of these feminist reconstructions of the relationship between public and private spheres into focus through consideration of the multitudinous ways that battered women have responded to the violence in their lives and to efforts to make that violence subject to public censure.

In chapter 4 I seek to illuminate the various ways that law has functioned to both mirror and constitute cultural assumptions about the appropriateness of violence within the familial sphere by analyzing the patterns of legal interventions into domestic violence in the United States from colonial times to the present. In the final portion of the chapter, I argue that although the effectiveness and frequency of legal interventions on behalf of victims of domestic violence have increased dramatically, these legal reforms do not pose a serious challenge to the cultural construction of domestic violence as a private problem. The narrow focus of the legal interventions not only limits their effectiveness but also serves to construct domestic violence as a private dispute between two individuals instead of as a widespread social problem warranting public attention and action.

The theoretically and historically based discussions presented in the first four chapters are brought into the realm of practice in chapter 5 through an analysis of the experiences of individuals who directly deal with domestic violence on a daily basis. Data for this chapter derive from interviews I conducted with forty-five such practitioners. Included in the interview pool were legal advocates for battered women; activists lobbying for changes in legislation; policymakers at both the legislative and bureaucratic levels involved with issues of domestic violence; volunteer and professional shelter workers; prosecutors; and police officers.

The one- to two-hour interviews were loosely structured around questions designed to elicit information from the respondents on whether concerns over privacy and the nature of public responsibility arose in their work, and if so, how they understood and dealt with such matters. The hypothesis that drove the interviews was that interventions in domestic violence will inevitably generate tensions around the privacy interests of the victim and the perpetrator and around the nature and limits of the public's responsibility to stop the violence. I assumed that in order to deal with such tensions, individual interveners would naturally develop their own approaches to the challenge of determining the proper relationship between public obligations and privacy rights. The interviews revealed that individuals in this field do in fact utilize sophisticated frameworks for negotiating the conflicts between public and private that they encounter. The first theme that emerged from the interviews revolves around the limitations of the law as a strategy for transforming domestic violence into a public problem. The second theme concerns the strategies discussed by the respondents for filling in the gaps left by a legally centered response to this type of violence. The articulation of these themes provides the basis for the alternative approach to public and private delineated in chapter 6.

In chapter 6 I argue that one of the most significant implications of the approach to domestic violence embodied in these two themes is the desirability of expanding the range of public responses to domestic violence by challenging the habitual association between "the public" and "the state." Building on such insights, I develop an alternative model of public and private that replaces the traditional dichotomy with a triangular relationship between the state, the family, and the community.

There are a number of fundamental differences between the model that I propose and the approaches to public and private that are critiqued in chapters 2–4. The differences arise from two primary factors. First and most obvious is that the proposed model incorporates "community" as a category in addition to "family" and "state." It is important to note that my inclusion of community (and the civil associations that define it) is not in and of itself new to discussions of public and private. In fact, as discussed earlier, theoretical treatments of this dichotomy have traditionally centered on the relationship between the state and civil society—with the family largely excluded. Clearly, close parallels exist between the category of "community" in the model and the concept of "civil society," a topic that I deal with in some detail in chapter 6. However, in my model, "family," "state," and "community" are accorded equal importance in the delineation of the boundaries between public and private in our society. As a result, my model provides the opportunity to consider how different components of society operate to shape one another and the meaning of public and private.

The second fundamental difference between my model and others arises in the methodological approach that I take to theorizing. As should be apparent, my belief in the importance of listening to the practical expertise of those who must grapple daily with the tensions between public and private significantly influences both the nature of the research presented here and the shape of the model developed from it. Because the model is grounded in empirical concerns that change over time rather than in abstract distinctions and categorizations, the approach to public and private that I propose is predicated on a fundamentally practical and evolving relationship between the state, the family, and the community. One important consequence of this practical emphasis is that boundaries cease to be understood as predetermined imperatives but instead are understood as the outcome of a process in which the three realms shape one another on an ongoing basis.

In chapter 6 I also discuss a number of notable implications of the proposed approach: in particular how the model will enable us to address more productively the tensions around privacy created by our efforts to address domestic violence. These benefits include the dual effect of de-centering the state as the solitary mechanism for addressing violence and moving us away from what has been a very heavy dependence on the victim in the effort to transform this into a public issue. Further, I discuss the effect that the model has on turning the relationship between public and private into a democratic one by refocusing our attention on boundaries as a product, rather than a precursor, of the democratic process.

I conclude with a critical analysis of the right to privacy and the process of drawing boundaries more generally. Here I discuss the importance of reconceptualizing privacy as a positive right that facilitates the ability of all individuals to relax, develop autonomy, and enjoy intimacy. I argue that turning away from the habit of reducing privacy to a "right to be left alone" makes us better able to evaluate whether the boundaries we have established are really functioning to facilitate the values that drive our commitment to privacy in the first place. I also highlight the desirability of including an appreciation for the relational qualities of privacy.

Next, I turn to the valuable role that principles can play in our efforts to renegotiate where we want to draw the boundaries between family, state, and community. One of the subthemes in the interviews concerned the widespread sense among the interviewees that principles such as justice, equality, and fairness were of limited use in terms of their ability to help people to see why domestic violence should be viewed as a public concern. That assessment, although accurate, should be understood not as a product of a fundamental questioning of the usefulness of principles per se but, rather, as a result of the widespread tendency to express them in an overly abstract manner. In this light, I make a series of recommendations for how we might approach principles so that they are more closely connected to the specific social issues to which we seek to apply them. I conclude with an argument as to why I believe the findings of this research support a general approach to legal and political theory that begins, rather than ends, with the social practice it seeks to describe.

Before concluding this introductory chapter, I would like to describe the two central concerns animating the research. The first is my desire to contribute toward making things better for those whose lives are shadowed by the pain of domestic violence. This includes improving our ability to intervene and offer assistance in a manner that is helpful and respectful, as well as supporting present and future efforts to prevent such violence from occurring in the first place. My second concern revolves around my theoretical interest in the relationship between public and private and my desire to enhance our understanding of this relationship so that we are better able to address the tensions that arise from it.

Although distinct in focus, the two concerns are actually very closely related. As I discussed at the outset of this chapter, worries about privacy and widespread doubts about how to intervene in situations of domestic violence in a way that does not undermine the sanctity of the family or individual choices about personal matters have directly contributed to our inability to deal with and prevent this type of violence. Throughout the chapters that follow, I argue that a great deal of our uncertainty and confusion about how to proceed when facing such practical dilemmas can be directly traced to the presence of serious tensions within the conceptual frameworks that structure our interpretations of the proper boundaries between the public and private spheres. With this point in mind, it becomes much easier to see how the theoretical analysis and approach developed in this book, by improving our ability to understand the often contradictory assumptions that are embedded in conceptions of public and private, can contribute simultaneously to the philosophical investigations that surround this topic and to practical efforts to address specific social problems such as domestic violence.

Two

The Family as a Private Entity

THE PUBLIC/PRIVATE DISTINCTION STANDS OUT AS one of the most important and continuously debated concepts within liberal politics. As one of the first liberal theorists to systematically address this issue, John Locke played a fundamental role in structuring the way contemporary liberals seek to understand and negotiate the relationship between these two spheres. Locke's importance to this topic can at least partially be attributed to the clarity of his arguments about why a separation between public and private is essential to the pursuit of individual liberty and freedom. A close examination of the *Two Treatises of Government* reveals that beneath Locke's arguments about the meaning of these terms lies an extremely complex model of the relationship between them.

A good deal of this complexity comes from the fact that, although he embeds them within a single opposition, Locke ultimately ends up articulating two distinct models of public and private. The first model is premised on his exhaustive discussion of the difference between political and paternal power. Locke creates a picture of social relations in which the domestic realm is defined as paradigmatically private and the political realm of state power is defined as public. The second model arises from Locke's efforts to explain how individuals, who are born into a state of freedom and equality, are able to consent to a government without relinquishing the natural freedom that is theirs by God's intention. Locke resolves this dilemma by reducing the government's involvement in citizens' lives to that of a referee in cases of direct conflict between individuals. Within this second model, the family plays a crucial role: Locke depicts it as a relatively peaceful association that does not require the continuous presence of a neutral arbitrator with the power over life and death to maintain order. Thus, the domestic realm provides Locke with the conceptual and the physical space for individuals to realize their potential as rational free beings even after they have consented to partial rule by government.

Identifying the presence of these two models is important because both within Locke's theory and in other liberal constructions of public and private, they have been largely conflated. For example, when discussing privacy, liberals rarely specify whether they are referring to the privacy of the family or the privacy of the individual. The conflation rests upon the fundamental assumption that the interests of family units and the individuals that comprise them will rarely be in serious conflict. Locke's assertion that conjugal society does not require the continuous presence of a neutral party to resolve disputes and enforce compliance is closely connected to his vision of the family as a naturally peaceful and paternally run association. Locke attributes the relative lack of conflict between individuals in the domestic sphere to God's having created people in such a way that "Obligations of Necessity, Convenience, and Inclination" work together to provide them with the desire and means to come together in peaceful sociability.[1] However, such a state of affairs is an admirable *ideal;* the *reality* is that familial relationships often include a significant amount of friction.

When we begin with an assumption of familial conflict rather than peace, the duality between individual and family embedded within Locke's separation of private and public becomes problematic. Bringing these two models together illuminates the tensions that are produced in liberal societies by the competing desires for personal autonomy and social connection, on the one hand, and the practical necessity of pursuing individual interests within the context of social groupings, on the other. With these points of tension in mind, the question that will structure the remainder of this chapter is: What happens when we can no longer assume that the interests and rights of individual family members are compatible? As I argue below, the major limitation of Locke's model in particular (and of the liberal model of the family more generally) is that the presumption of a minimal amount of serious conflict between individual members results in a theory of politics that does not include an adequate account of how to deal with conflicts between individuals within the family—if and when they arise.

In addition to articulating Locke's development of this model, the pages that follow explore the implications of this dualistic liberal vision for the construction of the family as a paradigmatically private realm. Liberal theory presumes that the domestic realm will provide people with a private space to develop their individuality and their most intimate connections to others: yet examples abound in which the objectives of "individual autonomy" and "family unity" do not work well together. One of clearest examples can be found in instances of domestic violence. When one family member physically attacks another, it is virtually impossible to miss the gap that is created between the pursuit of individual interests and familial intimacy. In such instances, the victim's self-interest is clearly being violated. Furthermore, the violation occurs, at least partially, because of the privacy afforded by the familial context. Thus, in such situations the commitment to protecting the family as a private realm can contribute to a climate in which repeated acts of domestic violence go unaddressed.

As the example of domestic violence demonstrates, the liberal construction of the family as private is not always capable of satisfying the goals of protecting both individual and family interests. This is not to suggest that we should seek to find a resolution to this tension. Ultimately, such tensions are an inescapable product of the fundamental schism within liberalism over whether people should be understood primarily as autonomous individuals or as social beings. Moreover, *both* interpretations capture something important about the human condition: to reject one in favor of the other in the name of consistency would be to commit a serious error.[2]

Therefore, rather than seeking to resolve the tension, can we increase our understanding of how it operates so that we might be better equipped to deal with it productively? That objective prompts the following examination of the theoretical and historical origins of the construction of the family as a private realm in the writings of John Locke. In this analysis, I further elaborate the ways in which Locke's model accentuates the tensions between the goals of individualism and connection within the liberal family.

My intention in this chapter is not to provide yet another demonstration of the exclusion of women in Western political thought, to prove that Locke's was an inherently sexist theory, or to suggest that Locke approved of husbands battering their wives.[3] Nor is this engagement an attempt to discern in Locke's theory formulations that can be "updated" and then used to provide answers to contemporary struggles around domestic violence. However, although I do not think it is wise to attempt to transport Locke in time to solve problems that are particular to our society, I do believe that revisiting the original formulations of liberalism can assist us by providing insights into the often unstated and unacknowledged assumptions that we have inherited from this tradition.

The relevance of Locke's theory of the family to present day approaches to addressing domestic violence derives from a number of key areas of influence. First, his theory of politics has played a critical role in structuring the way contemporary liberal thinkers understand the relationship between public and private. Locke was one of the first liberal theorists to analyze explicitly why the family should be viewed as distinct from politics, and thus his thinking provides many important insights into the continuing tendency to characterize the family as a strictly private association. Further, Locke's ideas on the social contract and his emphasis on the natural rights of individuals are the foundation of later arguments about why a private sphere is essential for the development of individual liberty. Most important, however, it is in Locke's discussion of the family that we find the origins of the liberal assumption that the private family could provide people with a space in which they could simultaneously develop their sense of individuality *and* satisfy their need for connection to others.

Political and Paternal Power

Central to Locke's *Two Treatises of Government* is the distinction he draws between paternal and political power. Locke's distinction can be understood as an effort to make sense of the transition occurring in seventeenth-century England from a kinship society toward a society organized around economic markets.[4] Locke was offering a philosophical justification for the separation between private and public spheres that the transition was producing. Basic to this justification is Locke's construction of the family as a strictly nonpolitical form of association. This position ran counter to the reigning patriarchalist position enunciated most forcefully by Sir Robert Filmer, who supported the absolute power of the monarch on patriarchal grounds by identifying political power and familial power as equivalent.[5]

According to the patriarchal worldview, all social relations could be understood in terms of a model of the household in which the father was the absolute master. From Filmer's perspective, all of society, beginning with Adam and Eve, could be viewed as a single household. Just as Adam was made master of all his domain by God, so the king of England should be master of his domain as the literal father of his own biological family and as the figurative father of the body politic. Filmer's defense of absolute monarchy depends heavily on his notion that political power could be derived directly from the hierarchical relations of the family in which the father was the final authority on all matters. Filmer makes no distinction between "familial" and "political" or between "private" and "public." As Gordon Schochet points out, when Filmer talks about the king as the father of his people, he is not speaking metaphorically. Filmer literally believed that political relations and family relations should be understood as coming out of a singular hierarchical order. For him, paternal and political power are not just similar, they are indistinguishable.[6]

Locke directly challenges Filmer's conclusions about divine right by contending that there are major differences between the familial and political spheres. The *Second Treatise* begins with a bold statement: "The Power of a *Magistrate* over a Subject, may be distinguished from that of a *Father* over his Children, a *Master* over his Servant, a *Husband* over his Wife, and a *Lord* over his Slave" (II, 2). Locke's discussion of the differences between a familial and a political association enables him to establish the clear distinction between paternal power and political power upon which his arguments against Filmer depend.

According to Locke, the origins of society can be located within the family. In his version of the state of nature, human beings, in addition to being born into a state of freedom and equality, are born with a strong inclination toward sociability. This inclination, along with necessity and convenience, causes men and women to come together voluntarily in conjugal society (II, 77).

Locke's primary method for differentiating conjugal society and political society is through a comparison of ends. The chief ends of conjugal society are procreation and the rearing of children. Because human infants are helpless for a long period of time and because a woman can conceive again before her first child is independent, human procreation requires that a man and woman stay together until the children are reared and independent (II, 80). Although children are born as free and rational beings, Locke indicates that these qualities are not fully developed prior to adulthood. For this reason and this reason alone, although children are dependent, they are ruled by their parents. However, in contrast to Filmer's view that all people are born into and forever remain under the authority of some paternal power, for Locke this state of subjection is only temporary. Once children reach adulthood, they are as free as their parents (II, 55). Accordingly, the temporary nature of this subjection allows "*natural Freedom and Subjection to Parents*" to exist together (II, 61).

Locke utilizes this argument about parents' need to exercise authority over their children as one means of demonstrating that Filmer's model of patriarchal rule is misguided. After all, if paternal authority and political authority were the same, it would not be possible for parents to "retain a *power over their Children*," for all of that power would necessarily reside with the monarch (II, 71). The fact that the bearing and rearing of children necessarily entails a period of parental authority over children is proof to Locke that Filmer's conflation of paternal and political power violates the natural order. Locke is adamant when distinguishing the two types of authority:

But the two *Powers, Political* and *Paternal, are so perfectly distinct* and separate; are built upon so different Foundations, and given to so different Ends, that every Subject that is a Father, has as much a *Paternal Power* over his Children, as the Prince has over his; And every Prince that has Parents owes them as much filial Duty and Obedience as the meanest of his Subjects do to theirs; and can therefore contain not any part or degree of that kind of Dominion, which a Prince, or Magistrate has over his Subject. (II, 71)

Contradicting Filmer, Locke asserts that authority within the family, rather than belonging exclusively to the father, is shared with the mother. As Locke points out in the *First Treatise,* Filmer's argument that the political authority of a monarch originates in his role as begetter makes little sense once we remember that the mother has an equal, if not a greater, share in the act of procreation (I, 55). According to Locke, once we acknowledge the existence of shared authority within the family, Filmer's equation of the absolute authority of the king with a father's absolute authority over his children that is his by natural right breaks down.

In addition to being temporary and shared, paternal power in Locke's family is also limited because it does not include the power over life and death (II, 86). This limitation is extremely significant because it too serves to set paternal power apart from political power. *The* defining characteristic of political power for Locke is the power of the sovereign over life and death. The meaning and purpose of this power for Locke's definition of political relations can best be understood through a consideration of why Locke believed men originally chose to exit their natural state of freedom and enter political society.

Recall that according to Locke, at the beginning of human history people existed primarily in widely dispersed family groups. Because they lived simply and with minimal possessions, it was possible for the father of each family to resolve whatever disputes might arise among its members. However, with an increase in population and greater accumulations of wealth and property, the inadequacies of this simple form of political association became readily apparent.

The major weakness is that because decision-making is concentrated in the hands of a single patriarch, there is no way to separate his private interests from the interests of his subjects. As a result, the sovereign could easily abuse his political authority to accumulate wealth and power for himself. Locke believes that people faced with such an unacceptable state of affairs would naturally seek to dissolve this form of government and look for one more in accord with their natural rights (II, 111). Although the option to live without a government (and thus to return to a state of nature) exists, Locke does not believe that individuals who are endowed with reason would choose it because the individual's control over "his own Person and Possessions" is "very uncertain, and constantly exposed to the Invasion of others" (II, 123). People would rationally choose to "unite for the mutual *Preservation* of their Lives, Liberties and Estates, which I call by the general Name, *Property*" (II, 124).

Government's chief purpose is to preserve property. To do this, the government must be equipped to perform three functions: to pass laws, to interpret the law so as to settle disputes, and to punish lawbreakers (II, 124–26). Additionally, it will be necessary for all persons who have consented to live under that association to relinquish two important natural rights: the right "to do whatsoever he thinks fit for the preservation of himself and others within the permission of the *Law of Nature*" and the right "*to punish the Crimes* committed against that Law" (II, 128). Both of these rights are to be assumed by the legislative government and upheld through the enactment and enforcement of laws—which brings us back to the power over life and death.

According to Locke, the legitimacy and power of any government depend on maintenance of exclusive control over the power over life and death. His underlying logic is that if the subjects retained this power, the government would be incapable of enforcing the laws and chaos would result. Thus, although parents may have absolute authority over their children until they reach maturity, parents can never have the power to kill a child, no matter the magnitude of his or her disobedience. The absence of power in the family to bring an end to a life, more clearly than anything else for Locke, marks domestic society as a nonpolitical entity.

For Locke, the ends of political society justify the state's exclusive right over life and death. Similarly, the ends of domestic society explain why such a power is unnecessary within families. For procreation to occur, the structure of familial relationships must meet several requirements.

First, a man and a woman must have a "Right in one another's Bodies" (II, 78), a right that is obtained through the voluntary consent of each to marry the other. Although Locke characterizes marriage as a contract, it is a contract qualitatively different from the social contract that forms the basis of government. The social contract requires that all persons give up their right to punish transgressors, transferring it to a neutral authority. Conjugal society, on the other hand, is a voluntary exchange involving mutual affection and need. The proof of this characterization can be found in the fact that its ends of procreation and the rearing of children can be accomplished without either party's retaining the right to determine life and death (II, 83).

The assertion that conjugal society does not require the continuous presence of a neutral party to resolve disputes and enforce compliance is connected to Locke's assumption that familial relations will not be marked by the type of intense conflict that potentially threatens order in civil society. Locke attributes this relative lack of conflict to the fact that God created people so that they have both the desire and means to come together in peaceful sociability (II, 77). He concedes that a "Husband and Wife, though they have but one common Concern, yet having different understandings, will unavoidably sometimes have different wills too" (II, 82). Locke argues that when this situation occurs, the power to make final decisions "*naturally* falls to the Man's share, as *the abler* and *stronger*" (ibid., emphasis added). His reliance on God-given characteristics and a biologically based hierarchy to maintain order in the family stands in sharp contrast with his description of the origins and qualities of civil society, which is premised on convention, free will, and reason. The contrast here is not accidental, as it highlights the distinction between paternal and political power.

Paternal power, which is natural, God-given, and not dependent on the power to determine life and death, is properly exercised in the family. Although paternal power establishes a natural hierarchy of authority (with the husband at the top and the wife, children, and servants below), Locke does not believe that the hierarchy conflicts with his assertion that all people are born equal and free due to the limited nature of paternal power. As noted, Locke viewed the authority of parents over children as continuing only until the children have obtained the reason required to become the free and equal individuals that is their natural right. In the case of the wife, the father's position as final authority applies only to matters that are of "common interest and property." From Locke's perspective, this qualification serves to leave "the Wife in the full and free possession of what by Contract is her peculiar right, and gives the Husband no more power over her Life, than she has over his" (II, 82). The freedom of a wife is further evidenced by her ability to separate from her husband in accordance with the terms of the marriage contract and the laws and customs of the country (ibid.).

Finally, the exercise of paternal power is jurisdictionally limited. In keeping with his insistence that paternal and political power are distinct, Locke specifies that the only way to maintain the integrity of each is to keep them separate—conceptually and in practice. This point directly challenges patriarchalist theories such as Filmer's that assume that paternal and political power are interchangeable. Even more important, however, Locke's differentiation of paternal and political power serves as the foundation for a new approach to government which includes a strong presumption against the imposition of political power within the familial context. By positioning this distinction as a central focus for his theory of politics, Locke became the first political theorist to articulate explicitly the modern liberal separation between public and private.

Two Models of Public and Private

Although Locke's theory is premised on the single distinction between paternal and political power, a closer examination of the theory reveals two distinct models of public and private. The first, outlined above, separates the family from politics; the second separates the individual and the state.

As we have seen, in his attempt to undermine patriarchal theories of government, Locke deems the family a private association that will not require the level of mediation and rule-setting between individuals in political society that government is equipped to provide. If something is "not necessary to the ends for which it is made" (II, 83), then it should not be included in that realm of society.

Locke's separation of "the domestic" from "the political" was not new. Beginning with Aristotle, political theorists have contrasted the function and nature of familial relations with those of politics. In the theorist's eyes, the importance of the family has less to do with its actual attributes than with the ways it highlights the unique characteristics of politics. The theoretical focus is not really on the family at all but, rather, on the political realm. In the *Two Treatises of Government,* Locke clearly distinguishes why the family is not political in this same way.

Still, it would be incorrect to characterize Locke's theory of the family as performing this negative function only. Once we consider his second model of public and private, it becomes clear that the understanding of family provides far more than a contrast to political power. The second model of public and private arises from Locke's effort to establish a clear division between the private lives of individuals and the public sphere of politics and the state. The domestic realm provides Locke with both an intellectual and an actual space for his arguments on behalf of individualism.

Behind Locke's attack on Filmer lies his rejection of Filmer's assertion that all humans are born into and forever remain in a state of subjection to a higher authority. Locke believed that if "we consider what State all Men are naturally in," we see that it is a state "of *Equality*, wherein all the Power and Jurisdiction is reciprocal, no one having more than another," and thus people "should also be equal one amongst another without Subordination or Subjection." The only authority that all men must obey is God, whose will is expressed through the "law of nature," which can be discerned through the exercise of reason. Therefore, it is through expanding our capacity to reason that we develop the ability to rule ourselves. "The *Freedom* then of Man and Liberty of acting according to his own Will, is *grounded on* his having *Reason*, which is able to instruct him in that Law he is to govern himself by, and make him know how far he is left to the freedom of his own will" (II, 7). God-given rationality serves many crucial functions in Locke's theory: it defines us as uniquely human; it enables us to live according to our own authority; and it gives us the ability to consent to governmental authority.

Locke's challenge was to devise a system of government that would be capable of protecting men from one another while still preserving their natural freedoms. As we have seen thus far, a central component of his solution was to distinguish paternal from political power and, through the articulation of this distinction, to develop a model of society structured on a clear separation between the private realm of the family and the political realm of politics. As we will see below, Locke's construction of the family as a nonpolitical realm serves to bolster the separation that he seeks between the individual and the state in a number of important ways.

First, the premise of a peaceful family shows that prior to the existence of governmental authority, people were able to live together in harmony. According to Daniella Gobetti, the peaceful family resolves a central dilemma for Locke by providing an illustration of situations wherein people are not dependent on the presence of an all-powerful ruler to get along. Locke's description of the family becomes itself an argument against conflictual characterizations of human relations such as that put forth by Thomas Hobbes, who argues that according to the laws of nature, when human beings "live without a common power to keep them all in awe, they are in that condition which is called war; and such a war, as is of every man, against every man."[7] As long as Locke can provide one example of absolute power's not being a prerequisite for the maintenance of peaceful social relations, he can propose limitations on the ruler's power without exposing his political theory to the criticism that it will eventually lead to an anarchical state.[8]

Second, by depicting the family as a realm that can remain largely free of government, Locke creates a physical space in which individuals can exercise the rights and freedoms that government was designed to preserve. One of the most important functions of the family in this respect is the cultivation of the all-important ability to reason, the key to individual freedom.[9] Locke believed that although the capacity to reason is natural, its exercise requires both cultivation and practice. Furthermore, Locke views the moral education of children as critical in order to prevent the natural state of freedom into which all humans are born from becoming a "state of license" to do whatever one pleases regardless of the consequences.[10] Significantly it is to the family that he assigns the all-important task of providing children with the moral education that they require to realize their reasoning potential. Locke states repeatedly that it is the obligation of all parents "to inform the Mind, and govern the Actions of their yet ignorant Nonage, till Reason shall take its place" (II, 58). Once this reason has been developed, the authority that parents have over their children will be spontaneously suspended and the "*Child* comes to be as *free* from subjection to the Will and Command of his Father, as the father himself is free from subjection to the Will of any body else" (II, 66).

Because paternal power is of a nonpolitical nature and is guided by "the Affection and Tenderness, which God hath planted in the breasts of parents, towards their Children" (II, 170), it is ideally suited to the task of providing children with the guidance that they need in order to realize their own rational powers. In contrast, political power would not be appropriate, for it includes the absolute power over life and death, which can legitimately be exercised only over those who have consented to it. Children, because they have not yet developed the reasoning powers necessary for consent, would therefore not be appropriate subjects of such power (II, 170).

Even after the ability to reason has been developed, the family continues to contribute to its cultivation by providing adults with a realm in which they can exercise their reasoning powers. In what was certainly a radical notion for his time, Locke indicates that as long as procreation and the rearing of children are secured, a man and a women should be free to organize their association through contracts of their own making (II, 83). This echoes the position that he develops on the importance of individual autonomy in matters of conscience in *A Third Letter for Toleration*. There he forcefully argues for the preservation of a realm where individuals are free to organize their affairs according to their own rational assessment of what is best for them:

In private domestic affairs, in the management of estates, in the conservation of bodily health, every man may consider what suits his own conveniency, and follow what course he likes best. . . . Let any man pull down, or build, or make whatso-ever expences he pleases, no-body murmurs, no-body controles him; he has his liberty.[11]

Third, Locke's depiction of the domestic sphere as nonpolitical bolsters the separation between the individual and the state by providing men with a mechanism for transferring and exchanging their property that does not necessitate government intervention. Although Locke argues that men agreed to leave the state of nature so that they could set up a central power "for the Regulating and Preserving of Property" (II, 3), he nevertheless insists that this in no way implies governmental authority either to take a man's property or to tell him what to do with it. Such prerogatives would defeat the very end for which the government is formed: "For a Man's *Property* is not at all secure, though there be good and equitable Laws to set the bounds of it, between him and his Fellow Subjects, if he who commands those Subjects, have Power to take from any private Man, what part he pleases of his *Property*, and use and dispose of it as he thinks good" (II, 139). The importance of the nonpolitical domestic sphere to the preservation of the individual's right to "use and dispose" of his property "as he thinks good" arises primarily from the family's role in providing a natural mechanism for inheritance. In his discussion of paternal power, Locke states that as long as a father fulfills his familial obligations, he may "dispose of his own Possessions as he pleases . . ." (II, 65). The right of a man to dispose of his own property before and after his death ensures that he will not be subjected to a situation where the state controls that which by natural right is his (II, 138).

Locke and Domestic Violence

Locke's discussion of the state of nature draws a picture of human relations that is paradoxically both peaceful and conflictual. As we have seen, his recognition of the inevitability of conflict between individuals led him to suggest that despite "all the Privileges of the state of Nature" (II, 127), humans would rationally seek to relinquish their God-given powers to interpret the laws of nature to a government that would then be empowered through their consent to resolve disputes between individuals. As a result, Locke states:

The Community comes to be Umpire, by settled standing Rules, indifferent, and the same to all Parties; and by Men having Authority from the Community, for the execution of those Rules, decides all the differences that may happen between any Members of that Society, concerning any matter of right; and punishes those Offences, which any Member hath committed against the Society, with such Penalties as the Law has established. (II, 87)

However, it is important to note that Locke limits the government's role as "umpire" to resolving disputes between individuals who are in "*Political Society* together." As discussed previously, Locke went to great lengths to demonstrate that domestic relations are not *political* in nature. Furthermore, as we have seen, Locke's efforts to preserve a space where individuals pursue their own interests free of government control depend heavily on the preservation of the family as a nonpolitical, and therefore private, realm.

All of this raises a thorny issue: how to protect individuals within the family from both state intervention *and* unwanted interventions by other private individuals. Not surprisingly, this is not a new issue: it has been raised repeatedly in feminist critiques of John Locke and of liberal theory in general. Rather than providing us with a solution, Locke and other liberal theorists avoid the issue entirely through their continuing acceptance of a patriarchal model of family relations, which subordinates the interests of the family to that of a single individual, the father. As Teresa Brennan and Carole Pateman point out, "*Logically*, there is no good reason why a liberal theorist should exclude females from this category; *in practice*, and in most liberal political theory, for three centuries the 'free and equal individual' has been a male."[12]

At first, the assertion that Locke's theory is patriarchal may seem puzzling. After all, central to his arguments in the Treatises is an attack on Filmer's patriarchal theory. The problem is that the term *patriarchy* has a number of meanings. The literal meaning of *patriarchy* is "rule by the father."[13] Within societies organized along patriarchal lines, power is passed from father to eldest son, and the family kinship system serves as the model for all social relations. Within this model, the leader of a community, although not the literal father of his subjects, can position himself as their metaphorical father. A wide variety of rulers throughout history have buttressed their rule by encouraging a comparison between the leader and a kind and protective father.[14] Filmer took this analogical strategy to an extreme when he argued that the king of England, as a descendent of Adam (the first father), should be viewed as the literal father of his subjects and therefore should be granted the same absolute power to rule that God had granted to Adam. It was this interpretation of patriarchy that Locke sought to undermine when he argued that paternal and political power could not, and should not, be equated.

Today the meaning of *patriarchy* has expanded. In addition to describing a family in which the authority resides in the father, the term also denotes those social and political structures that enable men to dominate women. It is in this second sense that Locke's theory can be interpreted as supporting patriarchy. Locke vehemently attacks Filmer's defense of a patriarchal political system but leaves virtually unchallenged the patriarchal structure of familial relations.

Zillah Eisenstein makes a similar point when she characterizes Locke's theory as "patriarchal antipatriarchalism."[15] Eisenstein argues that Locke's purpose in drawing a distinction between political and familial rule is "to free the market from paternalistic, aristocratic relations, rather than to free the family from paternal rule."[16] Thus, when Locke counters Filmer by pointing out that both a mother and a father have parental power, his intention is not to establish equality between husband and wife but to undermine Filmer's assertion that political rule can be derived from the father's absolute authority as the male parent. What results is a picture of the family that, although no longer characterized by the absolute rule of the father, nevertheless represents the wife as the subordinate partner.[17]

It is not difficult to see that a patriarchal familial model might not be good for women who are subjected to violence from their husbands. Even Locke's "liberal" version of the patriarchal family contains many troubling patterns. At the most basic level, Locke's theory, which is explicitly designed to maximize the natural liberty of all individuals, fails to challenge the accepted right of men to chastise their wives.[18] As we have seen, Locke assumes that the family is generally conflict-free, but in families where there is disagreement, he assigns the final authority to the "naturally abler and stronger" husband (II, 82). In theory, Locke believes in cooperation between husbands and wives; in actuality, by placing the lion's share of the power in the hands of the husband, he comes down on the side of patriarchal ordering.

In fairness to Locke, it should be acknowledged that he does place unprecedented limitations on power granted to husbands. For example, he insists that the male head of the household, although retaining final power, never has the power over life and death. This qualification is very important to any discussion of battering. Although the numbers of women murdered by their husbands each year in seventeenth-century England is unknown, current evidence that battering was then common (when combined with the contemporary numbers of women killed by husbands) suggests that contrary to Locke's optimistic generalizations, many husbands did in fact assume the power over life and death.[19]

Moreover, Locke's theory of the family provides no enforcement mechanism that might limit the power of the family patriarch. What makes this oversight particularly serious is that the absence of external checks on the husband's power is a central component of the argument he makes against Filmer. As we have seen, Locke was very eager to demonstrate that Filmer's political theory was based on a misguided conflation of paternal and political power. To bring this point to its logical conclusion, Locke needed to construct the family and politics as completely separate and autonomous realms. An unavoidable component of this conceptual distinction is that it generates a strong presumption against the use of political power to regulate the family and vice versa (II, 83). The unfortunate consequence of such a presumption for many battered women is that they are effectively denied the presence of a neutral arbitrator with the power to control the abuser's attacks.[20]

Locke's conception of marriage as both a natural and a contractual institution provides another possible source of protection for wives. Men and women naturally come together to procreate and to rear children, and through the marriage contract they formally agree on the terms of their relationship. Locke's views on the possible variations within a marriage contract were somewhat unorthodox. For example, he included divorce among the alternatives as long as the main ends of conjugal society (reproducing and rearing children) had been accomplished (II, 82). Another unconventional idea was that a man and a women might freely organize their marital relations in whatever manner they desired as long as it did not violate the customs of their society (II, 83).

The flexibility and freedoms that Locke includes in his discussion of marriage seem to provide women with the tools to prevent domestic violence from occurring in marriage and to escape the relationship in the event that violence were to occur. Yet, upon examination, the actuality is less promising. Locke's primary mechanism for limiting the freedoms within conjugal relations is the mechanism he relies on to secure these freedoms in the first place: the contract. A substantial amount has been written outlining why the marriage contract serves to disadvantage women. Several elements of these critiques are particularly relevant to this chapter.

The most telling criticism is that the marriage contract does not meet the minimum requirements of a legitimate contract. By definition, a contract requires the free consent of all parties. Many feminists have argued that for women the "choice" to marry is not really a choice at all, for there are few alternatives for women in our society. This point, in many ways still true today, was especially true in the seventeenth century. At that time, the vast majority of occupations were closed to women, and those that were available, such as servant, were less than desirable. To support herself, a woman needed a husband. In addition, there were social pressures that compelled women to believe from childhood on that the only truly honorable vocation for them was that of wife and mother.[21]

Another criticism of the marriage contract is that even if the decision to enter into a marriage is freely made, the terms of the contract remain closed to negotiation, which devalues the freedom that ideally forms the basis of the association. Although Locke allows that a man and a woman can develop a marriage contract according to their desires (as long as they do not interfere with the procreational end of marriage), he endorses traditional marriage, in which the husband is given the power "to order the things of private Concernment in his Family, as Proprietor of the Goods and Land there, and to have his Will take place before that of his wife in all things of their common Concernment" (I, 48).

However, once again the equality and freedom of choice which Locke promises by means of a contract remain merely theoretical possibilities that, all too often, were not actually available to women. Further, the lack of freedom for women within marriage raises yet another question about the legitimacy of the contract itself: Why would a rational woman ever freely consent to enter into a contract that entailed her subjection?[22] The answer is her dependent position and the lack of alternatives.[23] Either way, the elements of "choice" and "freedom" that Locke develops through his articulation of the marriage contract become much less likely to be realized for women once these questions are considered.

A final criticism of the marriage contract has to do with the process of exiting it. Locke explicitly included the possibility of divorce in his discussion of marriage: "The *Wife* has, in may cases, a Liberty to *separate* from him; where natural Right, or their contract allows it" (II, 82). The question that needs to be asked is to what extent divorce was a realistic possi-

bility for women who were being brutalized. In seventeenth-century England, Locke's qualification that divorce would be permissible when the
marriage "contract allows it" amounted to a statement that divorce would
not be allowed. In the event that a woman used the Lockean argument
that her "natural right" to bodily integrity had been severely violated, the
legal sanctification of chastisement would most likely have undermined
such a plea.

In her study of feminist reform efforts in Victorian England, Mary
Lyndon Shanley suggests why the liberalization of divorce laws ultimately
had such a limited impact on the choices actually available to women:

Obtaining the right to leave an abusive or grossly negligent husband, however,
was hardly the door to freedom for a woman without property. Enforcement of
maintenance orders must have been extremely difficult, and the legislation did not
touch the main source of the grinding poverty of many widows and separated
wives, their low wages and the paucity of jobs available them. Children, as well as
the prospect of poverty, must have tightly bound many women even to miserable
marriages, for to appeal to a court for custody ran the risk of losing one's children
altogether.[24]

Although conditions for women have certainly improved, even today
wives face great difficulties when seeking annulment of their marriage
contract. The lack of available shelter and employment opportunities,
combined with the need to care for children, often means that even
women who are severely brutalized do not feel that they can realistically
leave their abuser.

The limitations on government that are developed in Locke's critiques
of Filmer in the *Two Treatises of Government* have played an important
role in supporting many of the freedoms we enjoy. As long as conjugal society lives up to being the primarily peaceful association that Locke believed it to be, the privacy that Locke's distinctions between paternal and
political power make possible can indeed provide a precious respite from
the exposure and demands of civil society. Still, in situations that fall short
of Locke's assumptions about the relative peace and tranquility of family
life and that feature instead violence, domination, and abuse, the liberating potential of this separation diminishes dramatically.

Violence in the home is an important test of Locke's model of familial
and political separation. According to Locke, the separation of the two
realms is a key factor in the development and maintenance of a social
order that supports the individuality and freedom of its citizens. The reality of violence in the family reveals that the separation, in addition to hav-

ing a liberating potential, can also contribute to the vulnerability and isolation so often experienced by victims of domestic violence. Locke certainly puts forward a number of propositions to address this possibility:
His limitations on the powers of familial patriarchs, however, are deficient
as realistic alternatives.

One possible response to these critiques is that the gender assumptions in Locke's depiction of the family are an unavoidable component of
the historical period within which he wrote, and the assumptions should
not be used as a justification for rejecting the theory in its entirety.[25] However, although this single element does not warrant an outright denial of
the value of Locke's thinking about families and the public/private distinction, the presence of such assumptions should give us pause. It goes
without saying that in today's society Locke's method for dealing with
conflict through deferring to the male head of the household as "the abler
and stronger" is no longer widely acceptable. Taking this into account,
some have suggested that we simply extend to women the individual
rights and freedoms that Locke posits for men in the private sphere.[26]

The major limitation of the proposal to extend these rights and freedoms to women is that it fails to address what is to be done in cases of
conflict between adult individuals within the family.[27] One option would
be to rely on the state as a neutral arbiter when there are disagreements,
just as Locke suggested for disputes within the public sphere. The problem is that this option would serve to disrupt the boundary between the
private realm of the family and the public realm of politics and state authority that Locke worked so hard to construct.[28] The presence of state
authority in familial relations would also threaten their special intimacy
that, according to Locke, makes them so different from political relations.

Such violations of Locke's theory are not simply problems for purists
within the tradition of political philosophy. The argument put forth by
Locke and other liberal theorists after him—that the family should be preserved as a private realm shielding individuals and intimate associations
from public scrutiny—has become an essential component of the cultural
and political landscape of the United States. We have inherited the tension
that exists within his theory between maintaining that privacy and the
need to resolve conflicts between individuals in a manner that does not involve the arbitrary subjection of one class of persons to another. Furthermore, over the past two hundred years, this tension has only increased as
our commitment to honoring the individualism of all family members has
become stronger. Finally, as Linda Nicholson has observed, our adherence
to Locke's sharp separation between the public world of politics and the

private world of the family in the face of this rising individualism should be acknowledged as especially problematic for women because "it is women whose identity has been more closely tied to the family, it is women's lives, particularly over the last two centuries, which have more acutely expressed the conflict between an expanding individualism and an older conception of the family."[29]

Individualism versus Connection

Nowhere are the dilemmas produced by the tension between the dual imperatives of individualism and connection within the family more vividly illustrated than in situations of domestic violence. During the past twenty years in the United States, largely as a result of the efforts by activists within the battered women's movement, we have seen a dramatic increase both in the general awareness of the problem and in the desire to do something about it. In addition to generating many important changes in the institutional and legal responses to family conflicts, the movement has also encouraged us to face the contradictions implicit in the twofold function of the private family: to provide people in liberal societies with a sense of connection and at the same time a sense of individuation. When violence occurs within the context of these competing goals, a wide range of troublesome questions results. For instance, should a victim's primary concern be to protect herself by leaving, or should she stay to try to work things out so that the family is not torn apart? How far should the government go to protect victims or potential victims from violence? What is the role of neighbors, the church, or the community more generally in addressing instances of domestic violence? If a victim does not want to leave or prosecute her abuser (even in extreme cases), should she be allowed to stay in a situation even if it means subjecting herself and her children to continued abuse?

To make matters even more complicated, these and other questions involve multiple tradeoffs between deeply held values about privacy, family, individualism, and community responsibility. Instead of facing these questions head-on, the discourse surrounding domestic violence has attempted to reduce or avoid their complexity through reliance on stereotypical and oversimplified interpretations of the issues. Most speculation has focused on the individual recipients of abuse. The emphasis is not surprising, for the victim most clearly embodies and expresses the associated tensions. The battered woman who protects her abuser by denying the abuse (sometimes even after *she* has called the police for help) embodies the contradictions that occur when an individual seeks simultaneously to protect herself and her family. The apparent irrationality of such behavior rivets our attention on why she responds in the manner that she does.[30] Many people simply are not able to get past such questions as, Why does she stay? and What did she do to cause a person who loves her to commit such violent acts?

These questions fail to recognize adequately that violence between people who love each other does not readily lead to what the average person might commonly think of as "rational behavior." Unfortunately, the widespread lack of awareness about the nature and depth of the frequently unresolvable tensions that are inherent in domestic violence has made it easier to blame the victim than to acknowledge our own confusion about what is happening.

Blaming the victim can take a number of forms, including holding her directly responsible for causing the violence or distancing ourselves from the situation with thoughts like "I would never allow it to happen to me." Another common reaction is to explain domestic violence as the product of external factors such as unemployment or substance abuse. Although external factors may contribute to particular instances of domestic violence, such explanations are fundamentally incomplete. These accounts fail to appreciate the tensions that are embedded within the origins of the liberal construction of the family as a private institution. The development of a working knowledge of the derivation and operation of these tensions is crucial to contemporary efforts to address domestic violence. When we replace the idealizations of the family that presume familial peace, which recur in Locke's theory, with an understanding that the domestic sphere is a site of significant conflict or repetitive acts of violence, the need for an understanding of the relationship between public and private that is capable of accommodating the paradoxes and contradictions that arise in instances of familial conflict is undeniable. Failure to fully engage these tensions results too easily in a pattern whereby the interests of some individuals are systematically subordinated in order to achieve a level of clarity that simply may not be possible.

Three

Feminist Re-Visions of the Public/Private Dichotomy

THE LIMITATIONS AND PROBLEMS ASSOCIATED WITH the liberal division between the private and public spheres have long been topics of concern for feminist theorists. As Carole Patemen has argued: "The dichotomy between the private and the public is central to almost two centuries of feminist writing and political struggle. . . . It is, ultimately, what the feminist movement is about."[1] With this in mind, the focus of this chapter is on the question of whether feminist theory can provide the basis for an approach to these boundaries that will be more supportive of contemporary efforts to address the problem of domestic violence.[2]

The importance of feminist theory to a new approach grows out of a number sources. First, many of the most thorough and interesting critiques of the liberal distinction between public and private can be found in the work of theorists who treat gender as a central category of analysis. Because the operation of women's power has been historically restricted to the domestic realm, feminist theorists have been especially attuned to the negative implications of defining familial relations as inherently nonpolitical and private. This has resulted in insightful discussions of the operation and impact of the distinction, as well as in a range of alternative visions as to how these boundaries might be approached in a manner that does not so predictably disadvantage women.

Feminist discussions of the public/private distinction are also particularly pertinent to the specifically gendered nature of domestic violence. Although men are occasionally victims of domestic violence, the evidence strongly suggests that the vast majority of victims are women.[3] Furthermore, many of the patterns associated with domestic violence are closely connected to gendered roles of domination and submission.[4] The part that the sharp demarcation between public and private has played in both generating and reinforcing such patterns has been a recurring topic among feminists. Of particular relevance are the feminist theorists who have explicitly considered how the delineating boundaries of these spheres might be altered so as to decrease the incidence of violence against women within intimate relationships.

The Problem

Despite the wide range of feminist approaches to this topic, one point characterized by significant agreement is that a dichotomy between public and private does exist. Political theorists such as Carole Pateman, Susan Okin, and Jean Elshtain have traced it from the ancient Greeks through twentieth-century theories of liberalism.[5] Going further afield, anthropologists Michelle Rosaldo and Sherry Ortner have located this dichotomy in non-Western cultures, even in all known human societies.[6]

A related point of consensus has to do with the assertion that women are most closely associated with the private realm of family, child rearing, and the performance of household tasks; and men with the public sphere of ritual, culture, and politics. What dismays many feminists about this assertion is that men are encouraged to move between the public and private spheres, but women have historically been hindered in this regard. The source of women's exclusion from the public sphere has been widely interpreted as originating in the biological capacity to bear children. According to Zillah Eisenstein, the capacity has been systematically transformed into a cultural expectation that they should also be responsible for rearing their offspring. Nature is used to mystify this role and the "institutionalization of public/private domains on the political level" makes the role very difficult for the majority of women to escape.[7]

The assignment of women to the private sphere has been identified by feminists as problematic for a range of reasons. One is that the exclusion of women from the public domain denies them the opportunity to function fully as citizens. Embedded in this point is the assumption that meaningful citizenship depends on public engagement with issues that transcend particularistic concerns. Hence, when women are hindered from full participation in the public sphere, they are prevented from maturing into truly responsible members of the community.

Beyond missed opportunities for maturation and self-development are the arguably more immediate feminist concerns about how women's absence in the public sphere impacts the political decisions made there.

Susan Okin, for example, has suggested that "the people in positions of power in our society are people who gain the influence they have in part by never having had the day-to-day experience of nurturing a child."[8] She believes the impact of this state of affairs has been that programs associated with the care for dependents in our society have been chronically underfunded and undervalued. Even as politicians hail the nuclear family as the cornerstone of our society, they put very little effort into enhancing the quality of family life.[9]

Another category of problems associated with the designation of women as belonging to the private sphere brings us back to domestic violence. The evidence clearly establishes that women are frequently hurt in the private sphere. To illustrate, according to the American Medical Association, among women aged 15–44, battering is the leading cause of injury, outnumbering both automobile and household accidents.[10] Furthermore, because the abusive incidents leading to these injuries usually occur within a familial context, they are often assumed to be private matters that should not be subject to state interference.[11] One of the consequences of such assumptions has been a pattern of nonintervention that, according to many feminists, has served to intensify the vulnerability and isolation that many women experience within the private realm. As Anne Bottomley writes: "Private ordering can only be detrimental to women. Economic, social and psychological vulnerability all militate against the image of the equal bargaining situation which is presumed to be present."[12] A related point is made by feminists who argue that repeated decisions to "look the other way" when there are problems occurring within the private sphere devalue women by implying that they are not important enough for legal protection. However, whether they make such symbolic arguments or not, most feminists agree that a noninterventionist approach to domestic life has functioned to protect the privacy of men at the expense of the safety of women.

A more benign criticism of the public/private split made by some feminists is that women are harmed by the distinction because of exploitation and inequality they face in the private sphere. Although many women now work outside the home, they are still expected both by their male partners and by society to fill domestic roles. Studies indicate that even in the most "liberated," dual-income couples, the women continue to do the bulk of child care and household activities.[13] The double burden leaves millions of American women exhausted, and when that fact is merged with the fact that men typically earn more and are better educated, it produces the prerequisites for serious inequality in the home.[14]

Inequality within the domestic realm connects very closely to the cycles associated with domestic violence. Studies on interpersonal patterns associated with violence between intimates have repeatedly identified as one of the most powerful and consistent causal determinants of the violence the abuser's belief that he has the right to dominate and control those subordinate to him.[15] In addition to reinforcing such attitudes, inequalities in both the home and marketplace negatively affect the ability of many women to exit violent relationships that provide essential economic support for themselves and in many cases for their children.

The Ideological Nature of the Public/Private Split

Thus far, the feminist arguments that have been presented as to why the public/private division has disadvantaged women in our society are all fairly straightforward. Each harm is easily described and documented. Other arguments are less susceptible to quantification. They are not based on identifiable harms to individuals but, instead, arise from reasoning as to why the maintenance of the public/private split is invidious to any project to free women from the oppression and violence that they face within the family. These arguments center on the assertion that the dichotomy functions as an ideological construct. A definition of ideology that works particularly well in this context is provided by Zillah Eisenstein, who defines ideology as "a set of ideas that helps to mystify reality."[16] Carole Pateman echoes the definition: "The term *ideology* is appropriate in talking about public/private because the profound ambiguity of the liberal conception of the private and public obscures and mystifies the social reality it helps to constitute."[17] More generally, the "reality" that the public/private split mystifies is the domination of women by men. In keeping with this definition, the first step taken by many theorists toward disempowering ideology is to unmask it by demonstrating that it conveys an artificial and inaccurate depiction of how our society functions.

One of the most favored defenses of maintaining a strict separation between public and private is that given women's biological function as the bearers of children, the split is nothing more than an outgrowth of the "natural" order of things. One response to this position, as mentioned above, comes from Eisenstein, who points out that such a naturalistic justification relies on a conflation of the *physical* act of giving birth and the *social* act of rearing. Technically, childbearing need engage a women for only the months of pregnancy and the time required for delivery, recovery, and an optional period of breast feeding. According to Eisenstein, once we consider the facts of childbirth, the notion that women should remain primarily in the private sphere for the fifteen to eighteen years following the relatively short period associated with physical act of giving birth is revealed as a social construction. The ideological role of the public/private split is to mystify the origins of this construction and reinforce it through the "institutionalization of public/private domains on the political level."[18] The construction of the public/private dichotomy as "natural" supports its maintenance despite the violence and inequalities that women experience in the private sphere. As long as the split is understood as biologically based, it can be presented as inevitable, thereby shielding those in political power from pressures to accept responsibility for the problems associated with it.

A second approach to unmasking the ideological character of the public/private division is to demonstrate its lack of empirical validity. This is accomplished either by showing that the public is influenced by the private sphere or, more commonly, that the private sphere is heavily regulated by the public sphere. In this respect, Frances Olson argues that "because the state is deeply implicated in the formation and functioning of families," the language of intervention and nonintervention has the effect of obscuring the policy decisions that the state makes constantly with regard to so-called private families.[19] Linda Gordon makes a similar point in *Heroes of Their Own Lives*, in which she traces the history of the regulation of family violence in Boston. She concludes that even prior to the emergence of the welfare state, family autonomy was a myth, given the evidence that a high incidence of regulation from relatives and neighbors has always existed.[20]

Feminist scholarship on the family such as that of Olson and Gordon illustrates the ways that failures to acknowledge the heavy regulation and state control of the family can operate to undermine society's capacity to deal openly with problems that occur within the familial context. A related argument is that in addition to justifying the inaction of outsiders, the construction of the division between the public sphere and families as natural, inevitable, and just isolates those who suffer inside particular families.

Within the ideological framework of the public/private split, when an experience is privatized, it is also depoliticized. According to critical legal scholars Richard Gabel and Paul Harris, the impact of this isolation and depoliticization is to undermine radical political consciousness and stunt our ability to "imagine alternatives."[21] But critical legal scholars are not alone in making this observation. To a large extent, the consciousness-raising efforts within the feminist movement during the 1970s were designed to circumvent exactly this dynamic. Current efforts to address domestic violence continue to challenge the perceptions of many victims that they deserve the abuse or that there is no alternative.

Because of the strong association between women and the family, the primary focus of feminist discussions of the public/private dichotomy has been on its influence on the *private* side the equation. However, in recent years an increasing amount of attention has been paid to how the split influences what is possible or not possible in the public sphere as well. For example, Iris Marion Young argues that the public sphere can maintain its image as impartial and rational only by channeling needs and desires into the private sphere. The public citizen, in turn, is defined in "opposition to the disorder of womanly nature, which embraces feeling, sexuality, birth, and death, the attributes that concretely distinguish persons from one another."[22] Young insists that in the absence of a public/private split, policymakers would be unable to avoid messy and contentious issues—domestic violence for one—that are currently labeled "private." Even more dramatic would be the need to respond to the issues and concerns of the persons who have been largely limited to the private realm. Relatedly, Pateman suggests that as long as we continue to let the ideology of public and private structure our thinking, we will be incapable of grasping what it takes to participate in the public realm. Such an understanding "demands at the same time an understanding of what is excluded from the public and why this exclusion takes place."[23]

Feminist Alternatives to the Public/Private Division

There is no single critique that can be labeled *the* feminist position on why the public/private split is problematic for women, and particularly on how the split contributes to violence against women within the domestic realm. However, there is significant consensus that the split exists and is harmful to women, and that it is a social construction that frequently serves ideological purposes. Once we consider proposals on how to address the associated problems, however, disagreements and contradictions abound. To make sense of this debate, it is instructive to look at some of the chief positions taken, particularly relative to efforts to redraw the boundaries of public and private as a means of reducing violence against women. Three sets of solutions—radical, conservative, and liberal feminist—each provide a distinct reformulation of the public/private split.

Radical Feminism: Overcoming the Oppressions of Privacy

The most dramatic solution to the problems of the public/private division is simply to do away with it altogether. This is the suggestion of two of the most well-known radical feminist thinkers: Shulamith Firestone and Catharine MacKinnon.

In *The Dialectic of Sex,* first published in 1968, Firestone builds her argument around a Marxist framework but with several significant revisions. First, she replaces economic class with sex class as the driving force of history. Second, she displaces capitalism by sexism as the principal oppressive ideology to be surmounted. Third, the material basis for oppression is located in the biology of reproduction rather than in economic conditions of production. Firestone concludes that the source of women's oppression as a "sex class" can be located in the fact that only females are capable of giving birth. As a result, the survival of the species has become dependent on women remaining subordinated in the private sphere to bear and then rear the next generation. With this analysis as her starting point, Firestone asserts that the only way for women to escape oppression and the physical violence associated with it is to do away with biologically based reproduction. The state would take over responsibility not only for producing children but also for ensuring that they are reared by adult volunteers.[24]

The work of Catharine MacKinnon represents a more recent strand of the radical feminist position on the public/private split. Like Firestone, MacKinnon begins with a Marxist framework but then replaces the economic analysis of Marxism with a sex-based analysis of why women are subordinated to men in our society.[25] The primary difference between the two scholars is that where Firestone emphasizes the facts of childbirth, MacKinnon emphasizes heterosexual sex as the material basis of women's oppression.[26] In large part, MacKinnon's analysis stems from her critique of the First Amendment doctrine, which has made the regulation of any public expression, including pornography, subject to strict constitutional scrutiny. One of the major impacts of the United States Supreme Court's reluctance to permit state regulation of pornography has been to reinforce our understanding of sex as private. Because MacKinnon views heterosexual relations as the source of women's oppression, she believes that sex must be treated as a politically significant act no matter where it takes place. From her perspective, when sex that subordinates women[27] takes place in a publicly distributed film, the Court's refusal to acknowledge its political character becomes itself an act of repression by the state. MacKinnon's solution is to use the legal system to regulate pornography, thereby eliminating its status as a private activity.

If the state regulation of sex and procreation suggested by MacKinnon and Firestone were to come about, the private sphere (as it is currently understood) would cease to exist. Domestic violence would no longer be treated as a private dispute between a man and a women but as a manifestation of an unacceptable pattern of domination meriting political action. The elimination of activities now treated as presumptively private would not disturb either theorist, for each views the distinction between public and private as little more than an ideological construction designed to naturalize and disguise the exploitation of women as a class. From this perspective, whatever benefits might accrue from keeping the state out of the realm of familial and sexual relations become irrelevant in the face of the violence and subordination that women inevitably experience when such activities are left unregulated. MacKinnon makes this point explicit: "In feminist translation the private is a sphere of battery, marital rape, and women's exploited labor; it is the central social institution whereby women are deprived of (as men are granted) identity, autonomy, control, and self determination."[28]

The majority of feminist theorists who have given their attention to the public/private split are in agreement with MacKinnon's basic argument that privacy, at least in its current configuration, has significantly contributed to the subordination of women in general and more specifically to unacceptable rates of violence against women within the context of intimate relationships. The aspect of her work that receives much less support is her assertion—made also by Firestone—that the oppression of women will *always* result from strict boundaries between public and private, and therefore the distinction should be eliminated.

Conservative Feminism: Moralizing the Private Sphere

One of the strongest attacks on radical interpretations of the public/private split has come from Jean Bethke Elshtain.[29] In *Public Man, Private Woman,* she argues that if the remedies proposed by Firestone and other radical feminists were to be actualized, the result would be fascism. Relying on H. P. Stern's study of Germany's Third Reich, she declares that "fascism begins and ends with an overpersonalization of politics." Elshtain believes that the radical feminists' rallying cry, "The personal is political," embodies exactly this type of "overpersonalization."[30] By collapsing the distinction between public and private, radical feminists risk creating a situation in which "one no longer speaks as an autonomous individual but as woman-identified woman, fused with others, seeking union finally with the Great Mother."[31]

Elshtain sees this utopian vision as akin to fascism for several reasons. First, radical feminists have overstated the extent of women's oppression and victimization and have ignored the many historical examples where women have been empowered and active participants in Western culture. Radical solutions become inevitable and reasonable only when placed against a distorted and exaggerated assessment of a problem. Were such "utopias" to be realized, all of the many men and women who do not feel oppressed by the old system would need to be reeducated so as to see their true victimizer and victim roles. Because Elshtain thinks that very few people really believe the assertions of radical feminists, their desired outcome would necessarily entail a highly coercive and brutal reeducation process.

What makes radical feminist solutions most dangerous for Elshtain is the threat that they pose to the existence of the private family. According to her, elimination of the private family would entail nothing less than the destruction of our ability to function as social beings. This argument is connected to her belief that it is only in the private family unit that children can experience the primary attachments to specific adults who are essential to development of the skills needed to connect productively with other individuals. Citing examples of neglected children in the communes of the 1960s and a "wild" boy who grew up alone in France and was subsequently incapable of living in society, Elshtain makes the strong case that the family must be understood as a "categorical imperative of human existence."[32] Further, although she concurs with many of the feminist positions as to why the current configurations of the public/private split hurt women, she maintains that feminists must subordinate their concerns as long as there is any danger that the proposed solutions will interfere with children's need for long-term, intergenerational ties with specific adults.

The feminist political thinker must similarly ask at what price she would gain the world for herself or other women, utterly rejecting those victories that come at the cost of the bodies and spirits of human infants. Unless this reflexivity is ongoing and central, feminism is in peril of losing its soul. The feminist concerned with a reconstructive ideal of the private sphere must begin by affirming the essential needs of children for basic, long-term ties with specific others.[33]

Elshtain is certain that the best place for children is in a familial context protected from the pressures of the public world. In keeping with this view, she is adamant that feminists should support maintaining a clear split between private and public.

It would be easy to infer that what Elshtain is proposing is nothing more than a return to a patriarchal model of public and private—with women relegated to the domestic sphere and men occupying and controlling the public, political sphere. Relative to domestic violence, it is difficult to see at first glance how Elshtain's suggestion that traditional arrangements be preserved could represent anything but a worsening of the violence. However, examination of her argument reveals that a principal objective of her analysis is the empowerment of women *through* their central position in the private sphere. Along with maternal feminists such as Sara Ruddick, Elshtain holds that it is in their capacity as mothers and homemakers that women can have the most profound impact.[34] The notion, developed most fully by Ruddick, is that the mothering of small children requires women to develop uniquely maternal values, such as compassion, humility, attentiveness, sensitivity, and a strong orientation toward preserving life.[35]

The connection between mothering and the public sphere derives from maternal feminism: rather than trying to adopt the individualistic and competitive attitudes that characterize that sphere, women should use their maternal perspective to transform the conduct of politics. According to Elshtain, accomplishing the latter would not only improve the quality of government and citizenship—creating what she calls the "ethical polity"—but would also help to bring about a much needed reevaluation of the private sphere and the activities therein.

Although Elshtain never goes so far as to advocate a policy of absolute nonintervention in cases of domestic violence, she manifestly thinks feminists are mistaken in locating the primary source of the violence in private familial structures. Instead, her analysis suggests that violence within familial relationships is more likely the result of the conflicts and frustrations that are generated when adults leave the family to engage in activities associated with citizenship and employment. As Elshtain describes it, when parents return home, they bring their stress and anger with them; and as a consequence, "conflicts that originate 'outside' get displaced 'inside,' perhaps into the very heart of the family's emotional existence."[36] Contributing to the potential that such pressures will result in physical violence is the erosion of values such as gentleness, connection, and responsibility that were traditionally instilled (by women) within the context of the private family. For example, in Elshtain's view, the "diseases of nonattachment" that "lead to the inability of the child to modify his or her aggressive impulses" can be traced to a failure to provide the child with the intense emotional ties required as an infant.[37] Thus, according to this frame of reference, feminist responses to violence against women that call for the politicization of familial relations paradoxically threaten to further devalue the very institution that stands as the best hope for addressing the root causes of many of the most serious social ills, including violence.

Liberal Feminism: Shifting Boundaries and Providing Protection

The third set of solutions explored in this chapter to the problems associated with the public/private split are those offered by theorists who identify themselves as liberal feminists. Given the prominence during the past three hundred years of liberalism as a guide to the structuring of political and social relations, it is hardly surprising that the range and number of liberal approaches to the public/private relationship are enormous. To accommodate this diversity, the discussion of liberal solutions consists of three parts: (1) an outline of the original liberal feminist position, taken by political theorists of the nineteenth century and suffragettes at the turn of the century; (2) a brief discussion of the various ways in which these arguments were revised by liberal feminists in the 1960s and 1970s; and (3) a review of the recent efforts by progressive liberal feminists to extend these arguments.

Broadly, it is fair to say that liberal feminists of all types are in agreement with Elshtain to the extent that they reject radical arguments about the need to eliminate all distinctions between public and private. For them, the solution to the oppression and violence that women experience in the private sphere is to work within existing institutional arrangements to ensure, simultaneously, equal treatment and empowerment by bringing women into the realm of politics as a force in their own right. For example, in his essay *The Subjection of Women,* which to this day stands as one of the clearest and most influential expressions of liberal feminist ideas, John Stuart Mill explicitly linked domestic violence to the failure to grant women a legal status equal to that of their husbands. According to Mill, the brutal treatment of women in the home was the predictable outcome of a system of laws that operated to establish their "legal slavery," causing men "to feel a sort of disrespect and contempt towards their own wife which they do not feel towards any other woman . . . and which makes her seem to them an appropriate subject for any kind of indignity."[38] An essential component of this "legal slavery" was that women were taught from a very young age that "their ideal of character is the very opposite to that of men; not self-will, and government by self-control, but submission, and yielding to the control of others."[39] Mill's solution was to give women the same rights that men enjoyed, which would entail equalizing relations in the private sphere through revisions to the marital contract and opening up the public sphere by granting women access to political and economic activities.

Although Mill believed that formal legal equality would have a beneficial impact on the formation of both men's and women's characters, he also assumed that even after women had become educated and politically active, their primary interest would remain (by choice, of course) within the domestic realm.[40] His assumption was shared by other liberal feminists of the period, including Mary Wollstonecraft, who in 1792 published *A Vindication of the Rights of Women*. She argued for women's rights on the basis that the activities of public citizenship would enhance a woman's ability to be a good wife and mother in the private sphere by facilitating the cultivation of her rational capacities.[41] In a similar way, the American suffragettes relied heavily on strategies that emphasized the moralizing impact that women would have on politics because of the natural virtues developed through caring for children and the home.[42] Significantly, the assumption that women would choose to stay within the domestic realm enabled these early liberal feminists to assert that the political enfranchisement of women would bring great benefits (including decreasing violence in the home) but not actually require a radical restructuring of existing gender roles.

The assumption within liberal feminist theory that the position of women as the primary caretakers of the home was an unproblematic "choice" underwent a significant change during what is now known as the "second wave" of the women's movement. Beginning in the 1960s, it became apparent to many women that although they enjoyed more legal rights than ever before, they confronted a multitude of serious problems within the private sphere that were going unaddressed. In her extremely influential best-selling book, *The Feminine Mystique*, Betty Friedan described what she called "the problem that had no name." Its symptoms, experienced most acutely by middle-class housewives, included isolation, unhappiness, guilt, and loneliness. Friedan attributed these feelings to the presence of a "feminine mystique" in American culture that operated to convince women that they should be completely satisfied by lives that revolved around taking care of the suburban household. In addition to a general feeling of malaise, Friedan and such other liberal feminists of the period as Elizabeth Janeway argued that the isolation, economic dependency, and social expectations of deference that accompanied their role undermined women's sense of self-worth and ultimately served to stunt the development of their rational capacities as individuals.[43] Although domestic violence was not the primary focus of these second wave liberal feminist discussions, one of the most serious consequences consistently attributed to women's isolation in the private sphere was loss of the ability effectively to challenge abuse or exit a violent relationship. Friedan wrote, "Only economic independence can free a woman to marry for love, not for status or financial support, or to leave a loveless, intolerable, humiliating marriage, or to eat, dress, rest, and move if she plans not to marry."[44]

The primary goal of the liberal feminist agenda during the 1970s and 1980s was to bring about structural and legal change that would enable women to experience what men already had: the opportunity to play *both* public and private roles. In keeping with this objective, the reforms proposed were concerned largely with ensuring equal access to, and fair treatment within, the public sphere. It is important to emphasize that these changes were *not* designed to alter the boundaries between public and private. Unlike the radical feminists, liberal feminists did not believe that there was something inherently oppressive about heterosexual sexual relations or the maternal role. They were oppressive only when they resulted in women's inability to explore and develop the public elements of their personalities. And, in contrast to Elshtain, many liberal feminists during this period sincerely believed that women could "have it all" without incurring serious costs to themselves or their children.

Liberal feminists have recently begun to express doubt about the second wave strategy of pursuing equal opportunity in the public sphere as a means of addressing the problems and vulnerabilities associated with the position of women as the primary caretakers within the familial realm. One of the earliest and most serious questions about this strategy arose from the recognition by a number of feminists that solutions centered on empowering women to move into the public sphere through the expansion of employment opportunities failed to take into account that working-class and poor women, who had always worked outside the home in large numbers, still encountered many of the same problems of vulnerability and powerlessness faced by full-time housewives. Additional doubts have emerged among liberal feminists with the growing realization that, despite some progress, women continue to earn substantially less than men and still find it very difficult to make it into the ranks of the most desirable and high-status professions.

Susan Moller Okin addresses these gaps and provides an example of a contemporary liberal feminist response. In *Justice, Gender, and the Family,* she states that the persistence of gendered patterns of inequality in the public sphere can be traced to a failure of liberal theory to account adequately for the vulnerabilities generated by the predominant assumption of both sexes that the woman will assume the primary caretaking and domestic responsibilities regardless of whether she engages in paid employment.[45] Because the decision to direct significant energy into mothering and household maintenance can be framed as a "free choice," it has been possible to avoid applying liberal standards of justice to the home.[46]

Echoing the arguments of Mill, Okin carefully shows how these "asymmetrical vulnerabilities" operate to generate power imbalances that exert a corrupting influence on all family members, ultimately creating a human relations climate in which "there is great scope for unchecked injustice to flourish."[47] Unlike Mill and other early liberal feminists, however, Okin does not think that simply extending legal rights to women will effectively address the patterns of domination and submission in the family. Furthermore, because she believes that inequality within the family and the public activities of work and politics are closely connected, she also questions the adequacy of second-wave liberal feminist strategies that focus chiefly on increasing women's participation in the public sphere.

According to Okin, to address problems such as violence in the family we need to ensure that the family is subjected to the same standards of justice that apply in the public realm of work and politics. As a liberal feminist, Okin naturally turns to state regulation as the means of choice. For example, included among her suggestions for reform is legislation that requires employers to divide a pay check between an employee and the employee's partner in cases where that partner contributes to raising children. Although the suggestion sounds radical, Okin counters that in most instances it would only codify what most people already recognize: "that the household income is rightly shared, because in a real sense jointly earned."[48] The major benefit of such an enactment would be to diminish the level of potential vulnerability that women expose themselves to when they commit a significant amount of energy to rearing children. Under such a system, full-time mothers would automatically have access to a reliable source of income. In addition to disrupting patterns of continuous financial dependency, formalizing equal allocations of income among adult family members would help to communicate a societal commitment to enhancing the status of caregivers within families. Okin contends that through such laws the state can play a more positive role in protecting women from asymmetrical power relations that contribute to such problems as domestic violence.

Okin's recommendations are representative of contemporary liberal feminist strategies that seek to shift the boundary demarcating the family from politics. Liberal feminists in the 1980s and 1990s continued to develop the connections between the personal and the political through the application of legal standards to more and more issues that were traditionally treated as private. In this respect, they do not share Elshtain's resistance to politicizing familial relations. Still, it is important to be clear that unlike radical feminist suggestions, the liberal feminist strategy of realigning the public and the private to represent women's interests and concerns more effectively is not a fundamental challenge to the maintenance of the family as a presumptively private association. To the extent that relations within the family become matters for the political realm within a liberal feminist framework, they are politicized through carefully circumscribed laws designed to protect specific rights of individuals according to broadly agreed-upon principles such as justice. By relying on established institutional mechanisms of intervention, liberal feminists are able to maintain their commitment to boundaries even as they challenge them.

Feminist Analyses of Public and Private

The varied feminist analyses of the public/private split provide conceptual support for efforts to combat domestic violence in a number of important ways. First, the delineation of how privacy can function to isolate women speaks to the experiences of victims and survivors who report feeling as if they had no choice but to deal with the violence on their own. Additionally, feminist articulations of how patterns of dependency and vulnerability within the family are variously reinforced by women's inadequate access to (and status within) the public sphere have contributed to a growing understanding of why some women stay within the relative "security" of abusive relationships. Also, feminist arguments about how the liberal ideology of "separate spheres" operates to obscure the political nature of problems that occur within private relationships help to explain why widespread domestic violence has for many years been virtually ignored as a major public policy issue.

Beyond simply explaining the status quo, however, feminist critiques of the public/private division have also positively contributed to concrete efforts to challenge the image of domestic violence as a private concern. The identification of battering as a "women's issue" was instrumental in creating momentum and solidarity around the fight to provide services to victims and to reform the laws regulating domestic assault. The positive effects of those efforts should not be underestimated. The United States has gone from not having a single shelter for battered women in the

1960s to having more than 1,800 community-based centers that assist individuals experiencing violence at the hands of those with whom they are intimate.[49] Domestic violence is now defined as a crime in every state, with the majority having significantly increased the penalties for persons who are convicted. Across the nation, there has also been a concerted effort to improve the quality of the police response to domestic violence calls.[50]

Still, despite such indications of progress, many challenges remain. Funding for shelters and victim services remains woefully inadequate. Many counties do not have a single shelter, and those that do are frequently forced to turn away women and their children because of lack of space.[51] Although domestic violence is no longer the "dirty little secret" that it once was, many victims continue to keep their experiences of abuse to themselves because of fear, shame, isolation, or all three.[52] Even so, although most people would now agree that family violence should not be ignored simply because it occurs within the private realm, such acknowledgments do not diminish the serious tensions that are created when the state seeks to intervene in events that have occurred within a familial context.

The continuing presence of tensions raises the question of whether the feminist reconstructions of the relationship between public and private can help in working through the difficulties and paradoxes that are associated with contemporary efforts to address domestic violence. There is no doubt that feminist analyses of public and private have helped to pave the way for significant forward momentum in terms of how we view this problem. However, the potential of these analyses for providing the basis for the development of a model of the public/private relationship that will be better equipped to address the dilemmas encountered by those who seek to intervene in cases of domestic violence is much less clear. The major limitations of the various feminist reconstructions of public and private arise from a reliance within each model on narrow and essentialist assumptions about the meaning of womanhood that are discussed in the following section.

Essentialist Foundations in Feminist Reconstructions of Public and Private Boundaries

The term *feminist* describes a category of theorists who focus on gender in their analyses. Within feminism, however, one finds great variation regarding both assessment of the main problems ensuing from the public/private split and the solutions proposed. One of the questions that this diversity occasions is: How is it possible for a group of theorists who fundamentally agree that the division harms women to come up with radically different, even contradictory, solutions? The answer can be found by posing yet another question: *Whom* do these theorists hope their solutions will benefit? At first glance, the question appears odd. After all, if the feminist motivation to reconceptualize or eliminate boundaries of public and private derives from a common concern over how the boundaries hurt women, should it not be obvious that "women" will be the starting point and main beneficiaries of any solution that is proposed? Intuitively, the answer is yes, of course. But there is more to this answer than meets the eye.

Take Elshtain, for example. Although she undoubtedly is concerned with the ways in which the public/private split hurts women, when it comes to proposing an alternative, she is adamant that the preeminent concern of feminists should always be the effect on children. Because she believes that children need long-term intergenerational nurturing and maintains, along with many maternal feminists, that women are uniquely suited to provide this type of care, it is hardly surprising that she argues that even as they pursue their own ambitions, the primary commitment for women should be to do what is required to preserve and strengthen the private family. Thus, we can see that the focus of Elshtain's search for a reconceptualization of public and private is not on women alone but rather on women and the children for whom they are responsible. To the extent that women fit into her vision for the future, it is first and foremost as mothers.

Likewise, the starting point of liberal feminist theories about how to alter the public/private division is not women but, rather, the "liberal individual." As prior discussions demonstrate, liberal feminist conceptualizations vary regarding the meaning of women's individuality and the significance of social context to its free realization. Historic changes and contemporary controversies mean that it is extremely difficult to pinpoint the liberal feminist position on the public/private dichotomy. Still, even within this diversity, there remains within liberal feminism an abiding and central focus on the issue of what we can do as a society to ensure that all *individuals* in our society have the opportunity to grow to their full potential. Significantly, although the particular concerns associated with being female are certainly considered by liberal feminists, their question is not, "What do *women* need in order to maximize their potential as individuals?" Rather, within these theories it is generally assumed that once women overcome the gender roles that have oppressed them, that special attention to their status "as women" can be left behind. In fact, as we have

seen, one of the major criticisms that liberal feminists have of the pub-
lic/private split is that it artificially exaggerates gender differences.

The resulting absence of embodied women in the liberal analysis of
and solutions to the public/private split is the basis for some of the
strongest criticism that radical feminists have of this position. For example, Catharine MacKinnon has argued that the "abstracted individual"
upon whom liberal theories are premised are (upon closer examination)
male individuals writ large and, therefore, such theories do not speak to
women's interests at all.[53] From MacKinnon's perspective, the best way to
avoid the irrelevance that accompanies such abstractions is to explicitly
make women central. This is accomplished by a singular focus on the fundamental characteristic that has historically differentiated women from
men: their sex. It is the sexual act and its consequences (that is, pregnancy) that have enabled men to dominate women since the beginning of
time. The only way to liberate women is to confront the implicit oppression of all heterosexual sexual relations and activities by exposing their political nature. Thus, according to MacKinnon's radical analysis, because
the liberal distinction between public and private functions to construct
sex as an intimate (and therefore apolitical) activity, it should be approached by feminists as a powerful obstacle to women's freedom that
should be challenged.

The differences among feminist theorists concerning the public/pri-
vate split can be traced to a fundamental disagreement among them regarding the aspect of women's lives most in need of liberation. Is it
women as mothers, women as individuals, or women as sex objects? It
may be that the dichotomization of public and private harms women no
matter how they are classified, but as we have seen, the aspect of womanhood that is identified as most important to protect or liberate has a significant impact on the solutions that are proposed.

Thus in assessing the value of these reconceptualizations to the issue
of domestic violence, it is important to consider the views of a wide range
of feminist theorists who have raised serious questions about both the
utility and the accuracy of approaches that are developed around singular
conceptions of womanhood. For example, postmodern feminists have effectively questioned whether or not it is legitimate to assume even the existence of a unitary subject, let alone one that can be unproblematically
identified as "woman."[54] Other feminists such as Elizabeth Spelman have
emphasized the long-standing tendency within feminist theory to ignore
or paper over differences between women that derive from variations associated with race and class. In some cases, this tendency can be traced to

patterns of racism and classism within the women's movement which have resulted in the exclusion of non-white, working class, and poor women's perspectives. But as Spelman points out, even if feminists are able to successfully confront problems of racism and classism, they will still be left with the fundamental "paradox at the heart of feminism: Any attempt to talk about all women in terms of something we have in common undermines attempts to talk about the difference among us, and vice versa."[55] Finally, through the development and elaboration of the concept of intersectionality, black feminist theorists have emphasized the crucial importance of developing an understanding of gendered oppression and violence that is capable of accounting for multiple and overlapping impacts of racism, classism, and sexism on the lives of women of color.

Each of these approaches shares an acute awareness of the fact that women are constituted by multiple identities, including but not exclusive of the identity associated with gender. Also implicit in these approaches is the understanding that the majority of women play many roles simultaneously, adapting to the demands of wife, mother, and autonomous individual. In addition to the enormous amount of work that this balancing act requires are the complex and often heart-rending dilemmas produced when the demands of these multiple roles conflict.

Feminist Reconstructions and the Challenge of Domestic Violence

Domestic violence provides an excellent illustration of the various types of conflicts that can materialize as a result of multiple role identities. Some of the specific difficulties that are routinely faced by victims of domestic violence also illustrate why the essentialist assumptions of feminist reconstructions of the public/private dichotomy weaken their potential to contribute positively to the task of developing strategies. Take, for instance, a battered woman's decision as to whether she should tolerate the abuse of her partner in silence, try to stop the abuse, or leave the relationship. According to a liberal feminist analysis, the fact that the violence has been traditionally defined as a private problem is going to circumscribe the options available. Given the liberal feminist objective of maximizing the liberty and freedom of all individuals, the best way to help the woman is to make sure that an effective system of public intervention is in place. This means that if she calls the police, they will arrive quickly, will look upon the violence as a criminal matter, and will arrest the batterer if the injuries are visible. Furthermore, when and if she decides to leave the relationship, public resources such as restraining orders, shelters, and support services should be available. In line with the liberal feminist analysis, the existence of such public responses functions to deprivatize domestic violence while maintaining the classical liberal boundary that protects the private realm of the family from unwarranted and potentially oppressive government intrusions.

The liberal feminist approach takes it for granted that if given the opportunity, *all* individuals will seek to maximize their best interest. Furthermore, there is an assumption that a rational pursuit of self-interest in this scenario will almost always mean leaving the abuser. The approach does not have the capacity to account for the actions of victims who fail to take advantage of resources once they are made available. It follows, then, that liberal feminist revisions of the boundaries that define certain problems as public or private, although potentially helpful to many women, do not provide a mechanism for asking why some victims choose to stay despite having legal recourse. Until such questioning becomes central, the reaction to failed efforts to help a domestic violence victim through state intervention is likely to alternate between blaming her for the violence or to giving up on her as "a hopeless case." What is clearly missing from these interpretations is an appreciation of the many legitimate reasons a victim might have for not turning to public officials for help.[56] Included among them are distrust of police and state authority; fears that bringing in outsiders will escalate the violence; love for the abuser; a desire to keep the family and relationship together; feeling shame about the violence; and wanting to avoid public disclosure and exposure.

Although a decision to remain within an abusive relationship might appear irrational or masochistic to an outsider, it can also be understood as the result of a careful evaluation by the victim of how to maximize the achievement of competing objectives and multiple roles. In the majority of cases, leaving the relationship appears to be best in terms of the interests of the victim. However, leaving might also be viewed as a betrayal of powerful societal expectations that women will take responsibility for maintaining the unity, peace, and privacy of the family unit. In light of this scenario, the points made by Elshtain regarding the need for feminists to make the well-being of children and families a priority are much more effective than the liberal feminist analysis in illuminating the seemingly irrational actions of victims who choose to stay for the sake of the family. This is not to suggest that Elshtain is advocating that victims of domestic violence should simply put up with abuse so that their children can remain within a conventional family pattern. Patently, families torn by domestic violence are going to be poorly equipped to provide the type of "long-term intergenerational nurturing" that Elshtain believes essential for children to develop into healthy adults. Still, in a situation where there are few alternatives, the prospect of homelessness may indeed convince many women that putting up with violence really is in the best interests of their children.

Elshtain's discussion of the distinction between public and private highlights the important insight that, for women in particular, the pursuit of individualism often requires serious and difficult tradeoffs. In this respect, her approach appears to be more sensitive than those of some liberal feminists to the fact that most women occupy many roles and (most important) the implicit demands of these roles can conflict. Despite such strengths, as with the liberal feminist approach, Elshtain's analysis of the relationship between public and private suffers from a number of key inadequacies as a framework for understanding and addressing domestic violence. Again, the primary source of the problems associated with this approach can be traced to a dependence on a particular view of womanhood and its central purpose.

According to Elshtain, feminist efforts to develop solutions to the many problems that plague the American family should begin with a commitment to revitalizing the private sphere through a more vigorous application of the familial values of care, compassion, and peacefulness that are already implicit in the tasks that the family is uniquely designed to accomplish. For her, the answer is *not* in subjecting the family to public standards and intervention. Her strategy would "unite rather than divide women" because the "transformative values" that Elshtain has in mind are especially well developed in women, who, as mothers, have historically had the most experience with protecting "fragile and vulnerable human existence."[57] Her arguments rely on the assumption that women do, in fact, embody the maternal values that she views as so potentially powerful.[58] But as statistics on child abuse and neglect by women show, not all women are the paragons of motherhood that Elshtain envisions. Skillful parenting takes more than just maternal instinct. Rearing children also takes economic resources, positive role models, healthy and supportive familial relationships, and community support. Elshtain reveals her understanding both of the importance and the absence of such social supports when she calls on feminists to harness the power of maternally based values to bring about "the structural changes in American life" that are necessary to revitalize the private family.

Where this analysis comes up short is in explaining what can be done, prior to revitalizing familial ideals, for those who currently lack the resources and tools to create loving and supportive familial relationships.[59] Further, because the driving force behind such changes are maternal ethics, the responsibility for healthy families is placed directly on the women, who embody these values. For women who have the resources and the ability to develop and express these maternal values, an increase in the worth ascribed to this perspective will certainly be empowering. However, it is highly doubtful that Elshtain's reconstructive vision for the family will serve to empower women who neither match the image of motherhood assumed nor who, for whatever reason, are simply not able to realize or express their maternal potential. Once again, domestic violence provides a clear example of some of the practical dilemmas that are implicated in this theoretical approach.

Research documenting the coping strategies employed by domestic violence victims has demonstrated that many of the most widely used tactics for preventing violent episodes revolve around the perfect performance of household duties. Over and over, survivors talk about what they now see as naive beliefs that the violence would stop "If only I kept the house clean," "If I could make sure dinner was always on the table," or "If I could just be the perfect mother."[60] The persistence of such strategies, in spite of their long-term ineffectiveness, is a testament to the strength of the pervasive message that women's power resides in their position as wives and mothers. Although the intention of maternal feminist arguments is undeniably empowerment, the basic assumptions that drive these theories tie directly into this narrow interpretation of womanhood.

The consequences in cases of domestic violence of reinforcing prevalent interpretations can be quite problematic. Most obvious is the effect on victims of battering who believe that they should be able to use their feminine powers and skills to maintain unity and peace in the home. Even when the impossibility of this goal is starkly obvious, many women continue to stay in abusive situations either because they hold onto the hope that they can change the batterer or because they are ashamed of their failure to do so. Reinforcing this pattern is the use by many batterers of alleged shortcomings in the performance of tasks associated with homemaking and mothering to justify specific acts of violence.

Other feminist scholars have repeatedly identified the ease with which domestic responsibilities can be used to keep women in damaging relationships as evidence of an important flaw in maternally oriented feminist theories. In the view of Joan Tronto and others, these conservative theories fail to take seriously enough that many of the characteristics that they portray as naturally arising from women's maternal nature may have been developed as strategies to compensate for and adapt to a position of relative powerlessness.[61]

In her discussion of the fight for female suffrage in the United States, Elshtain makes a related point: the political strategies utilized by the suffragettes, which often depended on assertions about women's special morality as the protectors of the private sphere, were easily sentimentalized in such a way that the political potential of women was completely undermined.[62] Despite the drawbacks, Elshtain herself nevertheless relies on very similar strategies, saying simply that feminists must "refuse to lapse into a sentimental rendering of the values and language which flow from 'mothering.'"[63] What is missing from Elshtain's theory is a place from which feminists might gain enough critical distance from the family to assess which feminine qualities might have transformative potential and which are simply a product of powerlessness within the family. As we have seen, Elshtain adamantly rejects both liberal and radical feminist efforts to challenge patterns of domination in the home by subjecting familial relations to a political analysis because of her conviction that they function to further undermine and weaken the already beleaguered American family.[64] Yet in her attempt to protect the family from politicization, Elshtain generates a theory that does not have the capacity to distinguish circumstances where traditional roles are empowering to women from circumstances where those same roles may be directly contributing to patterns of violence and domination within intimate relationships.

It is in the radical analysis that we find the most clearly articulated method for identifying the ways in which traditional feminine roles contribute to domestic violence. However, just as with the liberal and conservative feminist approaches, the radical feminist analysis of the public/private relationship is also ultimately undermined by its dependence on an overly simplistic vision of womanhood. The element of radical feminist theory that creates the most difficulties in this respect is the assumption that all women are oppressed by men and that they experience this oppression in the same way. As we noted earlier, radical feminists see the distinction between public and private in liberal society as a central mechanism through which this oppression is accomplished and justified. According to MacKinnon, privacy functions to support sexual coercion, inequality, and acts of violence by framing them as personal matters whenever they occur in private settings or within the context of personal relations. The significance of this designation is that within a liberal framework, when an issue or problem is viewed as personal or private, it becomes much more difficult to generate the level of public concern required in a representative democracy to justify political action to address it. For women, this dynamic is especially problematic because much of the oppression that women experience occurs within the context of private relationships.[65] MacKinnon therefore contends that one of the primary tasks of feminists is to undermine the liberal separation of public and private by demonstrating the political nature of "personal" problems.

The radical feminist approach has proved to be a very powerful explanatory tool in helping us to understand why problems such as domestic violence have received so little public intervention. However, the limitations of this approach become apparent when it is applied as a framework for developing practical solutions to specific problems occurring within the family realm. In the case of domestic violence, the radical analysis has included a dual emphasis: (1) exposing the political nature of battering and (2) developing a program of public intervention. During the early days of the battered women's movement, radical feminist theories often served as the basis for the development of shelter programs that were explicitly directed at changing women's consciousness about the violence in their lives. These activities were designed to help victims see that their experiences of abuse were widely shared and could be traced to larger patterns of male domination. Along with liberal feminists, radical feminists also supported efforts to transform domestic violence into a criminal matter warranting serious penalties.

Although such initiatives were (and are) steps in the right direction, they also have shortcomings. First, for many women, the radical assertion that "the primary oppression faced by all women is patriarchy" simply does not ring true. Even women who have experienced violence at the hands of male partners often feel intense loyalty to these men and find it very hard to conceptualize them as their primary oppressors. The radical feminist designation of all men as "oppressors" results in a theory of public and private that does not allow for distinctions among men. The absence of distinctions is significant because it results in a failure to acknowledge the reality that many minority men and men from the lower classes are also without power in our public institutions. Carol Brown, for example, relies on this insight to argue that we have transitioned from a private to a public patriarchy. Although men have less power to dominate women in the home, the dynamic of domination has not disappeared: it has simply been transplanted to the public sphere. Brown's take: "The power of higher level men over all women has increased while the power of lower level men over any women has decreased. Even higher level men have lost their personal control over their women but what they have gained is economic control over the larger society which subordinates women."[66] The radical feminist analysis is especially problematic for women of color, some of whom are likely to experience racism, not sexism, as the predominant source of oppression in their lives.[67] Likewise, women who are economically disadvantaged often find that the challenges they face in their day-to-day lives are more clearly connected to their class than to their gender status.

It could reasonably be argued that it is unfair to critique a theory based on the contention that it does not perfectly describe the internal experiences of all women. However, at least in the case of radical feminists, the criticism is justified by the universalism of their claims and solutions. The policy recommendations issuing from a radical analysis come directly out of the assumption that gender oppression is the source of *all* oppression and that women should therefore be eager to uproot patriarchal structures wherever they encounter them. As with the liberal approach, there is very little room in the radical analysis for victims of domestic violence who clearly want the violence to stop but are simply not willing to impose legal sanctions on their batterers to achieve that end. As a result, the very real fear felt by many women that going public with their problems could result in further victimization—by public officials who harbor racist feelings toward them or their abusers—is disregarded.[68] Also overlooked is the harsh reality that for many victims, leaving or having their abuser jailed is very likely to result in impoverishment and homelessness for themselves and their children.

What is missing from the radical analysis is an adequate appreciation of the variety of costs that can accompany politicization of issues that have traditionally been understood as private. The radical argument that problems such as domestic violence are *already* political because of their basis in patriarchal relations of oppression and dominance may in fact be correct. But accurate or not, there is still a substantial difference between reconceptualizing something in theory and transforming it in practice. Misguided or not, many battered women view their situation as intensely personal and are reluctant to make use of solutions that depend on the politicization of the details of their intimate relationships. Ultimately, the essentialistic assumptions implicit in radical theories eventuate in a scenario where women who do not fit or agree with these interpretations are left to fend for themselves when facing domestic violence. Ironically, contrary to the intention of radical theories, the outcome for such women is the reprivatization of the abuse in such a way that it can no longer be reached by political solutions.

Conclusion

John Locke's designation of the family as a naturally private association was intended to enhance the ability of citizens within a liberal polity to maximize both their individual autonomy and their ability to connect with others. Through their focus on the interests and status of women in our society, feminist theorists provide a compelling account of the many ways that this arrangement, though designed to optimize the interests of all citizens, has historically functioned to disadvantage women.

Despite their various limitations, the feminist critiques and reconceptualizations of the relationship between the private realm of the family and the public sphere of politics contribute to a larger objective: increasing our understanding of the implications of the dichotomy for contemporary efforts to address domestic violence. By highlighting the ways in which the designation of the family as a private association can isolate women, feminist analysis adds depth to efforts to explain why so many victims of domestic violence fail to report abuse and continue to live with it. Elshtain's arguments about the central importance of maternal responsibilities to large numbers of women provide insight into decisions to stay that are made with the best interests of children in mind.

Points made by liberal feminist theorists regarding the difficulties faced by women who seek to establish independence and authority outside the domestic realm are also very important. The relative inability of women to move back and forth between public and private spheres goes a long way toward explaining why, rather than serving as a source of liberty, Locke's dichotomization of public and private has persistently contributed to a situation where women's autonomy and their ability to get their concerns heard within the political realm have been undermined. The latter point, when combined with radical feminist arguments about the ways in which the public/private split has operated ideologically to obscure the political significance of domestic violence, also helps to explain why public officials virtually ignored such a widespread and serious problem for so long.

Still, despite the value of these feminist critiques, it is not clear that the proposed reconstructions are any more capable than the classical liberal model of *addressing* the complex dilemmas present in instances of domestic violence. The general applicability of these approaches is severely constrained by their reliance on overly simplistic and essentialistic assumptions about women and, at least in the radical analysis, about men as well. As we have seen, although quite different from one another, the feminist

reconstructions of public and private presented in this chapter are all developed from very particular interpretations of *why* women are oppressed
by the division between public and private and of *what* they need to do to
free themselves from the oppression. The rigidity of the approaches prevents their adaptation to the multitude of overlapping identities and commitments that characterize the lives of women. Consequently, rather than
providing a framework for engaging the tension between individualism
and connection, each approach seeks to resolve the tension by developing
solutions that are designed to liberate the particular aspect of a woman's
identity that is deemed most crucial.

The practical implication of these shortcomings is that none of these
approaches to the public/private division is likely to facilitate the development of a public response to battering that will be suited to the needs and
desires of a wide range of victims. The most probable prospect, consequently, is the perpetuation of the status quo: large numbers of women
will continue to believe that their best, or only, alternative is to deal with
domestic abuse on their own. Where, then, can we find a basis for an approach to this relationship that will be more amenable to the creation of
an effective public response to domestic violence?

Four

The Legal Regulation of Domestic Violence

I T IS NOT POSSIBLE TO CONDUCT A SUSTAINED inquiry into the boundaries that define public and private in the United States without eventually encountering questions that can be answered only by examining the legal system. The inevitability of legal analysis in this context demonstrates the profound influence that the law has on nearly all aspects of U.S. society, a phenomenon that can be traced to the American Revolution. As Paul Kahn describes it, "Americans believe they created themselves first through a violent, revolutionary break with an inherited, unjust, monarchic order and then through a positive act of popular lawmaking."[1]

Such early experiences of self-creation through lawmaking served to strengthen the constitutive power of the rule of law in the United States; a power that extends well beyond its obvious regulative function.[2] This means, among other things, that in addition to establishing and policing the boundaries between the public and private spheres, legal pronouncements give meaning and expression to the normative understandings about relations within the spheres that are embedded in the impulse to establish boundaries in the first place.

Although there is clearly a strong relationship between the process of boundary construction and the law, the nature of the relationship is multifaceted, including both regulative and symbolic elements. In its regulative function, the law plays a critical role in the demarcation of the boundaries between public and private because, in the United States at least, the enactment, interpretation, and enforcement of laws through democratically prescribed channels are the principal means by which the state exerts its authority. One of the main functions of state authority is to protect the autonomy and freedom of all citizens, and a key component of that task is the restriction of actions that are deemed to negatively impinge on the liberties of others. Thus, an examination of the historical patterns of state-backed legal interventions into domestic violence reveals the specific limits that have been placed on what is and is not allowed to occur within the realm of the family.

In addition to determining when the state can interfere in the affairs of citizens, the law also has a significant role in ensuring that state actors do not go too far in their efforts to regulate and protect citizens in areas traditionally marked as under the control of private individuals. Relative to domestic violence, the limits can be seen best in instances where a decision is made *not* to take legal action, despite evidence that the rights of one person have been violated by another (e.g., an abusive partner in the private sphere).

Finally, as the primary institutional mechanism for both limiting and exerting government authority over citizens, the law has become a symbolic marker in the United States of which topics and events should be treated as public and which should be respected as private. In this regard, the symbolic significance of the law can be distinguished from its instrumental function. As Joseph Gusfield argues, law can be viewed "as symbolizing the public affirmation of social ideals and norms as well as means of direct social control."[3] In keeping with this distinction, the following analysis of the significance of legal interventions for the status of domestic violence as a public problem in the United States will include an investigation of both the functional *and* symbolic impact that laws have had on how battering is conceptualized and approached. This analysis, in addition to enhancing our understanding of today's boundaries and providing insights into the norms and assumptions underlying those boundaries, represents an opportunity to reevaluate more generally some of the major advantages and disadvantages of a legalistic approach to this social problem.[4]

The Common-Law Approach to the Family

The story of the legal treatment of domestic violence in the United States begins with the common-law doctrine of marital chastisement in the colonies, which permitted a husband to subject his wife to moderate corporal punishment. The prerogative arose in the structuring of marriage, which assigned the husband authority over his wife. According to the laws of the day, marriage suspended a woman's individual legal status. In his 1765 commentaries on English common law, William Blackstone notes that "by marriage the husband and wife are one person in law: that is, the very being or legal existence of the woman is suspended in marriage."[5] This joining of persons was not merely symbolic but carried with it a number of very real consequences for both parties.[6]

For the woman, marriage meant that she could neither retain nor acquire her own property. She could not sign contracts, any earnings were controlled by the husband, and if the two separated, guardianship of their children was placed with the husband. For the man, marriage meant that he was responsible for his wife. He must provide for her and make certain that she behaved, publicly and privately, in a manner befitting a good wife. It was the latter responsibility that entailed legal authority to chastise her if necessary. Again, Blackstone's *Commentaries* provide insight into the common-law stance: "The husband also, by the old law might give his wife moderate correction. For, as he is to answer for her misbehavior, the law thought it reasonable to intrust him with this power of restraining her, by domestic chastisement."[7]

Chastisement was not an unlimited right. In fact, the positive function of the legal system in articulating this right was to specify when and to what extent chastisement was justified. As Blackstone tells us, "this power of correction was confined within reasonable bounds and the husband was prohibited from using any violence to his wife except as he may lawfully and reasonably do so in order to correct and chastise his wife."[8] Thus, the common-law rule on chastisement did not countenance unfettered brutality. To be "legally" justified, a husband's violence had to have higher ends, such as discipline and order. In this sense, the law of chastisement served to highlight the public significance of familial relations. The family, rather than being seen as completely separate from politics and order, through the rule of the patriarch played a fundamental role in the maintenance of public order.

Although originating in England, the body of common law exerted a tremendous influence on the structure of early American legal doctrine.[9] The influence is much evident in the laws dealing with marital relations that granted the American husband authority over his wife, including control of her property and earnings. The sanctioning of chastisement within marriage varied from state to state, with some states enacting legislation against marital violence[10] and others according it legitimacy.[11] Even in the former, there is little evidence to suggest active enforcement.[12] Still, during the nineteenth century, popular approval of domestic chastisement began to decline, and legal opinions mirrored the trend. By the latter half of the century, the courts were no longer openly expressing support for the common-law right of husbands to chastise their wives, and many judges began to object openly to marital violence. For example, in a 1883 case in Kentucky, the judge flatly declared, "The husband has no right to inflict personal chastisement upon his wife. She is entitled to the same protection from violence at the hands of her husband that a stranger is entitled to."[13]

A variety of explanations have been given for the eventual rejection of the law of chastisement in the United States. One possibility is the influence of the temperance and the women's suffrage movements of the nineteenth century. Both movements, albeit for different reasons, highlighted the horrors of abuse within the home. The temperance movement depicted domestic assault as one of the most vivid harms that could result from alcohol. Its extremely negative portrayals of drunken wife-beaters and husbands who drank away their wages may have undermined whatever positive association people had with moderate chastisement as an effective and humane route to household peace and order.[14] During roughly the same period, the suffrage movement pointed to the chastisement of wives by husbands as proof of the gross inequalities and abuses that were the lot of married women under common-law doctrines. However, suffragettes denounced domestic violence primarily as a means to highlight the necessity of granting women formal rights—such as the right to vote—that would empower women to protect themselves and their children.[15]

A related and probably more significant factor in the rejection of chastisement was the growing emphasis on the family as a realm where the objectives of order and obedience (originally the primary justifications for chastisement) were not appropriate or even necessary. Prior to the industrial revolution, the family, in addition to its role in reproduction, structured the economic and political activities of its members. An individual's position within the familial hierarchy essentially determined his or her position in society. However, with the emergence of a market-based economy and representative structures of governance, many of the activities previously within the domestic realm were conducted exclusively in such public realms as factories and legislatures.[16] The change had a profound effect on the definition of the family. The decline in its role in sustaining the economic and political ordering of society can be correlated with a growing perception of the family as a sentimental association. Americans began to view the family as ideally suited to providing the privacy, nurturing, and peace lacking in the competitive and impersonal worlds of the marketplace and politics.[17]

As the "angel of the house," the wife was to create an environment where children could flourish and men could find respite from the rigors of the outside world. A depiction of women who voluntarily devoted themselves to their household tasks out of love and duty replaced images found in the common law of wives as quasi-servants in need of regulation by their husbands. Within popular culture, the family was increasingly differentiated as a human association ordered according to altruism, cooperation, and self-sacrifice as opposed to the self-interested, competitive, and hierarchical values driving activities outside of its realm. Not surprisingly, the law of domestic chastisement did not fit well in this idealized family. The legal justification for chastisement depended on the supposed need to maintain an authority-based hierarchy within the household. That need was fading away—and with it, chastisement.

Entity Privacy and the Deregulation of Domestic Violence

The rejection of the legal doctrine of chastisement during the last part of the nineteenth century is significant in terms of what it tells us about changing conceptions of the family and its role within society. Ironically, the impact of the decline of the doctrine on the *incidence* of domestic violence is much less certain. It is necessary to acknowledge that asserting that the law should not grant husbands the right to hit their wives is *not* equivalent to believing that the government should employ legal force to prevent or stop violence in the home.

The decline of the law of chastisement, then, can at least partially be explained by a growing acceptance of the notion of the family as an association based on mutual affection and respect. This "modern" version of the family did not appear to require the formal grants of authority and regulation formerly provided by law. Thus, it is possible to see that the rejection of chastisement was not simply due to abhorrence of it: the rejection was part of a larger movement to remove legal regulation from the family. The pattern of legal response that emerged after the discrediting of chastisement supports this interpretation.

Out from under the rule of chastisement, judges faced a dilemma: How should they evaluate acts of violence in the home? By the turn of the century, most states had laws against family violence.[18] Although the laws served to clarify the emerging public opposition to state-sanctioned physical disciplining of wives, their enforcement created confusion. The primary difficulty was that the imposition of sanctions on perpetrators of domestic violence involved the state in familial relations to an unprecedented degree. The intervention ran counter to a range of still popular and important cultural norms about the nature of family relations. First and foremost, it threatened the status of the family as a private association. Although the meaning of family privacy varied dramatically depending on how the concept was employed, a number of elements stand out. One was the long-standing designation of the home as the proper location of the activities most closely associated with bodily functions, such as sexual relations and personal hygiene—activities increasingly construed as not to be seen by others. Additionally, as more families became able to afford homes with multiple rooms and doors that could be locked, the value of the family home in shielding certain activities from public view grew.[19] Thus, although the passage of legislation forbidding violence in the home may have been consistent with a rejection of chastisement, the realities of enforcement ran counter to a popular ideal of the familial realm as the space where the exercise of privacy should be inviolate.

But perhaps even more serious than the possibility of an occasional breach of familial privacy, enforcement threatened to undermine the basis for distinguishing between public and private relationships. The distinctions were critical because of the widespread practice of giving meaning to the content of particular interactions through the contrasting of opposites. "Public relationships" evolved out of the interactions with others in the course of earning money, obtaining necessary goods, contributing to the maintenance of the social fabric, and expressing views and interests through the political process. What the interactions had in common was that they were initiated by individuals to secure goods or services whose value is independent of the interaction. Such "public interactions" were continuously contrasted with "personal interactions," in which involvement with others was grounded in affection and mutual desire for intimacy rather than the desire to accomplish objectives outside the relationship. According to this schema, personal relationships require privacy because it is the ability to shut others out that gives meaning to our choices regarding our intimates. The privacy contributes to our capacity to reveal the most vulnerable elements of ourselves without fear of public shame or censure. During the latter part of the nineteenth century, the diminished role of the family in structuring the status of its members and economic production, and the corresponding shift toward it being a realm in which people could seek relief from outside demands, contributed powerfully to consolidation of the family as the site of intimate and private relations.[20]

In the decades following the demise of the chastisement doctrine, the need to preserve both a realm of intimacy and a clear distinction between public and private were invoked to justify a noninterventionist approach to cases of domestic violence. For example, in a case of wife battery in North Carolina in 1868, the state's supreme court included the following in its justification for a verdict of not guilty:

However great are the evils of ill temper, quarrels, and even personal conflicts inflicting only temporary pain, they are not comparable with the evils which would result from raising the curtain, and exposing to public curiosity and criticism, the nursery and the bed chamber. Every household has and must have, a government of its own, modeled to suit the temper, disposition and condition of its inmates. Mere ebullitions of passion, impulsive violence, and temporary pain, affection will soon forget and forgive; and each member will find excuse for the other in his own frailties. But when trifles are taken hold of by the public, and the parties are exposed and disgraced, and each endeavors to justify himself or herself by criminating the other, that which ought to be forgotten in a day, will be remembered for life.[21]

The disastrous results of bringing domestic violence into the public realm that are cited in this opinion reveal important assumptions about the appropriate usage of law in a domestic context. The assertion that "every household has and must have, a government of its own" conveys the message that the legal mechanisms that are designed to resolve objectively disputes between public citizens are not appropriate to the specialized and private realm of the family.

According to the 1868 North Carolina opinion and many others of the period, familial relations are unique because they are ruled by feelings of affection and duty rather than the self-interested and competitive spirit that predominates in other human endeavors. The characterization provides the basis for the reasoning that bringing adversarial legal mechanisms to bear on family conflict will necessarily distort the natural pattern of family relations, ending in situations where "that which ought to be forgotten in a day, will be remembered for life." The larger implication of such judicial statements is that for a family to function as it should, it must be left on its own to resolve disputes.

In her analysis of the North Carolina case and a number of others from that period, Reva Siegal argues that following the repudiation of chastisement, the courts utilized cultural conceptions about the privacy of the family "to justify giving wife beaters immunity from public and private prosecution." The cumulative effect was "a new doctrinal regime couched in discourses of affective privacy that preserved, to a significant degree, the marital prerogative that chastisement rules once protected."[22] Siegal notes that legal practitioners developed this "discourse of affective privacy" in both civil and criminal responses to domestic violence. In the civil context, assumptions about the nature of family relations were used to justify granting spouses immunity from attempts by their partners to seek redress by suing for damages. As with the criminal cases, judges frequently depicted legal sanctions as inappropriate and disruptive when applied within the domestic area. A statement made in a 1920 Minnesota case vividly illustrates such arguments:

By dragging into court for judicial investigation at the suit of a peevish, fault finding husband, or at the suit of the nagging, ill-tempered wife, matters of no serious merit, which if permitted to slumber in the home closet would silently be forgiven or forgotten . . . the welfare of the home, the abiding place of domestic love and affection, the maintenance of which in all its sacredness, undisturbed by a public exposure of trivial family disagreements, is so essential to society, demands and requires that no new grounds for its disturbance or disruption by judicial proceedings be ingrafted on the law by rule of court not sanctioned or made necessary by express legislation.[23]

What is interesting about the above statement is its exclusive focus on the requirements for the maintenance of domestic harmony and unity. Notably absent are considerations of what might be best for the *individuals* who make up the family.

The emphasis on marital unity was nothing new. In fact, both the original common law of chastisement and the patriarchal authority that it supported were widely justified as necessary to familial order. But what *is* different is the emphasis of the judiciary on promoting unity. Under common-law doctrines, legal institutions actively supported the authority of the husband by enforcing his right to control the wife's property, labor, and behavior. However, largely as a consequence of feminist activism during the latter part of the nineteenth century and the beginning of the twentieth, the practice of merging the legal standing of a man and woman through marriage (placing the husband in control) was discredited. Through passage of a series of "marriage and family acts," women slowly gained many rights within marriage previously denied to them by common-law practices.[24] Laws that had been written to provide institutional authority to a system of familial order based on a hierarchical relationship were being subjected to increasing critical scrutiny.

Nevertheless, although these reforms represented an increased appreciation of the family as composed of multiple rights-bearing individuals, they did not alter an overarching societal commitment to preserve the family as a unit free from government involvement. The distinct advantage of the common-law approach to marriage was that, by granting authority to the husband, familial unity could be maintained without excessive legal involvement.

The decline in the legitimacy of legally sanctioned dominance of one person over another presented courts with a challenge: how to respond to domestic conflicts in a way that would not require excessive involvement in the family. According to Siegal, the courts' solution was to replace the depiction of the family as properly ordered by obedience and hierarchy with a depiction defined by altruism and self-sacrifice. The major advantage of this solution was that in cases having to do with domestic violence, judges could simply defer to the necessity of minimizing state intervention so as to give couples the opportunity to forgive each other on their own terms. "It was no longer necessary to justify a husband's acts of abuse as the lawful prerogative of a master. Rather, the state granted a husband immunity to abuse his wife in order to foster the altruistic ethos of the private realm. In this way, laws that protected relations of domination could be justified as promoting relations of love."[25] Even when the state did become involved with instances of abuse, its approach reflected the emphasis on encouraging couples to work through their problems.

The Progressive Era ushered in a new optimism about the possibility of correcting social ills through rehabilitation and prevention. Social reformers commonly interpreted domestic violence as a "symptom" of a distorted family dynamic that could be "treated" by professionals trained in modern methods.[26] In keeping with this philosophy, domestic violence cases were channeled not to regular criminal courts but to "domestic relations courts," the purpose of which was reunification.[27] Couples were taught skills to resolve their problems without the assistance of government authorities. Police departments and police academies instructed officers in ways to defuse domestic conflicts before arrests were made: a common tactic was to "walk the abuser around the block" to give the couple time to calm down so differences could be dealt with rationally. Overall, the effect of the Progressives' initiatives was to define domestic violence as a problem that could not be addressed effectively within a legal framework. When legal intervention became necessary, it was limited to containing the violence and offering referrals so that the family (with or without the assistance of social service agencies) could work problems out on its own.[28] This approach to domestic violence was sustained until well into the 1960s.

The Revival of Individualism in Legal Responses to Domestic Violence

Beginning in the early 1970s, the legal response (or lack thereof) to domestic violence became the target of increasing criticism from, among others, feminists who had become active in the second wave of the women's movement. A major legacy of the political upheaval of the 1960s was the creation of the forums and language necessary for public discussion of many problems that most people had previously classified as private. Through a process of consciousness-raising, women gathered to talk about their "private" experiences, and it soon became apparent that one of the shared experiences was domestic violence.

The process of problem identification led to actions designed to provide battered women with resources to change their situation. As public discussion of the problem became more widespread and shelters and hotlines were established, more and more women came forward to identify themselves as victims of domestic violence. It appeared to many people that the problem had come out of nowhere: in actuality, what had happened was that the creation of public space where women could speak out served to make visible that which had been happening all along.[29] The outpouring of stories from those who had been touched by domestic violence challenged the long-standing designation of battering as a personal problem that impacted only a small number of deviant families. Because they provided designated places where victims could seek safety and support, shelters played an especially important role in feminist efforts to reframe domestic violence as a social problem meriting serious public attention and resources. As Elizabeth Pleck explains, "Shelters legitimized the issue of wife beating. If there was a place for battered women to go and if large numbers of women went there, then a social problem clearly existed."[30]

In fact, one of the major objectives of what by the mid-1970s had come to be known as "the battered women's movement" was to challenge the widespread cultural assumption that domestic violence was a private problem. A very important part of the strategy to deprivatize it was to push for reforms that would make the legal system take domestic violence more seriously. In an important sense, the efforts by advocates for battered women to improve the legal response to domestic violence fundamentally challenged many of the assumptions about the nature of the family and privacy that the minimizing of legal intervention depended upon. Rather than emphasizing the potential of the family to function as a unified *entity*, the battered women's movement began instead with an emphasis on the family as a grouping of distinct *individuals*. The emphasis arose naturally from the animating concern of the movement: the welfare and safety of individual victims of domestic violence. Through the lens of this "victim rights" perspective, the persistent stress within legal doctrine on the family as a private entity had effectively created a situation in which the rights of victims to state protection were being sacrificed in the name of family privacy.

Included among the "failure-to-protect" arguments were feminist-based concerns about a variety of negative gendered patterns implicated in the consistent noninterventionist stance of legal institutions toward domestic violence. The stronger versions of the arguments depicted the prevalent reluctance to sanction batterers as a thinly veiled attempt to preserve the *officially* discredited prerogative of a husband to control the members of the household as he saw fit. Even among the activists who did not see this as an *intentional* pattern, there was widespread recognition that the *effect* of a noninterventionist approach was to protect male privilege and power within the family.[31]

Such arguments serve to highlight the relations of power and hierarchy that operate below the surface of depictions of the family as a unified entity guided by feelings of love and affection. As discussed in chapter 3, from the perspective of many feminist theorists, this idealized notion should be understood as an ideological construction that obscures the problematic implications of women's historical relative powerlessness within the domestic realm. According to this feminist analysis, the lack of power of many women within that realm is the product of a complex of economic, social, cultural, and physical factors that can all be linked back to their gender.

Another element of feminist challenges to the notion that domestic violence should be resolved without legal interference concerns the argument that in liberal societies the things identified as "private" are deemed of lesser value. This type of argument is illustrated in a point made by Elizabeth Schneider and Nadine Taub, who have suggested that it is the delegalization and therefore the privatization of women's issues that has given women their subordinate status: "The rhetoric of privacy that has insulated the female world from the legal order sends an important ideological message to the rest of society; it devalues women and their functions and says that women are not important enough to merit legal regulation."[32] This association between privacy, the absence of legal regulation, and the failure to take women's concerns seriously is especially relevant to the plight of battered women. As noted, one of the major objectives of the battered women's movement in the 1970s and 1980s was to call into question the assumption that domestic violence was a private problem. The strategy came out of the recognition that as long as battering was identified as a private affair between husband and wife, its victims were not going to get the assistance needed to stop the abuse.

In the context of a liberal political system such as in the United States, one of the most important means of promoting the perception that wife abuse is a public issue is to frame the problem in legal terms. The enactment, interpretation, and enforcement of laws all occur in highly public settings. Laws circumscribe the actions that citizens may and may not take, and the legal system provides a valuable public forum to negotiate the roles and boundaries that structure society.[33] Because of the centrality of the law in providing both structure and content to the social framework of the United States, the presence or absence of an issue in the legal forum sends a message to the community about the significance of the issue.

Starting from the premise that the law *is* a principal means of assigning value in U.S. society, many activists in the battered women's movement have argued that failure to bring the force of law against batterers is, in effect, sending a message that their violence is not subject to punishment and is therefore an acceptable part of family life. A refusal by the state to become involved also serves to construct domestic battering as an individual act, one that is not connected to a systemic problem.[34] In line with these arguments, during the 1970s and 1980s, many advocates for battered women were convinced that bringing the violence into the purview of the law would empower victims. A strong legal stand was critical not only because it promised to provide some protection but also because it would "transform the violence from a private familial matter, for which many women blame themselves, to a public setting where men are made accountable for their acts."[35] Reflecting this belief, activists in the movement fought, and continue to fight, for legislation to protect victims from their batterers and to sanction perpetrators of violence. There has also been a very highly publicized effort to persuade jurors and judges to take the experience of battering into account when sentencing women who have been convicted of killing their batterers.

The legal reforms brought about by the battered women's movement are widely regarded as instrumental in bringing about a "public definition of wife abuse as a social problem."[36] The claim raises an interesting question: What does it mean when a problem such as domestic violence becomes a public issue? That we as a society are willing to take some responsibility for the causes and widespread practice of battering in our community? Or, that we are going to help individual citizens solve their private problems? Although it is true that increases in legal intervention during the past decades have brought the issue of battering into the public sphere, the way in which legal solutions are constructed can also operate to maintain battering as an individual problem. To illustrate this point, I examine two areas where the law has been utilized on behalf of battered women: (1) the battered woman's defense and (2) civil restraining orders. I also elaborate the ramifications of this individualization process for the models of public and private examined in previous chapters.

Defending Battered Woman

Every year, millions of women are battered by their partners,[37] and thousands die as a result. About one-third of all murders of women in the United States are committed by the men they live with.[38] Given such figures, it is hardly surprising that some women kill their batterers. Sometimes the killing occurs during a violent attack and can easily be termed self-defense. Sometimes, however, the killing does not coincide with a violent episode. In such cases, mounting successful defense arguments that are based claims of self-defense, diminished capacity, justifiable homicide, or temporary insanity will often depend on the ability of the defense attorney to convince the jury or judge that the woman's state of mind was such that she saw killing her tormenter as the only alternative available. In order to persuade the judge or jury that the woman's action was reasonable given her situation, the defense must construct a particular image of the battered woman. What needs to be explained is why she simply did not leave. Why did she resort to murder? The most common answer is that the woman was suffering from "battered woman syndrome," which destroyed her capacity to respond effectively to the violence, thereby trapping her in the relationship.[39] Expert testimony on the nature of the syndrome relies heavily on Lenore Walker's theory of "learned helplessness." Walker developed the theory from a psychological theory of Martin Seligman's, which was derived from laboratory experiments in which caged dogs were given random electric shocks. Eventually, the dogs stopped trying to resist the shocks and became passive. Significantly, when they were given the opportunity to leave their cages, the dogs refused to do so.[40] Walker believes the concept of learned helplessness allows us to understand why many battered women might begin to feel there is no escape from their predicament. "Once the women are operating from a belief of helplessness, the perception becomes reality and they become passive, submissive, helpless."[41]

Expert testimony on battered woman syndrome has increasingly gained acceptance as a legitimate strategy in defending victims of domestic violence who kill their abusers or who commit other crimes that can be linked to the psychological disruptions that result from ongoing experiences with intimate violence.[42] In cases in which women had been subjected to very extreme violence, the successful use of such a defense can contribute to significantly reduced prison terms. The importance of lighter sentences to particular defendants and their dependent children should not be underestimated. Beyond its value to individual defendants, the use of battered woman syndrome has helped educate legal personnel and the public about why some victims stay or enter into a series of abusive relationships, why there may be little prior documentation of abuse, and why victims may act in ways that appear abnormal or irrational.[43] The use of the battered woman syndrome in court cases has also served to publicize the horror of domestic violence, and in this sense it has contributed to efforts to reframe battering as a public issue.

Despite these positive impacts, Walker's theory has also been the subject of a significant amount of critical discussion, ranging from questions about its effectiveness to concerns about the image of battered women that it depicts.[44] A common theme within these critiques centers around the concern that the use of the battered woman syndrome by defense lawyers has served to undermine long-standing efforts by activists to turn battering into a political issue. According to these critics, expert testimony about the syndrome in murder trials serves to depoliticize domestic violence in a number primary ways. First, because of the intense focus on the behavior of the abused woman, there is a tendency to ignore the conditions that led to the killing. Lost in the shuffle are the actions of the abuser; and what remains is a syndrome that is associated with the victim, not the victimizer. In this respect, Christine Littleton points out that "translating women's victimization into a problem with women makes the pervasiveness and extent of men's ability to oppress, harm and threaten us invisible. It protects the legal system from having to confront the central problems of battering—male violence, male power and gender hierarchy."[45]

Second, a number of commentators have expressed concern that the defense may construct the battered woman as mentally unstable, pathologically weak, and lacking in the capacity to take responsibility for her actions.[46] In addition to the problems that this can create for the particular defendants,[47] the focus on the abused woman's psychology also yields a negative and extreme picture of what a battered woman is supposed to be like and often results in the reluctance of women who have experienced abuse to identify themselves as battered. According to Martha Mahoney, the legal and cultural images of battered women as dysfunctional, helpless, and dependent just do not match the self-images that many women have of themselves. The result of this disjuncture is an understandable resistance to applying the term "battered woman" to oneself.[48]

A refusal to identify oneself as battered is in direct contradiction to the process of politicizing domestic violence. A long-standing tenet of feminist consciousness-raising is that before women can fight back effectively, they must be willing and able to see that they have been victimized and that they do not have to tolerate violence. The construction of the battered woman as pathologically weak directly impedes this crucial identification process. It is important to be clear that the argument that battered women need to identify that they have suffered from a politically significant wrong is not the equivalent of advocating that they adopt the status of victim. As Susan Schechter rightly points out, "When women are viewed primarily as victims of male violence, it is more difficult for the movement to hold out the inspiration that attracts women to join in a political struggle."[49] Women need be able to see that they have been wronged, but that this experience does not entirely define who they are or can be. The extreme visions of disturbed and destroyed women that murder trials produce leave very little space for such a flexible and empowering self-perception.

Finally, the sensational nature of many of the trials of battered women who have killed their abusers is problematic in that it tends to generate a cultural definition of battering as an extraordinary event. The cases that receive the most publicity often involve abuse of grotesque proportions. When such cases stand as the primary representations of the problem, it becomes much easier for people to distance themselves from it. The abusers in these cases are often unrecognizable in their brutality. When people see made-for-television movies like *The Burning Bed*[50] as examples of battering, it becomes almost impossible to believe that the "normal" battering that may occur in their own homes fits into the same category. There is no intermediate category: it is "wife abuse" as depicted on the screen or it is not a problem warranting public notice. In this regard, Martha Minow has observed that "the denial of larger patterns of family violence seems to be linked to the dramatization of extraordinary cases."[51] What gets obscured by such denials are the relevant statistics: according to extremely conservative estimates, approximately one million women in the United States are battered each year by their partners.[52] Together, these real and fictional media-driven events contribute to an atmosphere where it becomes extremely difficult to foster a sense that battering is a widespread phenomenon in American family life and that the solution requires the development of a collective response.

It cannot be denied that the intense interest that has surrounded many of the trials involving women who have killed their batterers has served to raise public consciousness about domestic violence. It might seem that the publicity would contribute toward making battering a socially unacceptable practice that is subject to public scrutiny. However, awareness of battering as a public issue may mean very little if it is constructed as an event that happens only rarely, and when it does, happens to someone else. Martha Mahoney summarizes the dilemma: "Before the feminist activism of the early 1970s brought battering to public attention, society generally denied that domestic violence existed. Now, culturally, we know what it is, and we are sure it is not us."[53]

Civil Remedies

Restraining Orders

For most women who experience battering, the contact that they will have with the legal system will be not in the area of criminal but civil law. The most common legal intervention in a battering situation comes in the form of a restraining or separation order. Under a restraining order, police typically evict the abuser from the family home (if he is a cohabitant) and order him to cease contact with the victim. In some states, the imposition of a restraining order is accompanied by requirements to attend counseling and pay support. Violation of the conditions can be followed by a fine, imprisonment, or both.[54] Restraining orders are now widely available and represent a significant step forward in a number of ways. First, although a restraining order does not always work, it gives many women assurance that their batterers will not harass them. The space provided by restraining orders is essential for women who are actively trying to put their lives back together.

On a more symbolic level, issuance of a restraining order represents an important step away from the notion that forcing a man from his home constitutes a violation of his property rights.[55] As mentioned earlier, in addition to its regulative functions, the law has great symbolic force in American culture. A restraining order is a clear message that the actions of the batterer are extreme enough to warrant public action. The threat of imprisonment if the order is violated is a signal to the community that the behavior of the person in question does not accord with societal standards for acceptable conduct, even in the privacy of the home. As Lloyd Ohlin and Michael Tonry point out, "The language of blame and the machinery of criminal justice are necessary components of a societal response to serious family violence."[56]

Despite these positive effects, legal responses to domestic violence can raise serious questions about whether civil actions instill the sense that battering is an appropriate problem for the community to take on. First, as with the battered woman defense, a restraining order still treats the battering as a problem for an individual woman to deal with. This becomes more apparent when we consider the hardships that most women face after the separation and the fact that civil remedies do nothing to help women cope with such hardships.

Although an order that the batterer leave the home is often crucial to a victim's safety, it can result in impoverishment and greater economic vulnerability for the woman and her children, who are typically left in her care. For women who are undocumented immigrants, turning to the state for a separation order might result in deportation. But even in the absence of such constraints, many women simply are not willing to expose their families to the perceived shame that they believe "airing their dirty laundry" will bring. Michelle Fine has called it the "problem with going public."[57]

The associated hardships are highly relevant to an evaluation of the utility of legal remedies available to victims of domestic violence. If not addressed, they severely limit the ability to initiate and maintain separation. The power of these constraints is evident in the fact that even if a woman does find the strength to bring the force of the law to bear on her husband's or boyfriend's violence, the likelihood that she will withdraw her claim is very high. This failure of women to follow through with legal action can be very frustrating for legal practitioners, and frequently the response from judges is to dismiss the validity of the wife's claim if she does not remain steadfast in her decision to leave her batterer.

Two of the most common questions asked about a battered woman are: Why didn't she leave? or Why did she return? The problem with framing the discussion in this way is its narrow focus on the psyche of the battered woman. It precludes the more crucial question: What are the conditions that make staying or going back the best alternative?[58] Because legal proceedings having to do with a separation order also focus on the particular individuals involved, there is no opportunity to develop a picture of domestic violence that analyzes the implications of broader societal patterns of dominance and control. Additionally, the focus on the individual serves to de-emphasize the enormous barriers to separation faced by women who are trying to use the law to get out of a violent relationship. A failure to evaluate the negative real-life consequences that legal action entails for many victims serves to render their perspective invisible.[59] The result is that the frequent withdrawing of charges or, in counties where withdrawal is not an option, the adoption of a stance of uncooperativeness in an investigation is routinely viewed "as inconsistency or irresponsibility on the part of women, rather than possibly making good sense in the circumstances."[60]

Last but not least, apart from financial hardship, one of the most serious constraints faced by women who have separated from violent spouses is the isolation that can ensue.[61] When asked why they returned to their abusers, numerous women reply, "Because I love him." The reasoning is incomprehensible to many people, and expressions of love by battered women for their abusers have been commonly labeled as "masochistic."[62] Christine Littleton believes that such reactions are occasioned by a phallocentric bias that is unable to understand that a desire for love and connection can surpass all other concerns. Littleton's critique parallels the long-standing contention of many feminists that the nature of legal method, in general, implicitly utilizes a male standard to judge what is and is not reasonable or rational. In a review of reasons given for the retraction of legal actions against batterers, Littleton notes that an explanation that is rarely offered is that by staying, the women may be trying to rescue "something beyond themselves."[63] Because this alternative is not considered in legal proceedings, women's decisions to drop charges and/or return to their husbands are easily interpreted as proof of their masochistic desires.

It is important to recognize that for many battered women the desire to maintain connection will entail complex negotiations not only with their abusers but also with individuals who comprise the communities within which the relationship is conducted. As noted in chapter 3, women of color frequently report feeling hesitant about revealing the presence of violence in their lives due to fears that doing so will only feed negative racial or ethnic stereotypes. Domestic violence victims with strong ties to religious communities often describe experiences of turning to religious authorities or other church members and being warned against relying on legal mechanisms to address problems that are best resolved through prayer or through help and guidance obtained from within the church. As a result of such cross-cutting pressures, many victims must grapple with the perception that they must make a choice between seeking help from the law *or* preserving crucial systems of support that exist within the communities to which they belong.[64] Again, because of the individualistic bias of legal solutions, the complexities that are associated with a desire to preserve familial and community connections are rendered invisible.

Constructing the Problem as a Public One

As we have seen, although the current legal response to domestic violence is more effective than ever, it is limited because it constructs the problem as an individual one. That construction serves to isolate victims and to produce "solutions" of insufficient breadth. Beyond their implications for the effectiveness of particular legal solutions, the issues concerning the individualistic qualities of legal interventions are relevant to broader questions about the liberal division between public and private. Their significance derives from the observation that when the legal system operates to construct domestic violence as an individual problem, it effectively functions to preserve its traditional status as a private affair.

The contention that legal solutions are not currently capable of constructing battering as a public issue is premised on a definition of *public* that needs some elaboration. There are various ways to define a conceptually loaded word like *public*, but here I will utilize the definitions implicit in the work of feminist activists who have sought to make battering a public issue. A feminist perspective that is especially relevant in this regard is the belief that issues such as domestic violence, although personal, are nevertheless extremely political in terms of causes and effects. A related belief is that as long as women's concerns continue to be privatized, they will not be taken seriously as social problems in need of solutions. Thus, feminists in the 1970s sought to make battering a public concern, to bring about the recognition that to a very large extent battering arises from a patriarchal structuring of the family and that the harms suffered by individual women should be viewed as politically significant. They assumed that something is "public" if it is treated as politically important; if it is understood as causally related to societal structures in which all citizens are implicated; and if its solution is viewed as requiring a collective effort to bring about relief for the victims and reform to prevent recurrences.

It is true that the legal response to battering has served to publicize the problem. More people are aware that it happens, and there is a widespread feeling in society that battering is not acceptable behavior. However, if we use the above definition of *public* as a starting point, we can see that bringing battering within the purview of the law has *not* made it into a public issue. What has been publicized is a problem that individuals are having with each other. This is a point that Richard Gelles and Murray Strauss make when they observe that "interventions aimed at the individual level actually do little to change the societal organization that underlies violence in the family and allows an environment in which people can be violent toward loved ones." The legal construction of battering as an individual problem facilitates the denial that domestic violence permeates the entire society. In this view, as long as battering is something that only deviants do, people will generally remain unwilling to "see the violence as an outgrowth of the very structure of our society and family."[65]

However, the recognition that family violence is caused by structures in which we are all implicated, and that the structures must be reformed if the violence is to end, disappears under the dramatic stories of individuals who utilize the legal system. As Anne Jones asserts, "Domestic violence is a 'social problem' only in the sense that it affects an aggregate of those supposedly aberrant individuals."[66] One of the most troubling consequences of this emphasis is that many women who are experiencing brutality daily become unwilling to identify themselves as having anything in common with the dysfunctional individuals who must pathetically resort to the law to solve their personal problems. Because the law remains centered on individual needs, there is little acknowledgment by legal practitioners and policymakers of the crucial role that the availability or absence of nonfamilial community resources plays in the capacity of victims to effectively utilize legal solutions. Again, the result is a tendency to ask why a particular individual failed to follow through rather than to inquire into the social conditions that might be contributing to that failure.

Conflating Individual and Familial Privacy

There are several important areas in which the above discussion is relevant to larger questions pursued in this book about the relationship between public and private boundaries in liberal society. To begin, however, it is first necessary to take a step back from the historical details of legal intervention into domestic violence in order to highlight the general outlines of the various models of public and private that these patterns of legal response reflect.

One of the outstanding characteristics of the relationship between public and private as expressed by the common-law approach to the family was its focus on the husband as the sole source of authority within the family. The authority included integrally related rights and responsibilities.

Because the husband was the sole legal representative of his family, the common law held him accountable for the behavior and welfare of his wife and their children. As a means of executing such duties, the husband was granted legal control over the earnings and property of family members. Because it relieved the state of responsibility for regulating relations between individuals in the domestic realm, the common-law allocation of absolute authority to the male head of the household relates directly to a number of theoretical points developed in earlier chapters.

It will be recalled from chapter 2 that Locke depicted the family as an association that does not require the presence of government authority, and he therefore designated the domestic realm as private. A sphere free of government involvement is essential to the liberalism articulated by Locke on many levels. First, as the closest representative of the prepolitical "state of nature," the family provides individuals with a space outside government. Without such a space, every element of a person's existence would be potentially subject to government power, thus making the concept of consent to government authority logically impossible. Second, the privacy of the domestic realm provides liberal individuals with the freedom (and the physical space) to exercise and develop their God-given rationalism and free will. These capacities, in addition to their inherent value, are also critical to the ability of individuals to become effective citizens. Thus, it can be argued that by transferring the power to regulate the family to male heads of households through laws such as those having to do with chastisement, the common law served to mirror Locke's definition of the family as a realm that could remain largely free of government and legal intervention.

This liberal separation of the family from politics forms the basis of two distinct models of public and private that have historically been conflated. The first model grows out of the basic distinction, initially developed by Locke, between the family as a natural and therefore prepolitical realm and the rest of society. The second model defines the boundaries between the individual and the state. Locke justifies the latter set of boundaries through the delineation of specific privacy rights that enable individuals to exercise their powers of rationality and self-determination— capacities that are essential to a liberal political system wherein government authority is derived from freely consenting citizens. The conflation of these two models occurs as a consequence of the pivotal role that the family plays in this scheme in providing individuals with both the psychic and the physical space to exercise these privacy rights.

A key feature of this "individual-versus-the-state" model of public and private is that the privacy it produces is, by design, going to primarily accrue to only one individual in the family: the male patriarch. Because common law granted the husband control over the actions, property, and future of his wife, the advantages of individual autonomy and self-determination that went with familial privacy could not be officially claimed by women in marital relationships. The common-law right to chastisement serves to highlight that a wife's subordinate legal status within the family, far from being incidental, was a critical structural feature of this model. After all, it was the legal construction and legitimization of a hierarchical authority structure within the family that made it possible to talk about the privacy rights of the individual and the family as if they were one and the same.

Although significant in many respects, the eventual rejection of chastisement as a legitimate legal doctrine in nineteenth-century North America was not a departure from the important role played by legal doctrine in supporting the conflation of individual and familial privacy rights. The rejection of chastisement was *not* part of a larger shift toward separating familial privacy from individual rights, for there is no evidence that the approach to domestic violence that replaced the common-law support for chastisement was intended to protect the rights of *all* individuals in the family. On the contrary, the historical record reveals an increased emphasis by judges on the family as a singular entity whose members would be willing to subordinate their individual interests in the name of love and loyalty. Such a depiction of the family supported the growing perception that the utilization of legal mechanisms for resolving familial conflicts was not only inappropriate but could also seriously undermine the ability of family members to resolve their problems on their own.

The clear advantage of the approach adopted in the judicial decisions examined above was that the privilege accorded to the husband in domestic affairs was nowhere to be found. Gone were common-law justifications of moderate violence as a necessary prerogative of patriarchal authority. According to this legal and cultural construction of the family, it was up to *all* of the parties concerned to resolve their differences. The benefit of drawing a curtain of privacy around the family in this manner was that the benefits of doing so could be depicted as accruing to every person who valued a home life characterized by intimacy, altruism, and discretion. In a sense, judges during this period successfully resolved what had become an unacceptable focus on the rights of the patriarch by replacing the common-law hierarchical-authority-based model of family life with a model of the family that functioned to make the rights and needs of individuals secondary to the shared goal of a unified and loving family. One of the major outcomes of this development was that the conflation of individual and familial privacy, built into Locke's original construction of the division between public and private in liberal society, had been extended to the point where the two were now indistinguishable.

The subordination of individual needs to the maintenance of familial unity and the conflation of individual and family rights continued to influence governmental responses to domestic violence for more than half a century after the demise of the law of chastisement. This period, which was characterized by a strong bias against legal intervention in situations of domestic violence, finally came to an end in the 1970s when activists in the battered women's movement began to challenge the hands-off policies that this conflation made possible. Extending and building on feminist arguments about the political implications of personal problems, the activists criticized both patterns of nonintervention and claims about the importance of protecting the privacy of the family entity as directly contributing to the subordination of the interests and rights of some individuals, particularly women. These challenges eventually resulted in a range of legal reforms designed to: (1) provide victims with the understanding and services that they needed to put an end to the abuse and (2) transform domestic violence into a public problem.

Beyond improving the lives of countless victims of domestic violence, the reforms also pose a serious challenge to the conflation of individual and familial privacy embedded in the liberal construction of the boundaries between the state and the family. On one level, by drawing attention to the frequency and severity of domestic violence, activists in the battered women's movement unpacked the conflation by exposing the human and social costs of the assumption that individual and familial privacy rights could be treated as equivalent. Further, by demanding that the state deal with domestic violence through legal intervention, the activists successfully challenged the stance of nonintervention that had evolved out of this conflation.

One of the legacies of such challenges is that the modern model of public and private is much more complex than the one introduced by Locke,[67] which premises public and private spheres on philosophical distinctions that portrayed familial and political relationships as opposites. The push in recent decades to take the rights and needs of individuals within the family more seriously has effectively muddied that opposition by involving the state to a greater and greater extent in what are still widely regarded as private relationships. As a result, it has been necessary to extend the Lockean family/politics model to include the question raised by Mill through his elaboration of the "harm principle": When, where, and under what circumstance can the government intervene in the private affairs of citizens? As we have seen throughout this chapter, in liberal societies the question is answered primarily through articulation of legal rules and procedures.

These changes have produced a model of public and private that continues to idealize the family as a realm characterized by nonpolitical relationships ill-suited to government intervention while simultaneously acknowledging that because individual interests do occasionally collide in this context, mechanisms for intervening in carefully specified circumstances should be in place. This model is both a departure from and a continuation of Locke's. It departs from Locke's model in the sense that it treats the rights of all individuals with more gravity, and thus has a greater capacity to acknowledge conflicts when they occur. Even so, the model remains incapable of addressing the fundamental tension created by the assumption that the private family will provide individuals with a realm where they can realize and experience both individual autonomy and altruistically driven connections. However, we now have a situation in which, rather than obscuring individual rights by treating husband and wife as a single person under the common law or by invoking images of the altruistic family, the dependencies inherent in familial connections are obscured by a legal discourse that is tightly focused on individual rights and responsibilities. Thus, we see that although earlier versions of the model avoided the tension by simply assuming that individual and familial interests could be treated as equivalent, the contemporary model sidesteps the tension through a focus on individual rights and responsibilities when there is violent conflict within the family. In both models, the tension is resolved by designating either connection or individualism as less important or as inappropriate to the questions that surround state intervention in the family. Efforts to assist victims of domestic violence that come out of such simplified models are not equipped to address the vexatious dilemmas and multiple loyalties that victims of domestic violence regularly confront. Even more problematic is evidence that the inability to incorporate these tensions into a model of state response becomes translated as a deficiency in the victim's response rather than as a blind spot in the approach being taken to the problem.

I do not mean to suggest that the law is an inappropriate site of action to address the problems faced by battered women. Legal intervention does provide many with desperately needed assistance. However, the law should nevertheless be understood as extremely limited in its ability to challenge traditional boundaries between public and private in our society. Is there an alternative approach to formulating this relationship?

Five

The Power of Participation

T HE THEORETICAL AND LEGAL APPROACHES TO THE relationship between public and private examined in the preceding pages, although varied, share a problematic characteristic: a limited capacity to address the wide range of paradoxical and complex dilemmas that are faced by victims of domestic violence. That common shortfall is closely connected to a distinct and more deeply embedded aspect of these approaches: an incomplete ability to balance the fundamental tension between the liberal goals of protecting the rights and needs of particular individuals while at the same time preserving the family as a realm where individuals may retreat from public scrutiny.

To say that a tension exists between these two objectives is not to suggest that they are necessarily incompatible. After all, for a great many people, the domestic realm *is* a space where intimacy and privacy can be pursued in relative safety. The social problem of domestic violence, however, stands as a historically recurring scenario that reveals the flaws in the assumption that familial and individual privacy interests are always mutually beneficial. These shortcomings have serious implications for the various theoretical and legal approaches to the public/private relationship discussed in earlier chapters. As we saw, rather than engaging the tension, each approach eventually manages to sidestep it by either presenting "family unity" or "individual rights" as primary. None is able to adequately account for the dilemma of a battered woman who frequently faces the need to protect herself as an individual and the need or desire to preserve her family. To understand and therefore help victims of domestic violence, it is essential to develop an approach that works *with* this tension between the individual and the family rather than collapsing one into the other.

My primary purpose in developing such a model is to improve our ability to take the complex needs of victims of domestic violence into account as we seek to balance the liberal value of privacy with harm prevention. The objective of taking victims' situations seriously is not the equivalent of trying to resolve the tensions between individualism, familial connection and privacy, and harm prevention that are elaborated throughout this book. It is my position that such tensions can never be fully resolved once and for all. However, as I argue in chapter 6, I do believe that the model that I develop is better equipped than others for the task of working productively with these tensions within a public policy context.

Theoretical critiques are useful in helping us to see the problems and gaps in many of the assumptions we tend to take for granted. Still, no matter how useful critiques are in this respect, there is always the lingering question: What is the alternative? There is widespread agreement in the United States today that domestic violence is wrong and that something should be done to stop it. This relatively recent emergence of a consensus lends urgency to the development of approaches that will "do something" while still respecting our fundamental commitment to the privacy and rights of both the individual and the family.

This chapter and the next outline an alternative approach to understanding and renegotiating public and private boundaries that more effectively balances familial and individual privacy with the need to reframe battery as a behavior subject to public sanction. The proposed alternative is not based on a theoretical analysis of the public/private relationship or of the nature of the individual and the family. Instead, my analysis and the alternative model derive from an empirical examination of how individuals actively involved in the effort to stop domestic violence address and experience the tensions that occur around privacy in their work. My initial interest in seeking out the perspectives of individuals who are working directly with the problem of domestic violence was driven by my belief that all individuals, regardless of their interest (or lack thereof) in theoretical issues, utilize conceptual frameworks to make sense of the experiences that they encounter. More specifically, my expectation was that individuals who work in the area of domestic violence are likely to have had many direct experiences of confronting the tensions between public and private associated with this problem; and that these experiences would require them to develop their own approach toward the challenge of determining the proper relationship between public obligations and privacy rights.

Methodology

The concept of privacy and its relationship to protection is a complicated issue. It involves layers of meaning and nuance that would be missed
in the absence of a verbal exchange. I wanted my interviewees to define
and explore this relationship in a way that would allow the ideas and issues
to emerge with as little prompting as possible. Because I believed that verbal accounts would be the best means of getting at the issues I wanted to
examine, interviewing constituted my primary data-gathering technique.

I conducted forty-five interviews in northern California between 1997
and 1999. Interviewees included a wide variety of people who are involved in addressing the problems of domestic abuse. The general groupings of individuals that I interviewed were: (1) legal advocates for battered
women; (2) activists lobbying for changes in legislation; (3) policymakers
in the legislature and bureaucracy; (4) shelter workers (some of whom
were volunteers); (5) attorneys who handle domestic violence prosecutions; and (6) police officers responsible for intervening when violence has
occurred and issuing and enforcing orders of protection.

The criteria used for selecting the interview pool centered on the potential of the prospective interviewees to provide information about the
ways in which privacy concerns manifest themselves and are negotiated
when domestic violence is brought to the attention of public officials or
service providers.[1] Interviewing persons involved in a variety of levels and
stages of the reporting and treatment process provided an opportunity to
consider whether or not privacy issues vary in importance depending on
the context within which they are encountered.[2]

I identified twenty-seven themes from the transcribed interviews,
which fit roughly into two categories: (1) themes involving the limits of
legal intervention and (2) themes related to the gaps created by the limitations of a law-centered response and how they are being, or could be,
addressed. I analyzed the data in four steps. The first was a thorough reading of the transcripts, during which I recorded my impressions and noted
patterns and themes as they became apparent. The next step consisted of a
second detailed reading, during which I coded the data according to the
thematic elements identified during step one. I sought to verify the existence of these patterns in step three, which involved physically moving
discrete statements into sections that were marked by the major themes
that I had identified.

In the final step in the analysis, I compared the dominant themes and patterns identified in the interviews to information that I had gathered through participant observation and archival research. To generate additional data, I engaged in a number of different participant observation activities. First, I volunteered one day a week at a shelter organization near my home. Second, I took every available opportunity to attend professional conferences, hearings, and academic conferences where the issue of domestic violence was being discussed. Two conferences in particular were very important to clarifying the results that I obtained in the interviews. One was a small conference in Washington, D.C., where approximately twenty-five law professors and activists gathered to discuss approaches to domestic violence and domestic violence law clinics (which are designed to train prospective lawyers in working with domestic violence clients). The other was a policy conference held in Sacramento, California, that was attended by more than five hundred activists, medical personnel, law enforcement officers, and policymakers. Its objective was to discuss current challenges in the effort to develop a public response to domestic violence. The foregoing activities were also supplemented with research in the archival records of congressional debates; the documentation of training strategies for judges and police officers relative to domestic violence; literature distributed by a wide variety of domestic violence agencies; media reports on the issue; and books and articles pertaining to domestic violence.

Although interviewing is a powerful tool, it involves a number of limitations that I would like to briefly address. As Robert Dingwall points out, because an interview is a social encounter, the data that is generated must be understood as "the outcome of a socially situated activity where the responses are passed through the role-playing and impression management of both the interviewer and the respondent."[3] Of course, an interview is not just any social encounter but is one that is directed toward obtaining specific types of information. As Dingwall puts it: "A key feature of the framing of interviews is that the interviewer defines what the parties are going to talk about and what will count as relevant."[4] One of the dangers of a social interaction where one party is asking all of the questions is that the person who is being interviewed may well feel pressured to produce answers that will satisfy the requirements and expectations of the interviewer rather than answering in a manner that more accurately reflects his or her actual experience. Although I entered each interview with a series of questions designed to elicit reflections on topics relevant to issues of privacy, I intentionally kept the interviews largely open-ended and avoided leading questions. This technique allowed my interviewees to speak freely and in their own words and provided me with the flexibility to pursue relevant topics that I may not have anticipated.

Despite such precautions, it was clear to me in some of the interviews that the nature of the questions I was posing was having the effect of getting the interviewees to think about issues relating to privacy and domestic violence in new ways. For example, a number interviewees indicated that the interview had been enjoyable because, as one activist put it: "Normally I am so busy with the things that need to get done every day that I don't have the chance to think about these kinds of issues." Although it is important to remain attuned to the way in which interviews serve to illicit certain responses, they still have considerable value. As I stated earlier, my premise prior to conducting the interviews was that assumptions about the public/private divide, although they are usually not explicitly acknowledged, are an important part of the conceptual frameworks that structure patterns of intervention in domestic violence situations. The interviews were designed to encourage the respondents to articulate ideas and assumptions that are usually taken for granted.

My objective in drawing attention to these assumptions and exploring their implications is not so that I can provide a neutral snapshot of the way that all practitioners view these matters. Indeed, I have serious doubts about the possibility and utility of providing an accurate or neutral photograph of the way that practitioners view the problem of domestic violence.[5] Nor is it my intention to produce a theoretically based blueprint for action. Instead, my goal is both more modest and more ambitious: to integrate the knowledge of the interviewees with a theoretical analysis of the relationship of public and private in a way that serves to illuminate the problem in a new and helpful way.[6]

The Limits of Law

One of my central objectives in conducting the interviews was to learn how survivors and individuals working with domestic violence viewed the law.[7] As I argued in chapter 4, an examination of the legal response to domestic violence is an ideal starting point for analyzing the degree to which we define this problem as a public or a private issue. Again, the importance of the law to this topic derives from the observation that within a liberal framework, legal institutions are the primary mechanism through which the boundaries of state authority are delineated.[8] Laws serve not only to establish the authority of government in areas previously controlled exclusively by private citizens but also to protect the rights and privacy interests of the individuals that make up the liberal community. In these respects, the legal system plays a critical role, first in determining and then in enacting the boundaries between public and private in our society.

The importance placed on legal reform by the battered women's movement during the past two decades testifies to the prominence of the law in the construction of domestic violence as either a public or a private problem. As we have seen, the push to enact reforms in the laws pertaining to domestic violence which began in the early 1970s was largely based on the recognition by activists that battered women were simply not getting the protection from the government that they desperately needed and had a right to. The focus of these activists was primarily on redefining domestic violence as a criminal assault warranting meaningful police intervention and possible arrest. Such redefinition was a dramatic departure from the prevailing view of battering as a familial matter, in regard to which the role of the police officer was often simply to calm the aggressor.

The effort to improve the legal response to domestic violence continues today, but there have been some significant changes in the approach of those involved. Because domestic violence has been largely established as a serious violation warranting formal legal sanctions and intervention, the emphasis has now shifted toward the specific details of formulating the most *effective* legal response. An important piece of this process has been an ongoing evaluation of what has and has not been effective and what still needs attention. In addition to revealing where reforms in the law still need to occur, this evaluation process has resulted in a growing recognition of the limitations of a legally based approach.

The inescapable constraints on what legal institutions can realistically accomplish constitute the focus of this chapter. The identification and sorting of themes from the interviews made clear that a significant number involved a general concern about constraints associated with legally based strategies for achieving certain objectives. These critiques provided the framework for the second major category of themes: those describing gaps in the legal responses—frequently caused by the constraints identified—and those centering on suggestions for supplementing existing approaches.

As noted in chapter 4, within the liberal structure of the American political system, legal institutions play a critical role in the process of delineating the boundaries and meanings of public and private. The importance of the law to this process is made manifest in cases of domestic violence: legal intervention transforms what was previously a "private problem" into one that is subject to state authority and public scrutiny. In light of the centrality of the law, a consideration of the drawbacks of legal interventions as they were expressed in my interviews serves to illuminate the limitations of the general liberal approach to determining the proper relationship between public and private.

The Importance of the Law

Although the interviewees reported significant limitations of legal interventions, they nevertheless believed that maintaining a visible and serious legal response to domestic violence remains very important. There was consensus that the effort to criminalize acts of abuse resulting in visible injuries has been and continues to be absolutely essential. The interviewees conveyed their belief in the importance of criminalization in a variety of ways. For example, many framed the issue in social-contract terms: the failure of the state to intervene when someone is being assaulted, regardless of where the assault occurs, violates the state's promise to protect its citizens. Patricia, a lobbyist with an interest in domestic violence legislation, provided a very direct description of the state's obligation: "One of the basic functions of government is to keep people from resolving disputes violently. Thus when violence occurs, the state has an obligation to use the law to stop the violence and to punish the person who has committed it."

Others termed the widespread failure to impose legal sanctions in cases of domestic violence a lapse in logic. As Louise, an attorney, put it: "An assault is an assault; why should it be treated differently just because it has occurred within the family?" Both comments share a view of the law as the symbolic embodiment of the state and its obligations. In this context, the interviewees interpreted the fact that the state did not bring the force of law to bear in cases of domestic violence as denial of the victim's entitlement to protection.

Also emphasized was the importance of the law as *the* primary mechanism for defining what people can and cannot do and what society accepts as appropriate behavior. The interviewees repeatedly linked the significance of arrest to its power to signal that the state does not tolerate the behavior in which it is intervening. The symbolic value of the arrest was described in the interviews as extending to both the perpetrator and victim. For the perpetrator, arrest represents the activation of a process that is designed to hold him accountable for his violent behavior. This accountability is established in several stages, first when the police officer makes the initial arrest and then once again when he must face a judge.

Paula, a probation officer, explained it this way: "Standing in front of a judge is very different from going home and facing someone who is afraid of you anyway. For the victim, on the other hand, a consistent policy of arrest demonstrates public validation that what has been happening to her is not acceptable."

The above interview excerpts and others in the same vein, when taken collectively, reflect a persistent and consistent presentation of the law as a key mechanism for bringing public commitment and values to bear in cases of domestic violence. The primary function attributed to the law in this respect varied. Some interviewees emphasized the state's obligation to protect its citizens; others spoke of the more nebulous role of the law as a public marker establishing which kinds of behaviors are out of bounds. What these depictions of the law share is a characterization of legal mechanisms as fundamentally implicated in the redefining of domestic violence from a purely private affair to one subject to rules and norms derived from public commitments. This characterization comports with the generally ascribed view of legal institutions as key in the construction of the boundary drawn in liberal societies around the private realm of the family.

Yet one must acknowledge the law is just *one* piece of this complex process. Further, it is a piece subject to powerful limitations and constraints that can weaken the effectiveness of legal intervention in the effort to penetrate the shroud of privacy that can shield domestic violence from public scrutiny. The interviewees clearly supported this point by consistently portraying legal intervention as both essential *and* extremely circumscribed.

Problems within Legal Institutions

The focus of the following discussion of the limitations of legal institutions is on laying the groundwork for an investigation of the strategies most commonly suggested by interviewees for filling the resulting gaps.[9] I orient the discussion toward the strategies for filling the gaps rather than toward the limitations themselves in light of my central objective: to generate insights that can be used in developing a new approach to the questions and dilemmas that have been raised in this book.

The persons interviewed discussed the limitations of legal institutions in a variety of contexts, but their comments can be categorized. The first category is the most diverse and involves "limitations" deriving from the structure and operation of legal institutions. Common problems include limited resources; lack of coordination between civil, criminal, and family courts; insensitive judges and court personnel; and a court process that is "too slow," not only creating difficulties for victims "who often cannot get the time off of work to see the trial through" but also "giving the couple time to fall back into the honeymoon period and then the cycle of violence [begins again]."

What the above limitations share is that, with the exception of resource constraints, they all arise from limitations that can largely be remedied within the legal institutions themselves. In fact, when mentioning the limitations, many interviewees talked of reforms in other states that had been crafted to ameliorate the limitation in question. Although many of the limitations are serious and difficult to address, they are comparable to a mechanical problem with an engine. Usually, when a car makes a strange noise or breaks down, the first question is: How can I get this problem fixed so I can use my car again? Although certainly less common, it is also possible to react with another question: Is it necessary to be so dependent on a car in the first place, and are there steps that I can take to lessen this dependency? The latter question implies a much deeper critique, and it is to this level that I now turn.

Access Limitations

Those who seek to use legal institutions as a tool of empowerment do not always find the law equally accessible. Sociolegal research has repeatedly demonstrated that access to the law and success with using it are much greater for those who have the most resources to begin with.[10] The results of my interviews are consistent with this research in the sense that a large number of interviewees expressed serious concerns about the accessibility of the law for people who are in abusive situations. For example, many of the interviewees talked very specifically about the costs of utilizing the law when seeking to exit an abusive situation. According to Katherine, the director of a legal advocacy program for battered women, "To hire an attorney to get a restraining order costs between $1,600 and $1,800. Clearly, poor people or those who are economically dependent on their batterer and who frequently are without skills or a job are not in a position to afford such fees."

The widespread recognition within the battered women's movement of such costs has resulted in the establishment of restraining-order clinics that assist women in obtaining the orders for themselves. Legal aid is also made available to women who need an attorney for more complex matters, such as custody. Although the programs are clearly an important step in the right direction, their existence is the exception rather than the rule. Reflecting this reality were the persistent comments throughout the interviews about the plight of victims who are left with few alternatives when dollars are in short supply or absent altogether.

The interviewees also consistently referred to daunting legal fees when I asked what they thought of the option of utilizing civil law to sue either unresponsive police departments or batterers for damages. Although nearly all felt that the strategy could have very positive effects, their optimism was carefully qualified: because of the expense, a civil suit was an option only for the battered who could afford it. A comment from Katherine illustrates this point:

Some women do get empowerment from making him pay, but there are limitations to this approach. First, many batterers are judgment-proof because they don't have jobs. Second, it is very expensive and time-consuming to bring a suit against someone. The harsh reality is that in the legal system it takes resources to get resources.

Another point repeatedly made in a variety of contexts concerned the reluctance of many people to turn to the law for help because they mistrusted government or feared the police. These attitudes were identified as especially salient among immigrant populations[11] and people of color, who have a history of mistreatment by government authorities. The following remarks made by Nancy, an activist, are typical:

Nowadays, given the current political climate around criminal justice, we need to be very cautious about relying only on arrest as an emergency response mechanism. For example, because of fears of police brutality among people of color, they are less likely to call the cops in when abuse is taking place. Depending only on the police to intervene means that we are basically putting into place an emergency response for the middle class.

Complicating the picture even further were accounts of wealthy victims who had failed to call the police because of either shame or fear that no one would believe that their prominent husbands were capable of such brutality. Yet another victim cohort mentioned in the interviews were homosexuals. David, a social worker who volunteers as a domestic violence advocate for gay men, noted that "homosexuals are frequently afraid of police homophobia if they disclose that it is a romantic relationship. When they do call, it is usually only when the violence is severe, and then they usually say they are friends or roommates."

No matter what the particular barrier, the essential problem remains:

many victims of domestic violence are not willing to call on the law for help. Although a significant number of interviewees made this point, not one concluded that it meant that we should abandon legal channels of intervention in cases of domestic violence. Instead, the conclusion generally drawn was that in light of the barriers perceived to exist for many populations, we need to be very cautious about relying "too heavily on law to fix this issue."

The above opinions are significant because they demonstrate the sensitivity of the interviewees to the fact that victims of domestic violence, although they share the experience of being subjected to physical abuse, are very different in other respects. When these differences are given appropriate weight, the shortcomings of legal channels become very clear. In theory, the law protects all individuals equally. Unfortunately, the ideal of equal protection fails to take into account the reality that each person has a different relationship to the laws that are passed to accomplish the ideal. As numerous interviewees pointed out, the inability of many victims to pay for legal services—or fears of the power of the law to take away their freedom—dominates their relationship to legal forms of assistance. For such persons, the option of bringing their abuse into the public realm through legal channels either does not exist or is not perceived as a realistic or desirable alternative.

The Importance of Prevention in Bringing About Attitudinal Changes

Many interviewees saw legally based approaches to domestic violence as inadequate because of the limited ability of legal mechanisms to alter fundamental cultural attitudes toward the problem. A number of such attitudes were mentioned over and over as interfering with our ability to cope with domestic violence, including: "It is a private matter and not really wrong"; "It is the victim's fault"; and "It is really only a symptom of other problems such as alcohol and drug abuse or unemployment."

Among those interviewed, I found a clear sense that the law carried a great deal of symbolic power. However, they persistently qualified this opinion with statements suggesting that, *in practice,* legal mechanisms are of little use in the effort to significantly change deep-seated attitudes toward domestic violence. The following comment made by Lisa, an activist in the battered women's movement for over twenty years, summarizes the point well: "Our initial focus on law was based on a belief that if we could just get society to see it as a crime then it would stop. Now we realize that this is just the first stage. Now we have to go further and get people saying and believing that it is intolerable so that they will actually do something about it." Or as Frances, an assistant district attorney, put it: "People tend to conflate the statements that 'it's against the law' and 'it's wrong,' when really they are two separate and different statements."[12]

It is important to note that the argument being made here is *not* that laws have no impact on how we as a society view a particular action. We have only to recall that from its very inception, the movement to stop domestic violence included a major emphasis on legal reform as a key component in bringing about social change. However, even as they continued to view the law as an important site of struggle, interviewees also clearly recognized that legal reform can take us only so far in our efforts to change attitudes. According to many with whom I spoke, the next step, only recently begun, is to address cultural attitudes toward domestic violence. Along with Lisa, the activist quoted above, a significant number of interviewees believed that taking the step requires a shift in focus toward community. Susan, who is employed by a nonprofit group that is devoted to addressing domestic violence, explained that for her organization this shift has meant putting more and more energy into "creating community-based and community-rooted sanctions that are part of people's daily lives and part of the value system of the community in which they operate." The gist of the most frequent observations about the limits of the law to enact cultural change was that laws do not operate independently of prevailing attitudes. After enactment, laws need to be obeyed, enforced, and interpreted. As Elinore, who works for a state agency on the issue of domestic violence, observed: "Simply having a law on the books does not say that we are doing anything about domestic violence. It does say that there is a public entitlement to protection, but it does not address the problem of people failing to use or enforce that protection. Community education is what starts doing this."

When interviewees were queried as to what they saw as the major barriers to stopping domestic violence, one of the most common designations was personnel in the law-enforcement and judicial systems, some of whom have no grasp of the nature and seriousness of the problem. The following comment, again from Elinore, is representative: "Good laws and policy are in place, but what is not happening is an attitude shift. There are still key players in the legal system such as police and judges who have not altered how they look at this problem." According to many I talked to, the absence of an "attitude shift" on the part of certain court and law-enforcement personnel means that despite major changes in the law, many victims continue to encounter trivialization, blame, and disinterest when they seek to make use of the justice system to stop the abuse.

In this respect, judges were cited by some interviewees as especially ignorant and insensitive about the issue of domestic violence. There were a variety of reasons given for this situation, but the following comment summarizes the most common: "Of all the players, judges are the hardest to get to in terms of attitude adjustment. This is because they have the most discretion, they are not required to participate in trainings on the issue, and they are immune to lawsuits."

Even more challenging than educating legal personnel is the need to bring about a shift in the wider community where the violence is actually taking place. A strong feeling was evident in the interviews that although domestic violence is now officially illegal in every state, the notion that a certain amount of violence in the home is natural and acceptable persists among some portions of the populace. Typically accompanying this observation was the contention that until society faces up to and addresses this undercurrent of toleration for abuse within the confines of the family, we will be caught in a never-ending cycle of violence followed by legal intervention.

Although interviewees acknowledged the usefulness of the force of law to bring about a decrease in domestic violence, they typically also referred to the limitations of the law, which cannot be brought into play "until something actually happens" in an abusive relationship. At first, this observation appears so obvious as to verge on being trite, but once we consider its implications, its meaning deepens. If we are going to see diminishing numbers of individuals who become involved in violent relationships, some sort of intervention needs to occur before the first blow is struck—or at least before a pattern of violence is established. As Richard, a psychotherapist who facilitates domestic violence offender groups, explained:

We are waiting too long for intervention to take place. Typically, long before anything is done, many batterings have already taken place. But delayed intervention is a very difficult problem due to the fact that domestic violence is usually hidden so we don't even know that the offenses are taking place until they escalate to the point where they come to the awareness of neighbors or police.

The primary means mentioned in the interviews to reach people prior to such escalation is through prevention programs. Prevention came up again and again as the most important missing piece of a long-term plan of action to stop domestic violence. Debra, a legislative analyst specializing in domestic violence, suggested a range of vital prevention activities: "teaching children and adults that violence is not a good way to deal with things; teaching people not to put themselves in a situation where they are going to be hit; what warning signs to watch for; and providing at-risk families with help so that they don't enter into a cycle of abuse."

Although interviewees obviously believed that prevention is a critical component of any viable approach to the problem of domestic violence, they nevertheless recognized as well that "direct services always have to have top priority." Or as Claire, a battered woman's advocate, put it: "We definitely need to pay more attention to prevention. Right now, because of resource constraints, we are too focused on stopping the bleeding, but you can't really go on to prevention until that bleeding has been stopped."

The law has shown itself to be an invaluable tool to "stop the bleeding." However, as the interviewees' comments make clear, even as we celebrate our success in stopping violence when it occurs, we must not forget that a real solution must include a strong preventive component. Because legal intervention is designed to respond to discrete incidents, many of the interviewees deemed the law ill-suited to achieving preventative objectives.

The critique of the law as being of limited utility in the prevention of domestic violence is far from damning. After all, it is not reasonable or realistic to expect legal intervention to accomplish more than it is designed to do. Moreover, legal intervention is not the only arrow in society's quiver. Still, many criticisms went much further, suggesting that the legalistic approach has actually functioned to narrow the options for addressing domestic violence to those that fit neatly within a punitive law-and-order framework. The argument was made most commonly when the topic of prevention came up in the interviews. Several interviewees working in the California legislature spoke of a strong preference there for domestic violence legislation that entails an increase in penalties. As Patricia, the above-mentioned lobbyist, put it, "Bills that are not punitive have a hard time getting through." Many of the community activists I interviewed also expressed concern that a law-and-order framework can limit the range of strategies that we develop. As David observed: "These campaigns tend to be focused on punitive solutions. Jail can be useful, but it fails to articulate a meaningful strategy for prevention and treatment for offenders. If we, as a movement, don't do this, who is going to?" A rush to punish means that other essential components of a long-term solution, such as prevention and education, are being overshadowed.

Gaps between Theory and Practice in Legal Intervention

The last category of legal limitations that emerged strongly in the interviews had to do with the common disparity between the theory of legal intervention and its practice. These concerns went beyond the above-mentioned problem of personnel in the judicial system whose biases or ignorance about domestic violence function to obstruct what are essentially good laws. Controversy currently rages among those who seek to shape domestic violence policy about the efficacy of arrest as a factor in stopping or decreasing incidents of domestic violence.[13] With this in mind, I questioned all of the interviewees on whether they felt a policy of mandatory arrest was a sound idea. Their answers, rather than being strongly pro or con, were characterized by thoughtful ambivalence. The majority agreed with a policy of mandatory arrest, at least in theory. Among the positive elements cited were that an arrest "communicates that this is criminal conduct and not private"; that it "takes the onus off the victim to make the arrest, thus making domestic violence more like other crimes"; that it "gives the victim time to get out of the situation"; and that it functions to "bring the batterer into the system, where he can receive assistance in stopping his behavior."

Despite their positive tone, the comments were almost always qualified or prefaced with reservations. A common concern centered around fear about what would occur when arrests were made, in what was uniformly portrayed as a "less than ideal legal system." Debra, an activist, provides a representative statement of this ambivalence:

I have mixed feelings about mandatory arrest. In theory, I agree with it, for it accords with my view of the criminal justice system as the state protecting its citizens, and part of this is definitely the need to arrest. However, I hesitate because of the flaws in the system and my accompanying doubts about forcing someone into a system that is so screwed up.

One of the most frequently articulated fears about arrest centered on what can happen when a policy of mandatory arrest is enacted without the requisite police training to identify a "primary aggressor" in the conflict. According to a number of comments, the failure to train police to make the identification repeatedly results in situations where both the victim and the perpetrator are arrested—or, even worse, where only the victim, who may have harmed the aggressor in self-defense, is arrested. Another common concern of interviewees was that mandatory arrest would probably not help in situations where "the perpetrator is released very quickly or where the sentence is meaningless." Overall, the strong feeling among interviewees was that policies such as mandatory arrest are "only as good as the supports that you put in place behind them." Without personnel training, appropriate sentencing, support for the victim, and follow-up counseling and tracking, mandatory arrest has the potential to do more harm than good.

The above concerns, although important in their own right, also demonstrate a more general pattern in the interviews. Subjects persistently made distinctions between theory and practice, the ideal and the reality. The pattern was especially pronounced when the discussion turned to legal institutions and their utility in stopping domestic violence. Over and over again, when asked about the law, interviewees would begin by chronicling the many improvements that efforts to reform the legal response to domestic violence had wrought. The praise was almost always followed, however, by a listing of the limitations on realizing the objectives that the reform efforts were seeking to achieve. Although the limitations varied by topic discussed, they all involved the "backup mechanisms" or "supports" required to give substance to the formal legal policy or requirement in question. Examples of such supports included training programs for legal personnel; money for hiring adequate staff to administer new laws; programs to assist victims in accessing the legal system; emergency assistance and shelter for victims who lack resources but who wish to leave their batterers; and additional funding of probation programs to support tracking and follow-up efforts after the initial legal intervention.

The above list is only partial, but even in its incompleteness, it effectively conveys the interviewees wide-ranging appreciation of a basic insight: laws do not operate in a vacuum. The interviewees raised concerns on a great variety of topics related to frequent difference between the theory and practice of legal intervention. They pointed out regularly that the effectiveness of a law in positively impacting the problem of domestic violence is always critically dependent on factors extending far beyond formal legal articulations.

Legal Intervention and the Construction of Domestic Violence as an Individual Problem

As noted at the end of chapter 4, one of the limitations associated with legal intervention is its tendency to construct the problem of domestic violence in an especially individualistic way. The observation that the law has an individualizing effect on how we view domestic violence is not particularly surprising. After all, laws are designed to attach to individuals, not groups. When we make a claim for legal protection, we do so based on the assertion that another person has violated our individual rights. Furthermore, when the police make an arrest, it is the individual taken into custody who will receive due process protection based on constitutional commitments to impartiality and equality. Thus, in a very important sense, the law's *individual* focus ensures that the state will not use it as a tool of oppression. The emphasis on the individual can also operate in a manner that seriously constrains the power of the law as a tool to fight domestic violence. The first two themes discussed in this chapter—access to the law and the limitations of legal mechanisms to influence entrenched attitudes—illustrate this point.

The problems associated with access to the law reveal the difficulties created when we operate under the assumption that all individuals are equally situated in terms of their ability or willingness to utilize the legal system. As many interviewees asserted, such an assumption prevents us from adequately appreciating that many people are neither capable nor willing to involve the law in their lives, even in the most dangerous of situations. Because legal solutions largely take access issues for granted, they rarely include provisions to address the very real differences in ability to seek protection from the law. The blind spots created led many of those who were interviewed to conclude that despite the obvious value of legal interventions, an overreliance on them was indirectly contributing to a situation in which only victims who matched the profile of a "rational person" would have access to help.

The second theme—the limited power of legal mechanisms to influence widely entrenched cultural attitudes about domestic violence—also connects to the individual emphasis of the U.S. legal system. In this respect, interviewees highlighted the role that the narrow focus of legally based solutions on particular victims and perpetrators plays in contributing to a general failure to address the larger patterns in American society that foster domestic violence. Although the majority of people will never become directly involved in domestic violence as victim or perpetrator, many continue to adhere to stereotypes and attitudes that effectively sustain the problem. Interviewees repeatedly emphasized the need to recognize that "the problem of domestic violence" neither begins nor ends with a particular act of violence. Before the fact, incidents of domestic violence frequently receive tacit support in communities through a climate of acceptance; and after the fact they are swept under the rug. Even after violence has been subjected to legal censure, this "cultural support" continues if legal personnel fail to take the abuse seriously because of personal attitudes about violence between intimates or resource constraints and competing priorities. Unfortunately, because legal intervention is necessarily focused on the individual perpetrator or the victim who seeks the intervention, it typically occurs only after a pattern of violence is well established. As a result, a legally based approach tends to leave cultural supports that facilitate domestic violence largely untouched.

It is important to emphasize that the critiques of the individualistic focus of legal intervention need not lead to the conclusion that we should reject the focus. On the contrary, the interviewees looked upon the focus as both limiting *and* necessary to the web of protection that helps ensure that legal intervention and state power are not brought into play capriciously. What such critics *do* call into question is the assumption that if we can just "get it right," a legally based response to domestic violence will take care of the problem.

Although attaching legal interventions to certain acts of individuals is a suitable and important constraint, even if all of the victims of domestic violence were willing and able to utilize legal channels to resolve their difficulties, this would not be enough. The interview themes are united by an appreciation that an effective response to domestic violence demands that we pay careful attention to *all* the elements that contribute to and perpetuate the violence. Legal mechanisms address many of the elements, but many others are beyond the scope of the current legal framework.

In terms of the questions regarding the public versus private status of domestic violence that are central to this study, several points stand out. Legal intervention can be understood as the primary institutional mechanism for representing and constructing the boundaries that define the meaning of *public* and *private* in our society. It is logical to assume, then, that legal intervention that is individualistically focused contributes to a distinction between public and private that is driven by the relationship between the state and the individual. For example, whether a particular act of abuse is subject to public sanctions is heavily dependent on the victim's views of her relationship to the state and its surrogate, the legal system. Does she believe that the law will help? Does she have the resources and knowledge to access the help that is available?

When considered in isolation, there is nothing fundamentally wrong with the law's emphasis on the individual. After all, determining the proper relationship between state authority and individual liberty is one of the most profoundly important activities that can occur within a liberal

democratic system. A problem becomes apparent only when we realize
how much is left out of this formulation. In terms of domestic violence,
what is left out is an appreciation of the substantial role that relationships
that do not fit into a state-individual model play in both perpetuating and
stopping it. Because the law focuses only on the individuals directly involved and typically takes place after the violence pattern is well established, legal intervention effectively abstracts the issue from its context,
where it must eventually be solved.

The interviewees' observations illustrate that the effort to provide a
public response to domestic violence depends on factors that extend well
beyond victim and perpetrator. The attitudes of legal personnel; the degree to which arrest is followed by appropriate sentencing, counseling,
and monitoring; and legal representation are only a few of the contextual
factors mentioned as crucial to an effective response. One of the major
implications of the limits of legal intervention identified in the interviews
is that we must enlarge our vision of a useful response.

Legal Limits and Community Solutions

A general theme running through the interviews concerned the need
to pay attention to the ways in which a legally centered approach to domestic violence creates a public response that is characterized by serious
gaps. The initial focus of efforts to address domestic violence was almost
exclusively on generating changes in the institutional and legal responses
(or lack thereof) to the problem. The early emphasis came largely out of
"the critical need for shelters and services" and from the need to reform
the laws governing domestic violence, which at the time tended to treat it
"as a purely personal matter between a man and his wife."

The interviewees were nearly unanimous in regarding the changes and
reforms as absolutely essential. However, the interviewees also clearly recognized that these signs of progress are only a first and limited step
toward alleviating domestic violence. The following words from Victoria,
an activist, are characteristic: "Some people seem to see the law as the answer to this problem, but I think this is a big mistake; law is just one piece
of a very complex puzzle." There was a strong sense that the major challenge is to match the formal changes in laws and institutions with what
one interviewee called "an attitude shift in how we see domestic violence." Another observed: "We have enough laws. Now we need community education."

What unites strategies for addressing gaps in the legally based approach is their emphasis on community participation in developing an effective response to domestic violence. The term *community participation* encompasses a range of specific strategies for increasing the number and diversity of individuals actively engaged in addressing the problem of domestic violence. The strategies are categorized as participation, coalition, and education, which are directly linked to the larger topic of the public/private dichotomy because of their potential contribution to the effort to transform domestic violence into a "public problem."

When citizens play a role in responding to domestic violence, either through intervening in specific cases or taking part in programs to prevent it, several important things can occur. For one, the involvement enables learning firsthand about the complex and often confusing dynamics that accompany violence between intimates. For another, the involvement contributes to people's sense that they have a stake in stopping the violence. Once these happen, the ability to frame domestic violence as a social problem warranting serious attention by policymakers rather than as a problem off-limits to government involvement is dramatically improved. Expanding the number and variety of persons directly engaged also has positive implications for the meaning and effectiveness of the current legal response. Far from supplanting legal institutions, the increased community participation recommended by the interviewees is intended to fortify existing legal strategies for addressing domestic violence.

The Importance of Community Involvement

The longing for community is pervasive in our society. However, because the word *community* is subject to many interpretations, people tend to articulate the longing in abstract terms. In sharp contrast to this pattern, the interviewees rarely couched their observations about community involvement in abstractions. Instead, they spoke very specifically about the negative effects the lack of involvement was having on various aspects of the current response to domestic violence. The most commonly attributed negative effect was the failure to bring into being a major cultural shift in how we see and react to domestic violence in our society. Over and over again, interviewees confirmed the point that even though domestic violence may have been established as a criminal act deserving of punishment, many people—including some victims and legal personnel—continue to believe that it is a private matter, not the "business" of outsiders.

The interviewees deemed the involvement of a wide variety of community actors essential for a number of reasons. Principal among them was the belief that without it we will continue to depend too heavily on legal interventions. As Sue, a longtime activist, put it: "In the beginning we achieved great success with legal reform. Now this is creating a sand pit for the movement and we need to go on." Jeanne, another seasoned activist, described the current state of affairs in this way:

We are relying too heavily on the law to fix this problem. It's not the panacea. Certainly we need to keep working on the legal system, but we also need to start paying more attention to creating community-based and community-rooted sanctions that are part of people's daily lives and are a part of the value system and the community in which they operate.

Of course, the assertion that it is even possible to be overly dependent on the law is premised on the belief that the law is in some sense inadequate to the task. I briefly return now to the above-mentioned limitations of the law in order to convey why many of the interviewees looked upon community involvement as a potential antidote to the limitations.

Community Involvement and Prevention

One of the most serious limitations of legal intervention raised in the interviews was that, by design, intervention occurs subsequent to a domestic violence event, and often not until after repeated beatings. Further, because most domestic violence takes place in the home, it is neither desirable nor constitutionally permissible to bring the force of the law to bear on the situation before an actual assault. A number of interviewees pointed out that intervention therefore is often "too little and too late." The suggestion of many was to circumvent the dilemma by developing a system of informal, community-based interventions that would occur long before a serious escalation in abuse. An example of this strategy: teaching people the importance of confronting friends and associates when they behave aggressively toward an intimate. As Jeanne declared: "What we need now is to get everyone to send the message that violence is just not socially acceptable, no matter where it occurs."

As a means to this end, the organization in which Jeanne works has produced a video composed of vignettes in which aggressive or violent behavior toward a partner is displayed. It demonstrates how others present can react so as to show disapproval rather than turn away in embarrassment. Their reaction tells the perpetrator that the behavior is out of bounds and subject to adverse consequences. Further—and perhaps even more important—the reaction communicates to the victim that abuse need not be tolerated and that support is forthcoming in the event that she decides to take measures to stop it.

In my interviews, neither the difficulty nor the potential danger of such community-based intervention was downplayed. On the contrary, there was deep awareness of the very real barriers and dangers faced by community members when they seek to intervene.[14] However, the sensitivity to the difficulty associated with intervention, rather than resulting in an attitude of "let's let the police handle it," translated into an emphasis on why it is crucial to support one another as a community in making our opposition to domestic violence known before it spirals out of control. This emphasis was also apparent in the interviewees' desire to enlist the wider community in long-term prevention efforts, which many felt to be a missing component in developing a solution.

General resource constraints also constitute a barrier to prevention efforts. Frequently, organizations that provide services to domestic violence victims cannot justify devoting appreciable resources to prevention as long as there are victims who are not receiving those services. Many interviewees talked of the need to bridge the "prevention gap" by involving the community more actively in violence prevention. Examples included actions as fundamental as "teaching your own children from a very young age that violence is not acceptable, ever." Many also spoke of the desirability of supplementing family instruction with programs in public schools. Jennifer, a legislative analyst, put it this way:

It would be nice if we didn't have to rely on schools to teach our children not to be violent, but unfortunately, we can't always depend on healthy functioning families. I learned not to hit not only at home but in school as well. Good teachers have always taught values, and today we seem to need that more than ever.

Of course, as the controversy over "sex education" in schools has amply demonstrated, presenting information on topics traditionally dealt with in a familial context can be very contentious. However, according to Richard, the above-mentioned psychotherapist, this only serves to underline the vital importance of educating the community about the need for early intervention. He explains: "Until the community is aware of the enormous potential of early intervention, there will be no momentum for getting approval and funding for domestic violence prevention programs in the schools."

Community Involvement and the Law

Interviewees, although frequently seeking to involve the community in the solution, did not assert that community-based actions were viable substitutes for legal interventions. Doubts about the accessibility and effectiveness of legal interventions were almost always accompanied by impassioned declarations about the profound importance of maintaining a visible and consistent legal response to domestic violence.

According to one interviewee, the law performs a number of vital functions, among which is setting "the tone for major attitudinal changes." Another stated that the law is "a starting point for dialogue about ethics and what we will and will not tolerate in this society." Noteworthy is that both comments conceptualize legal mechanisms as an important piece of a much larger process, but just one piece. Although setting a tone for and starting the dialogue is certainly crucial, unless members of the community engage the challenges and dilemmas that domestic violence raises, lasting change is unlikely. Jeanne had this to say:

When we look at patterns of social transformation, what generally happens is that it begins with a focus on policy change, which is then followed by the enactment of a lot of new laws. However, if these institutional reforms are not ultimately followed by some significant measure of community involvement, it is very unlikely that there will any meaningful long-term change.

The interviewees described citizen participation as helping in a number of ways to guarantee that relevant legislation is not reduced to "form over substance." First, involvement can be tremendously useful in the effort to ensure that laws are actually enforced. Often referred to in our sessions were judges, police, and legal personnel in general who act as though domestic violence cases are not worthy of their attention—legal reforms to the contrary. To counteract this disinterest, advocates have set up clinics to educate victims about the relevant laws and procedures so that they can know whether they are being treated appropriately. Another tactic has been to accompany victims when they go to court, which not only provides support but also makes court personnel aware that they are being monitored. Currently, a combination of paid staff and volunteers in the clinics perform these services, but a number of those interviewed talked about plans to involve more people by creating community watchdog groups.[15]

On a slightly more abstract level, interviewees also pointed out that community involvement is essential for helping people feel empowered by laws already on the books. When asked why people often "look the other way" when faced with clear indications that domestic violence is occurring, the most common answer was that "a lot of people do want to help but they are afraid or they don't know how." In light of the frustrating helplessness that many bystanders experience, numerous members of the interview cohort spoke of the necessity of providing citizens with a range of instructions, tools, and opportunities to assist them in developing a response with which they would be more comfortable. Taking *some* action, even if it is only calling the police, tends to make people more committed to the issue. Lisa, the above-mentioned activist, drew a parallel to the campaign of Mothers against Drunk Driving to call on people to serve as designated drivers. As she observed: "When you ask people to do something and then give them the tools so that they can, it creates a momentum that extends beyond that single event."

The Importance of Coalitions

The concern to create "momentum" around the issue of domestic violence pervaded the interviews. Here too, the key to doing so seemed to revolve primarily around maintaining a healthy balance between legally prescribed requirements and internally driven commitments from both private community members and persons who are translating legal provisions into effective practices.

A strong theme regarding momentum in the interviews was the need to develop coalitions as a central component of any long-term strategy. Although the trend toward coalition-building was unanimously supported, it is a fairly new phenomenon. According to a number of interviewees, during the 1970s and 1980s, when many fewer people were interested in the problem of domestic violence, a sense of territoriality frequently accompanied the work that was being done. The descriptions of territoriality were not offered as part of an attack on early activists but were framed instead as an understandable response to a situation in which many activists felt as though they were solitary voices. Carolyn, who began working with domestic violence as an activist during the 1970s and now works on the issue for a state agency, had this to say about territoriality:

Especially in the early days of the movement it was easy to feel like we were the only ones looking out for these women who were confronting what was often terrible brutality in their lives. For me at least, the sense that we were alone in our fight only strengthened my desire to vindicate and do for the victims what the system had failed to do, thus turning it into a kind of personal fight. As people dedicate their careers to this issue, it becomes part of who you are. Once this has happened, it can be very hard to relinquish control over how it is going to go to others.

However, Carolyn went on to argue that activists and professionals who are working to stop domestic violence simply cannot afford to treat the effort as a "personal fight" but must seek to develop productive partnerships whenever possible.

The sentiment that those who care about domestic violence need to find new ways to work together reverberated throughout the interviews. One of the most common reasons given for an approach based on partnerships is that it is simply not possible for a small number of individuals to carry out the daunting task of addressing the problem. A case in point involves Lisa, who had been involved in providing domestic violence training to police departments and court personnel for many years. Although she believed the training was successful, when she took a break after five years, she watched as the momentum that she and others had worked so hard to generate in those early years came to a halt. Partially as a result of such experiences, as well as a growing sense of "no longer wanting to stand in front of forty officers with a feeling of being burned out," the organization employing Lisa started to reorient its efforts toward working behind the scenes. Energy and resources previously spent on training were transferred to working to develop leaders within law enforcement agencies. Underlying the shift was the recognition that "if you want to change an institution you need to bring the insiders along." Now that specific leaders have been cultivated, Lisa is confident that even without the organization's constant attention, momentum on the issue will continue.

Another common reason given for the importance of developing a coalition orientation relates to the desirability of providing victims of domestic violence with a coordinated set of services. Victims have a range of needs, and in their efforts to deal with abuse, they frequently come in contact with a dizzying array of public agencies and institutions, including hospitals, shelters, transitional housing services, public schools, welfare agencies, law enforcement organizations, and courts of several sorts. In the absence of coordination, victims often need to repeat their stories many times, and services are frequently inefficient or contradictory. Many of the interviewees described situations in which, even after finally mustering sufficient courage to leave the abuser, the victim ended up returning because she was unable to thread through the complex process of obtaining support services to make it on her own.

The lack of coordination within the legal system, which has separate civil, criminal, and family courts, can be especially vexing. For example, a victim might obtain a restraining order and then a divorce based on the violence but, when seeking custody, find that the judge will not consider

documented patterns of violence in making the decision. Judges frequently mandate custody arrangements that do not include any accom-
modations for couples who have a history of violence.[16] In light of such
problems, a great many interviewees talked very specifically about the
need for greater cooperation and coordination among and within the various agencies, organizations, and institutions that routinely come in contact with domestic violence cases. The most frequent suggestions had to
do with the creation of coalitions. The following recommendation made
by Victoria, a shelter worker, is typical: "The most effective response to
domestic violence is one where you have an active coalition task force including representatives from the district attorney's office, probation, the
medical community, housing, and social welfare agencies so that [the vic-
tim] has what she needs to stop the violence."

The interviewees also viewed coalitions as very useful mechanisms for
the development of future policy directions in the treatment and prevention of domestic violence. One of the benefits associated with a coalition-
based approach the presence of a variety of perspectives, which helps to
prevent compartmentalizing the problem. Many of the interviewees
talked about the problems associated with conceptualizing domestic violence as an isolated incident or as involving a single individual, when in
fact it is usually accompanied by problems such as drug and alcohol addiction, child abuse, animal cruelty, sexual assault, mental instability, and
homelessness. Failure to appreciate such cross-cutting connections can
mean missing opportunities for early recognition of the problem. Com-
partmentalization can also create problems once interventions begin. For
example Claire, an advocate for battered women, noted that she persistently encounters circumstances where individuals working in different
parts of the system "end up talking past each other and doing things that
replicate or actually hurt each other's efforts."

Another benefit of coalition-building is the opportunities that collaborative strategies provide for sharing information and ideas. In this respect, many interviewees spoke of the potentially important role of academics in coalitions. There was some derogation of the scholarly
contribution ("academic work in this area is of limited value to practitioners"), but the comments were typically made in reference to academic research carried out with very little attention given to the needs of practitioners directly engaged in stopping the violence. Even so, it was made
clear that academics could play a much bigger role in a solution if better
linkages were established between research, teaching, and policy.

There was near-consensus on the value of a coalition-based approach for building people's sense that their work is part of a cooperative, community-based effort. This point relates to a theme discussed earlier: the momentum that is generated when people believe that they can actually *do* something effectual about a problem. Not only are people empowered by their participation, it is likely that the solutions they develop will be better suited to the particular needs and dynamics of their agency or institution. The following comment made by Carmen, an administrator for a domestic violence program, concerns the needs of counties:

We need more people who are committed to the idea of coalition. Part of this comes out of my hesitation with legislation at the state level. Counties have such different needs and communities are in a much better position to know their own needs. For example, the same approach that works in a rural area with one sheriff may not work in an urban area that has twenty.

Last, but certainly not least, are the psychological and personal benefits that derive from working cooperatively with others on a project. When interviewees were asked why they continued to work in the area of domestic violence, many cited friends, colleagues, and the feeling of connection as the reason they remained involved, despite the many difficulties and frustrations.

Reframing Battering: Making Connections between Private Violence and the Community

The arguments used by the interviewees in their efforts to generate increased concern about domestic violence also demonstrate their emphasis on the importance of community. One of the major strategies described in the interviews to get people to see domestic violence as an important social issue warranting public intervention and funding is centered on helping people to recognize that they have a stake in stopping domestic violence because of the serious social consequences that it produces.

Many consequences were cited in the interviews to highlight the residual effects of domestic violence. At the most mundane level are the monetary costs of battering. As Linda, a legislative aide specializing in family violence issues, noted: "People still don't have a real understanding of the tremendous impact that this type of violence has on our society. Beyond just being illegal, domestic violence costs us all a lot of money, hospital time, kids acting out and disrupting classrooms, workplace violence, and work days missed." Other oft-cited costs include the enormous amount of police resources required to break up domestic disputes; court expenses and backlogs that result from victims seeking restraining orders and the prosecution of offenders; and the dollars spent on incarcerating individuals who have killed or injured either their victims or their abusers.[17] Yet by far the cost most mentioned in the interviews—and one that many people overlook—is the multiplier effect of domestic violence on the general level of crime and violence.

Polls consistently indicate that crime is a primary concern among Americans. However, although domestic violence is now officially a crime in every state, many people continue to view it not as a crime but as a dispute between lovers. This blind-eye stance supports another pattern identified in the interviews: the dissociation of crime in the home from crime on the streets. The interviewees seek to challenge that separation by making people aware of the connection between domestic violence and other crimes.

Both common sense and social science studies were used in the interviews to make the point that children who grow up in violent households have a much higher probability of becoming violent adults who will not only hurt those with whom they live but also express their anger and pain by committing crimes against the general population. Frances, an assistant district attorney, put it this way: "Assumptions about domestic violence as just a slap in the face are wrong. It's much more than a slap, and what goes on in these situations needs to be seen as just as important as what goes on in the street. In fact, domestic violence often contributes to street crime." The perceived correlation between domestic violence and street crime challenges the mistaken assumption that if a person is not directly experiencing abuse, he or she is not being hurt.

Another common approach in the interviews was to frame domestic violence cases as "pre-homicide cases." Those who used the description typically relied on two sources of evidence to support their position. First, a pattern of escalation has been documented in domestic violence situations. Barbara, a county victim witness advocate, asserted: "In light of a very predictable escalation pattern once abuse has started, it is best to intervene as soon as possible before major trauma to the children or a murder occurs."

The second source of evidence consists of the tally of victims eventually murdered by their abusers. From the perspective of many of those I interviewed, the sheer number of people who are subjected to domestic violence and who are seriously injured or killed as a result is, on its own, adequate justification to frame this issue as one of grave public concern.

Significantly, when referring to homicide, interviewees did not limit themselves to the intended victims of the abusers. They repeatedly referred to the deaths of innocent bystanders caught in crossfire and to the deaths of perpetrators at the hands of their victims. Leaving victims to their own devices and failing to intervene were deemed the equivalents of being an accessory to a possible murder. As Jose, a police officer, noted: "We have to remember that these women are going through a private hell and are being terrorized. If we do nothing to help, we are contributing to situations where women feel so desperate that they kill their aggressor." Furthermore, from the perspective of many interviewees, there is a persistent tendency in the reporting of these events to play down the connection between killings and the often long history of preceding domestic violence. For example, according to a number of activists, there has been an effort in San Francisco to ensure that the local newspapers do not use such demeaning headlines as "Lovers' Tiff Leads to Murder."

What is common to all of these arguments—whether about the effect of domestic violence on the victim, the batterer, their children, or the general population—is that they are based on an effort to emphasize the connection between domestic violence and larger patterns of violence in our society. According to those who make the argument, highlighting this connection and the enormous social and monetary costs of domestic violence is the most effective way to arouse support for programs and laws to stop battering. The logic is that if one appeals directly to people's self-interest, they will respond. Establishing a link between that self-interest and the generalized consequences of domestic violence is a first step in developing a personal connection to a problem that people previously viewed—if they viewed it at all—as completely outside their lives.

Six

Reconstructing the Boundaries of Community Concern

THE THEMES RAISED IN CHAPTER 5 REPRESENT IN varying ways the struggle by practitioners in the field to transform domestic violence into a "public" problem. What ties the themes together is the belief that an effective response to battering requires the active participation of a wide spectrum of the populace. A good deal of the interviewees' emphasis on participation can be understood as a product of their awareness of the limitations of formal legal responses. Although they unquestionably viewed legal mechanisms as essential, they expressed doubts about the efficacy of formal rules and sanctions in bringing about improved understanding and treatment of domestic violence.

At the most obvious level, many of the interviewees' suggestions sprang from their experience of utilizing legal mechanisms. The suggestions are not rejections of the law but are part of an effort to generate the conditions necessary for it to function to greater purpose. The latter is a significant point in itself, for it challenges the classical liberal construction of the law as an abstract and neutral tool for the regulation of society. Rather than simply seeing the law as a means to act upon society, the interviewees recognized it as part of the society it is designed to regulate. Implicit in this perspective is the understanding that the law not only constrains but also constructs social behavior.[1]

The interpretation of the law as one component of a much larger process of social change necessarily involves assigning it a more modest role. This move serves to bring the status of the law as just one piece of a complex social interaction into greater focus. Furthermore, activists who maintain an awareness of the contingencies of legal regulation are much more likely to recognize instances in which legal reform is not the most effective means of bringing about significant changes in the status quo.

The emphasis in the interviews on decentering law as the predominant strategy for addressing domestic violence has important implications for how we approach the negotiation of public and private boundaries. Developing these implications is a first step toward the construction of an alternative approach to understanding the meaning of public and private boundaries as they relate to this type of violence.

Expanding the Meaning of Public Intervention

The first major implication of decentering the law for our understanding of public and private boundaries is the way in which it serves to expand the range of possibilities for defining domestic violence as a public problem. In the 1980s and 1990s, the primary strategy for challenging the status of domestic violence as a private prerogative was to impose public sanctions for such behavior through the promulgation of regulations. In keeping with this emphasis, efforts to evaluate the degree to which domestic violence should be treated as a public problem are frequently reduced to questions about which level of legal intervention can or cannot be justified.

The interviewees persistently challenged this conflation of "public intervention" and "legal intervention." Examples can be found in their critiques regarding the limits of a legally based approach and their suggestions for improving the response to domestic violence more generally. In other words, an *effective* public response to domestic violence requires much more than the passage of laws. Laws do not operate in a vacuum but depend on a range of individuals to enforce, obey, and utilize them. This deceptively obvious point is central to the discussion because it draws our attention to an important distinction: an interpretation of "public" as representing institutional rules and procedures versus an interpretation of "public" as an actual grouping of citizens. The interviewees made clear that it is the latter interpretation (public as citizens) that merits our energies. It bears repeating: the shared element of the suggestions presented in chapter 5 is the goal of involving people in greater numbers and of greater diversity in addressing domestic violence. When viewed in combination, the critiques and suggestions of how we might improve our response to domestic violence point toward a richer and much more complex understanding of what its transformation into a public problem would mean. According to this perspective, designating domestic violence a public problem requires that we change our approach to it at the institutional *and* individual levels.

A New Model of Public and Private

The interviewees' expansion of the meaning of public interventions moves away from the dualistic framework that has traditionally provided the basis for conceptualizing the relationship between public and private. Instead of adhering to a strict dichotomy, we can use this expansion to think about the relationship as operating according to a triangular formulation, with the state, the community, and the family as the three corner points. Now, three boundaries, rather than only one, distinguish public from private (see Figure 1). And because each boundary structures a different set of relationships, the shape and nature of each will also be distinct.

The first relationship is between the state and the family. The term *the state* refers to the individuals and institutions that are directly associated with state power and sanctions. Included within this category are courts, legislatures, law enforcement agencies, appointed and elected officials, social service agencies, and public schools (see Table 1).

The boundary defining the relationship between the family and the state correlates with the liberal model of public and private theorized by John Locke and reiterated in the liberal feminist alternative to Locke's distinction. The major function of this boundary is to protect individuals and families from unwarranted intrusions by the state. A web of institutional and cultural norms, constitutional rights, legislative mandates, administrative procedures, and institutional mechanisms constrains the degree to which government agents can become involved in the affairs of the domestic sphere and structure interventions when such involvement takes

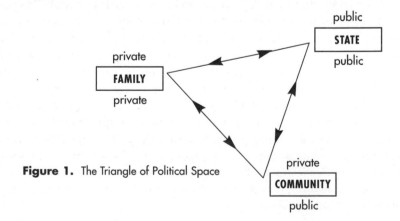

Figure 1. The Triangle of Political Space

Table 1. Groups included in each category of the triangular model that replaces the public/private dichotomy

State	Community	Family
Judicial institutions	Social movement organizations	Individual family
Legislative institutions	Political parties	members
Police departments	Special interest groups	Nuclear family
Social service agencies	Corporations and private employers	Extended family
City and town govern-	Neighborhood associations	Intimate relationships
ments	Religious institutions	Close friendships
Public schools	Philanthropic and service organizations	
	Health care organizations	
	Media outlets	

Table 2. The boundary between the state and the family

Public	Boundary Structures	Private
	Search-and-seizure laws	
	Due-process rights	
	Legislative mandates and programs	
	Property rights	
State	Contracts	Family
	Bureaucratic structures and rules	
	Administrative law	
	Police procedures	
	Physical barriers	

place (see Table 2). Throughout the interviews, approval for maintaining this particular boundary was widespread. Although the interviewees were unanimous that physical abuse in the home should be treated as a serious criminal matter, they repeatedly qualified this stance with equally strong statements about the importance of ensuring that all state-backed interventions in the home be made in accordance with the privacy and due process rights of the individuals involved.

The second element of the triangular relationship is structured by the boundary between the family and the community. In comparison to the institutionally driven boundary between public and private, this boundary is more informal and is less clearly defined. Its function is to distinguish what should remain completely within the discretion of individual family members from information or events that warrant some sort of involvement by members of the wider community. The community comprises a broad grouping of individuals and nongovernmental organizations, including neighbors, private employers, the media, churches, corporations, social activists, special interest groups, and health professionals (see Table 1). As this diverse list indicates, the term *community* is *not* being employed here to denote a set of values and commitments that are shared by the individuals and groups that make up this realm.[2] I do not assume the presence of unity within and among the communities that are discussed, nor do I wish to argue for the desirability of such unity.[3] In this respect I am using *community* in its descriptive, not its normative, sense.

One of the primary characteristics that distinguishes the community from the state is the absence of punitive sanctions backed by state power. The key difference between the boundary between the state and the family and that between the community and the family lies in the nature of the possible outside interventions that each is designed to mediate. When it comes to the relationship between the state and the family, the public/private boundary is intended to protect against interventions that carry with them the possibility of state sanctions and scrutiny. In regard to relationships between the community and the family, however, although some level of community-based censure might result, the imposition of state sanctions is not immediately at stake.[4]

Examples of activities that serve to involve the community in cases of domestic violence within the family include public education programs about how to avoid violence; provision of resources that enable victims to survive financially and emotionally without the abuser; informal actions and media-generated publicity communicating the unacceptability of abusive behavior; corporate contributions toward violence-prevention efforts and services; and development of workplace policies for assisting employee victims. Because such activities do not typically entail the imposition of state sanctions, the process of distinguishing between what should and should not remain private when it comes to community involvement tends to be less formal and less institutionalized.[5] Still, despite a greater amount of fluidity between the family and the community, there is nevertheless a boundary between them that preserves privacy by protecting the family and its members from excessive scrutiny. In addition to the physical barriers that shield family life from constant monitoring, the boundary is structured and mediated by property laws, civil rights, and cultural and community norms that pertain to privacy and family life more generally (see Table 3).[6]

The third side of the triangle is the relationship between the state and the community. One of the most important roles that the state plays in a democratic society is to ensure that the community does not impinge on

Table 3. The boundary between the community and the family

Public	Boundary Structures	Private
Community	Civil rights Legislative mandates/programs Property rights/contracts School boards Professional associations Ethical codes Cultural norms Religious principles Family values Physical barriers	Family

Table 4. The boundary between the state and the community

Public	Boundary Structures	Private
State	First Amendment Free speech Separation of church and state Civil rights Legislative mandates and programs Property rights and contracts Budget policies and procedures Taxes Government funding Economic regulation	Community

the rights of private citizens. In this regard, the interactions between non-state actors and individual citizens having to do with domestic violence are structured by bureaucratic institutions, administrative law, legislative bodies and processes, and social organizations (see Table 4). Activities that occur within these frameworks include the provision of funding, regulation and monitoring of state-funded services, education, research, reporting, public hearings, and the development and operation of coalitions designed to facilitate a more comprehensive and coordinated response to domestic violence.

The relationship between the state and community associations has been amply described in the extensive literature on civil society.[7] Although I do not wish to fully engage the complex debates about how civil society operates or should be defined, I would like to make several points about the relationship. Within my triangular model of public and private, the domain labeled "community" is distinct in that it is a hybrid, simultaneously public and private. In the relationship between the state and community associations, the latter are clearly private. When compared with familial relationships, their public nature becomes much more apparent. In this sense, the community side of the triangle serves as an important bridge between the definitively public sphere of the state and the private sphere of the family.

The fact that what I call "community activities" do not fit neatly into either category of public or private highlights the complexity and ambiguity of the two terms. Obviously, we should not take for granted that the private sphere refers only to the family. As noted in chapter 1, the majority of discussions of the relationship between public and private do not even consider the family but focus instead on the distinction between the state and private economic relations.[8] On the other hand, to automatically equate the public sphere with politics also invites oversimplification.[9] One possible consequence is that it becomes easy to forget that a great many of the activities that we commonly regard as "public" take place in voluntary associations outside formal political structures.[10]

The significance of determining the public or private status of the activities and groups within the community extends well beyond a technical interest in accurate labels. How we categorize particular activities or groups has far-reaching consequences because of the way in which responsibility is assigned in the United States. When an activity or group is categorized as public, certain procedures and consequences can follow. For example, according to the triangular model, when compared to the family, the community domain is designated as public. Accordingly, when individuals seek to intervene in a family, to some degree their intervention should be understood as public and thus subject to limitations that have been designed to protect the rights of individual family members from public intervention. To illustrate, if a church began printing names of alleged batterers as a means of sending a message to the congregation about the unacceptability of such behavior, the action would almost certainly be subjected to state scrutiny because of its potential to undermine our collective commitment to due process.[11]

Debates surrounding the provision of faith-based social services and their relationship to Title VII of the 1964 Civil Rights Act and the First Amendment's Establishment Clause provide an excellent illustration of the multiple stakes involved in the designation of an activity as public or private. For many years, religious organizations that provided social services were excused from Title VII's prohibition of religious discrimination and the First Amendment's requirement that the state shall neither hinder nor favor particular forms of religious expression. These exemptions were justified by the argument that to impose state standards of nondiscrimination on religious organizations would be the equivalent of forcing religious organizations to act against their beliefs when managing personnel. Significantly, these exemptions were dependent on the designation of religious organizations as private entities. In keeping with this distinction, religious groups that accepted public funding for the programs they administered were potentially accountable to the requirements of Title VII and to the establishment and free exercise clauses of the First Amendment. A case in point was a successful lawsuit filed against a Salvation Army domestic violence shelter in 1989 by an employee who had been fired because of her involvement in the Wiccan religion. According to the federal judge who decided the case, "Even though the religious exemption does permit the Salvation Army to terminate an employee based on religious grounds, the fact that the plaintiff's position as Victim's Assistance Coordinator was funded substantially, if not entirely, by federal, state, and local government revenue gives rise to constitutional considerations which effectively prohibit the application of the exemption to the facts in this case." As the opinion makes clear, it was specifically because part of the employee's salary came from government sources that the religious requirements imposed by the Salvation Army constituted a violation of the protections of the establishment clause against government advancement of religion.[12]

This approach to regulating faith-based organizations has been challenged by those who argue that it has a chilling effect on the creation of positive partnerships between religious organizations and the government in the provision of social services. Such concerns have resulted in a series of "charitable choice" initiatives, which include provisions allowing religious groups that receive public funds to discriminate on the basis of religion with regard to personnel matters.[13] Proponents of charitable choice legislation are implicitly challenging long-standing distinctions between public and private that revolve around the presence or absence of public funding. In this respect, the issue of charitable choice illustrates the significance of designations regarding the public or private nature of particular activities. It also highlights the ways in which these designations are themselves the products of current political, legal, and cultural debates.

One of the attributes of the triangular model that I propose is that it facilitates an appreciation of this aspect of boundary construction. It does so by providing a framework for understanding the way in which the meanings of *public* and *private* and the boundaries that are developed to uphold them are informed by the practical, political, and legal relationships that exist among family, community, and the state. The framework makes it possible to see how the three continuously shape one another. Because the model does not require us to define the three sectors or the individuals who move within them in a rigid or static manner, I believe that it is much less likely than the frameworks examined thus far to obscure the complexities of the relationship between public and private.

Benefits of the New Model

Decentering the State

Expanding the division between public and private to include a triangular relationship between the state, the family, and the community has important practical advantages. First, it counteracts the tendency to view the relationship between public and private as reducible to the maintenance of a single boundary between state power and private individuals. When the primary focus is on legal interventions, the importance of preserving that boundary will be paramount. After all, when the state intervenes in the family through the force of law, the stakes are necessarily going to be very high. Many of those interviewed were acutely sensitive to this fact, expressing strong reservations about the practice even when it was for a cause they believed in deeply. Although none of the interviewees suggested that we should back away from imposing criminal sanctions on abusers, there was strong consensus on the need to become more assertive about extending efforts beyond punitive responses.

The model of public and private that emerges from this approach is characterized by multiple points of exchange between the public sphere (now defined to include both the state and community-based interventions) and the private realm of the family.[14] The great advantage of this model is that it expands the meaning of public interventions to include actions that do not directly subject private individuals to state sanctions, thereby creating space for a somewhat less vigilant stance on the public/private boundary. In circumstances where state power is not directly implicated, the boundary can become more fluid. The interviewees' suggestions for ways to increase the range of intervention options available to those who wish to respond to, or escape from, a situation involving domestic violence stand as examples of the types of opportunities that are created when a more flexible approach is adopted.

It is important to emphasize that at the time they were interviewed, in the late 1990s, the dominant focus of the interviewees was on ways to in-

crease the opportunities for community-based, rather than state-based interventions.[15] Because they do not involve the direct imposition of state
sanctions,[16] such interventions are not required to meet the same level of
"probable cause" and thus can occur at a much earlier stage. For this reason, in many cases involvement by outsiders in domestic conflict *before* it
escalates to violence can help a couple address the abusive pattern early
enough to avoid physical abuse. Coalitions can be especially useful in this
regard by making available a network of community resources that do not
entail police involvement. As Margaret Borkowski writes,

Because privacy protects intimacy and because intimacy is an aspiration normally
expected to be satisfied in marriage, it is understandable that women, when first
experiencing marital violence and wanting to continue their relationship, should
turn to agencies such as doctors and marriage guidance counselors who are believed to have strict rules about confidentiality.[17]

Concerns about privacy are not limited to perpetrators who desire immunity: victims are equally subject to deep-seated beliefs about the private
nature of familial affairs. If the only recourse open to a victim is to call the
police, thereby involving the state directly and potentially subjecting the
partner to incarceration, many victims will choose to handle the violence
on their own. In light of the tensions between the goals of safety and privacy, the importance of the interviewees' emphasis on supplementing the
availability of assistance to include community programs and coalitions of
service providers becomes especially pressing.

Even in cases where state legal interventions do become necessary, the
presence of community-based sanctions and support can significantly contribute to the effectiveness of the state's measures. Domestic violence is an
extremely complex problem that extends well beyond the circumstances
of a particular incident. To expect that a single police intervention or even
multiple interventions will eradicate entrenched patterns of abuse is unre-
alistic.[18] The interviewees' recognition of the need to develop a social context in which violence is out-of-bounds and material and moral support
are available to victims mirrors the trend in law enforcement toward community policing. One of the principles underlying community policing is
the belief that the goal of police work is to prevent arrests rather than
make arrests. Proponents argue that the effectiveness of the police in reducing both the actual number of crimes perpetrated and the general level
of public fear is greatly enhanced when explicit efforts are directed at establishing and maintaining a good working relationship with the communities that they serve.[19]

In instances of domestic violence, there is an especially strong need for legal interventions to take place within a community-based framework. Because the perpetrator and the victim typically have a relationship of some duration, resolving a single incident rarely ends the violence. Accordingly, a range of coordinated services and support systems are essential to help the couple either to part or to resolve their difficulties. If these are lacking, it is very likely that the police will have to return again and again.

Significantly, in addressing cases of recurring domestic violence, some of the most serious tensions between privacy and protection arise. Lawrence Sherman tells us, "Given a choice between privacy and prevention . . . Americans choose privacy. The result is the chronic cases dilemma: preventing chronic violence is too intrusive, but ignoring it allows predictable violence to occur."[20] By reframing domestic violence as a problem that affects us all, involving more citizens in the effort to address it, and developing a coalition-based network of public service providers, the interviewees and others like them are helping to bridge the gap between these two options.

Finally, developing community-based responses has distinct advantages in dealing with the challenge of providing assistance to what is a very diverse population of women. As I have emphasized throughout this book, although there are certain commonalities that are of political significance, battered women vary considerably in terms of their immediate needs and their preferences about how to resolve the challenges that they face.[21] The fact that the community portion of the model described here is not a singular entity but comprises many different communities helps to direct our attention to the importance of providing a diversity of responses and highlights the presence of important variations in the population being served. The need for culturally specific services for battered women is particularly critical in the case of women of color and immigrant women, who are frequently not served adequately by existing services.[22]

Decentering the Victim

The second major advantage of the triangular model is that it diverts attention from the victim. One of the most common questions asked by people who have little experience with the dynamics of domestic abuse is, Why does she stay? The question has caused an explosion of studies, books, and theories seeking to explain victim behavior.[23] Some of the research has contributed positively to our ability to help victims, but there is a strong feeling among workers in the field that this is not the right question.[24]

The assumption that it is even possible to come up with a definitive explanation for why victims stay in abusive relationships indicates a widespread failure to appreciate the contradictions inherent in the liberal belief that the private family can simultaneously provide the greatest opportunity for both individuation *and* connection.[25] The most serious negative consequence of the question and others like it is that when a satisfactory answer is not forthcoming, it becomes very easy to distance ourselves from the dilemma by blaming the victim. Additionally, according to many of the interviewees, our obsession with what the victim did or did not do prevents us from asking the far more important question: What can *we* do to prevent this from happening again?[26] When generating new mechanisms for public involvement in domestic violence, this latter question is crucial.

As long as public interventions are chiefly defined within a legal framework, the primary focus will remain on the victim. One of the outstanding characteristics of the U.S. legal system is its individualistic basis.[27] Although it is no longer incumbent on the victim to press charges in felony cases of domestic battery, the burden on the victim to report the abuse and then to follow through with legal action remains very high. The great advantage of the interviewees' approach is that the public response is generated principally within the community itself instead of originating exclusively with particular victims. That is, whether domestic violence is going to be treated as a public matter no longer hinges so strongly on what its victims decide to do or *not* to do.[28]

Beyond simply taking the burden off the victim, increasing community participation can provide a firsthand perspective on the complexities and conflicting loyalties that are faced by individuals involved in a pattern of domestic violence. Coalitions are also very valuable in this respect. It came through in many interviews that when professionals come together to talk about the problems they encounter as the result of domestic violence, the magnitude and complexity of the victims' dilemmas are brought into sharp relief.

However, the objective of cultivating a greater understanding and empathy for the victims' dilemmas is *not* so that we can resolve them or make them disappear. As I have argued in the theoretical portions of this book, to a large extent these dilemmas come directly out of the conflicting objectives of the liberal family structure itself. But even without resolution as our objective, increasing our capacity to engage the dilemmas can enable us to see the connection between the actions of victims and the often "irrational" choices that we all make in the context of familial relationships.

In this regard, as Christine Littleton has suggested, when listening to victims, we should start with the assumption that the descriptions they provide of their experiences are accurate and reasonable, given the conditions within which they live. When we begin with this assumption, the tensions and contradictions in the descriptions give us a way to examine the conditions rather than a reason to invalidate the experiences or reactions that do not strike us as reasonable.[29] Instead of obsessively asking why she stayed or how this happened, we are much more likely to get on with the important task of supporting the victims and those who are working to stop the violence.

Producing Boundaries through the Democratic Process

One of the most significant theoretical implications of the interview themes for the construction of public and private boundaries arises in the role given to democratic institutions and processes. Throughout the interview responses, the determination of public and private boundaries was explicitly assigned to the democratic process. The centrality of democratic institutions is not surprising, given that one of my criteria in selecting interviewees was active engagement in efforts to address domestic violence through political and legal processes. Predictability aside, it is a significant departure from the theoretical and legal approaches to these boundaries that have been discussed in this book up until this point.

The major difference between the approach developed from the interviews and the models of public and private discussed in chapters 2, 3, and 4 is not the absence or presence of democratic commitments but, rather, the role that the commitments play in the formulation of the models. Although dissimilar in many other respects, the theoretical and legal frameworks discussed in those chapters share an approach to public and private that treats these boundaries as though their establishment was a *prerequisite* for rather than a *product* of democracy. Their underlying assumption is that it is possible to design an ideal division between the two spheres that will make the pursuit of the democratic goals of liberty, order, and freedom possible. The interviewees' approach reverses the sequence. The delineation of public and private spheres is not a necessary *precursor* of democracy but its natural *product*.

Two major interview themes are especially helpful in illustrating the emphasis on the creation of boundaries through the democratic process. The first theme revolves around the interviewees' insistence on the importance of education of the public as a tool in the treatment and prevention of domestic violence. For victims and potential victims, education was viewed as crucial in helping them "recognize the presence of a cycle of violence." The information could assist them to escape the cycle or, even better, to avoid it in the first place. For perpetrators and potential perpetrators, education, especially at a young age, could teach them that violence is never appropriate and train them in nonviolent methods of resolving conflict. Even for people who will never directly experience domestic violence, education is very important because of the great likelihood that at some point most people will come into close contact with someone who has experienced, or is experiencing, it. As one activist put it: "The most important factor to determine how well someone deals with domestic violence is not whether they are white or male, young or old, but whether they have been educated about it either through training or experience."

When I asked the interviewees about what they saw as the major barriers to resolving domestic violence, one of the most frequent answers given was "the ignorance, misinformation, and stereotypes about the problem that pervade our society." On a more positive note, many also spoke of the dramatic progress they had witnessed as a result of education efforts and the openness of a majority of people to becoming better informed. In this sense, education was portrayed as an ongoing process that even in its earliest stages has demonstrated enormous potential.

Interviewees manifestly used education in their attempts to transform domestic violence into a public problem.[30] Such usage places the construction of meaning around public and private firmly within a democratic framework. Education can be characterized as a paradigmatically democratic strategy because of its ability to facilitate a process in which people are able to arrive at their own conclusions.[31] Rather than telling people how they should approach domestic violence, providing relevant information can enable them to arrive at the well-thought-out conclusion that it is a problem calling for collective action. The following description provided by a legislative analyst of the use of education as a strategy in passing legislation provides an excellent illustration of the democratic basis of this approach:

A lot of the changes in the past years can be attributed to the slow process of educating the legislature on this issue. Most domestic violence bills don't make it in the first year or two, but as hearings are held where witnesses tell their stories and with constant pushing from women's groups and committed district attorneys, it is eventually possible to get people to change their minds. In my opinion, this is the legislature at its best.

The second thematic strategy in the interviews that marks the approach to domestic violence as democratic is an emphasis on participation. Community education and prevention programs, the push for coalitions, and the effort to help people to see the connections between private violence and their own concerns are all examples of strategies driven by a desire to increase people's involvement. Additionally, as the critiques of legal intervention make clear, when there is an absence of community involvement, formalized legal stands against the problem will not be effective in producing significant decreases in the rate or acceptance of domestic violence in our society.

The emphasis in the interviews on education and participation speaks to one of the central questions of this book: What does it mean to transform a private problem into a public one? In addressing this same question, Patricia Boling has suggested that finding an answer ultimately requires us to successfully engage the problem of "translating issues rooted in intimate life into perspectives and claims that are politically negotiable."[32] In a discussion of Hannah Arendt's fears that introducing private household and bodily matters into politics would serve to contaminate public discourse with their repetitive, self-centered, and mundane nature, Boling argues that the problem is not rooted in the nature of household matters per se but rather in their introduction into the public sphere in the "wrong spirit." As she explains, "the problem for democratic politics is not how to bar private matters from politics, but how to introduce those matters and the people who care about them to public life in a spirit that is conducive to democratic citizenship."[33]

Through their emphasis on education and participation as primary strategies for translating domestic violence into a public problem, those that I interviewed are taking important steps toward introducing the problem in a manner that is "conducive to democratic citizenship." In making this claim, I employ a definition of citizenship that derives from theories of participatory democracy which posit direct participation as a central feature of self-government. According to participatory theorists, it is primarily through direct engagement with others around specific concerns (rather than through indirect political activities such as voting) that citizens are able to realize their potential for collective self-determination.[34] Participation is not merely a means to an end but is an activity that serves to educate those who engage in it. As Hanna Pitkin puts it, it is through the process of participation that "I learn not only about the others, and thus about our collectivity, but also about my own personal stake in the collectivity, my stake in being a member of it and in the conditions of my membership. And I learn these in a context of responsibility, not in abstract thought, but in action which will have broad and tangible conse-quences."[35] The educational and participation-generating efforts de-scribed in the interviews are consistent with the process that Pitkin de-scribes. As noted in chapter 5, these strategies were not simply directed toward generating greater levels of understanding and compassion for vic-tims of domestic violence but were also explicitly designed to facilitate a direct appreciation for the ways in which domestic violence negatively im-pacts the entire community.

Another important aspect of the process of translating private matters into public issues involves the need to develop a mechanism for deperson-alizing private problems so that their political elements are exposed. Bol-ing describes the challenge very clearly in her explanation for why we need to find

a way to recognize and articulate problems first experienced in private or in isola-tion from others— perhaps because they usually occur in the context of the home, the family, friendships, or sexual relationships—not as personal problems of per-sonal biography (my problems because I am so unusual, neurotic, maladjusted), but as systemic problems that affect many or most people in the same situation, and are reinforced by social values and practices, as well as official sanctions, laws, and policies. When their problems are recognized and articulated in this way, people can begin to make claims about how they themselves ought to be treated, what they are entitled to, and what justice requires—claims that are negotiable as political claims.[36]

Boling's description of the nature of this challenge brings us back to the discussion of the ways in which legal interventions serve to individualize, and therefore depoliticize, the problem of domestic violence. When a problem is constructed as an individual one, the ties to the "systemic problems" that Boling refers to are effectively severed. As I argued in chapter 4, the individualizing effect of legal interventions operates to weaken the impact of feminist interpretations of domestic violence which are marked by their emphasis on the collective, institutional, and political elements of this type of violence.

Evan Stark and Anne Flitcraft have identified three major elements that distinguish feminist theories of woman battering from alternate inter-pretations. The first is the insight that battering is part of a larger pattern of coercive control that includes both discrete acts of physical violence and "an *ongoing* strategy of intimidation, isolation, and control that extends to all areas of woman's life, including sexuality; material necessities; relations with family, children, and friends; and work."[37] The second aspect of the feminist analysis of battering is the importance that is placed on "how structural inequalities mediated by institutional discrimination against women support interpersonal dominance by men."[38] Finally, a feminist analysis of battering is characterized by "a critique that links the gendered nature of male authority to the oppression of females at all stages of the life cycle, from childhood to old age."[39] These three elements are all directed at highlighting the ways in which systemic problems such as economic inequality, social roles, and gendered patterns of hierarchical power within the family reinforce domestic violence.

Interviewees were clearly sensitive to the many ways that gender roles and economic inequality contribute to the perpetuation of domestic violence. However, in the strategies and arguments that they used as part of their effort to transform domestic violence into a community concern, they repeatedly mentioned the importance of downplaying these structural issues due to their sense that many people are "turned off" or "overwhelmed" by them. Although these decisions about how best to frame domestic violence as a public problem were almost always presented as tactical concerns rather than philosophical beliefs, a more explicit acknowledgment of the feminist analyses of battering may be warranted, as the following discussion of the limits of community intervention suggests.

The Limits of Community Intervention

The interviewees repeatedly noted that, although legal reforms have challenged the perception that domestic violence should not be subjected to state sanctions, we are still very far from bringing about a widespread rejection of violence as an acceptable occurrence in intimate relationships. In this regard, the interviewees acknowledged the importance of addressing domestic violence at the level of morality. The need to explicitly engage fundamental community norms about the acceptability of interpersonal violence within the family is undeniable—especially if we are serious about prevention. However, framing domestic violence as a moral issue also has a number of potentially negative implications for translating it into a public problem that need to be considered. An examination of early patterns of nonstate intervention in situations of family violence provides insight into these implications.

During the latter part of the nineteenth century and extending into the Progressive Era, efforts to address family violence were dominated by charitable organizations and moral reformers associated with the temper-

ance and suffragette organizations. The reformers in this period emphasized cruelty to children, which was viewed almost exclusively as a problem of the lower classes and, in particular, of the immigrants who crowded
the urban centers during this period. Interpreting such acts as being committed by men and as the product of drinking, lack of self-control, and de-
praved habits imported from foreign cultures, social reformers sought to
"save" children either by removing them or by helping women to reform
their husbands by teaching them the proper norms and habits of middle-
class American families.[40]

In her analyses of the activities of "child savers" between 1880 and
1910 in Boston, Linda Gordon argues that the moralistic emphasis of
these early reformers enabled them to distance themselves from the social
problems that they were seeking to remedy. As she explains: "The emphasis on drink, and the envisioning of cruelty to children as something that
'they'—the immigrant poor—did, never 'us'—the respectable classes—allowed even anti-feminist moral reformers to include wife-beating within
their jurisdiction. They did not have to take the feminist message personally, so to speak."[41] Gordon's point about these early community interventions is very pertinent to my claims about the potential of community-
based interventions to help citizens translate domestic violence into a
public problem and thus to understand the connections between the violence and themselves. When domestic violence is constructed as a problem of moral deviance, as it was during the period of intervention described by Gordon, the likelihood that citizens will be inclined to identify
themselves as connected to the problem is reduced significantly. To the
extent that connections are made, they are likely to be focused exclusively
on the ways in which the violence is likely to infect the moral community.
This was case with the nineteenth-century moral reformers, who "considered child abuse not only a moral wrong but also a kind of pollution, poi-
soning the stock of future citizens and the daily order of civil society."[42]

A moralistic approach to community interventions is also problematic
because it impedes another important element that is crucial to the process of translating a private problem into a public one—a recognition of
the connections between violence in the family and systemic and structural problems such as poverty and discrimination. Because of their focus
on alcohol and moral depravity as the causes of family violence, upper-
class social reformers, Gordon argues, were consistently blind to the role
that poverty and severely limited opportunities played in contributing to
family violence and to the inability of women to escape it.[43]

Although well-intentioned, the activities and attitudes of child savers in the late nineteenth and early twentieth centuries serve as a cautionary example of the limits of community interventions that are premised on morally based assessments of family violence. I do not wish to suggest that there is no room for moral analyses of battering. Clearly, domestic violence stands in violation of many commonly held moral standards, and community-based interventions are in many respects better suited than legal regulations to address the problem at this level. Attention to the moral dimensions of domestic violence only becomes problematic when it operates to obscure other important elements of the problem.

One of the major advantages of the model I propose is that it facilitates our ability to account for the complexity of domestic violence in terms of both its causes and its solutions. The model is grounded in the recognition that different actors will see the problem of domestic violence through the lens of their particular interests, capacities, and constraints. Just as legal interventions are limited by their individualistic orientation, so too are community interventions likely to be limited by the perspectives and biases that they bring to the problem. For example, when a church offers assistance or education, the understandable focus on religious beliefs will almost certainly obscure elements of the situation that this focus cannot account for. Such limitations are also clearly evident when interventions are provided in accordance with therapeutic, social, or clinical objectives. Although battered women can clearly benefit from (and often are in desperate need of) the services that professionals provide, the norms and assumptions that are instilled as part of professional socialization can serve to blind social workers, medical personnel, and psychologists to important elements of the problems created by domestic violence that are not amenable to their particular expertise.[44]

Others have highlighted the presence of a serious tension between the professional and political objectives that individuals bring to their work with battered women.[45] This tension has repeatedly manifested itself in disagreements about whether victims should be treated as potential activists in the battered women's movement or as clients whose interests may or may not be in accordance with movement goals. Patricia Gagne's seven-state case study of the clemency movement for battered women who have been sent to prison for killing their abusers provides an illuminating look at some of the real-life consequences that can follow from decisions about whether to treat survivors as clients or as members of a political movement. For example, in a discussion of a struggle to gain clemency for a number of women in California, Gagne suggests that the failure of movement activists to call Governor Pete Wilson on his decision to deny clemency to three women in 1993 could be explained by the fact that the political "momentum that had built as a result of the Ohio and Maryland clemencies was dissipated in California by private attorneys who insisted that the petitioners be treated as clients rather than activists and that their problems be held private, rather than challenging the boundaries between public and private."[46]

The impact that relying on government funding or grants from private organizations can have on the way that domestic violence is framed and addressed has also received critical attention.[47] For example, in a discussion of the effects that government funding had on the battered women's movement during the late 1970s, Susan Schechter makes the following observation: "Just as the government bestows legitimacy on an issue, however, it can also change the parameters of how it is defined. In the pamphlets, brochures, and newsletters of the Office of Domestic Violence, HUD, and LEAA, battered women disappear to be replaced by spouse abuse and intra-family violence labels, a form of professional objectivity and a renaming that masks the sexism a grassroots movement would uncover."[48]

Although I harbor no doubts about the value of engaging in a process of evaluating both the adequacy and the political implications of specific intervention strategies, I highlight these partialities not in order to provide an assessment of their *limitations*. Instead, I would like to emphasize the *positive potential* of these partialities by returning to my earlier discussion of the linkages between democratic participation and the construction of domestic violence as a public problem. Nancy Fraser's reconceptualization of Habermas's "idea of 'the public sphere,'" which is centered around the idea of a "multiplicity of publics," provides a helpful staring point in this regard.[49] According to Fraser, "The ideal of participatory parity is better achieved by a multiplicity of publics than by a single public." This, she argues, "is true both for stratified societies and for egalitarian, multi-cultural societies, albeit for different reasons."[50] "Multiple publics" have a range of advantages. In multicultural egalitarian societies, they make it possible for "groups with diverse values and rhetoric" to participate together in public deliberations and, ideally, to "talk across lines of cultural diversity."[51] In stratified societies, the development of what Fraser terms "subaltern counterpublics" provides an opportunity for individuals who are part of subordinated groups to "invent and circulate counterdiscourses, so as to formulate oppositional interpretation of their identities, interests, and needs."[52] The ability of subaltern counterpublics to facilitate an oppositional discourse resides in their "dual character." As Fraser explains it, "On the one hand, they [subaltern counterpublics] function as spaces of withdrawal and regroupment; on the other hand, they also function as bases and training grounds for agitational activities directed toward wider publics. It is precisely in the dialectic between these two functions that their emancipatory potential resides."[53]

If we apply Fraser's analysis to the issue of domestic violence and to the triangular relationship between the state, community, and family, the value of having multiple publics generating (partial) solutions to the problem of battering is easy to see. As I have asserted throughout the preceding chapters, the meaning of domestic violence varies across time and among individuals. Despite this variability, the recent trend toward the development of coalitions designed to address domestic violence has made it much more probable that people with very different perspectives on this issue can collaborate in pursuit of common goals. Coalitions are typically made up of members from a range of professional and activist communities, including law enforcement, social services, shelters, and hospitals.[54] It is likely that each of these groupings will instill certain shared assumptions about the causes and solutions to domestic violence. Significantly, coalitions do not require participants to leave all of their differences at the door. On the contrary, value is added precisely from the diversity of perspectives that members bring to the table.[55] The enthusiasm for coalitions among the interviewees reflects their understanding that as they work to develop a public response to domestic violence, it is wise not to define "the public" as a single entity such as the state or as a unified community that speaks with one voice.[56]

The importance of "subaltern counterpublics" to generating alternative venues for deliberation, and thus to developing perspectives that run counter to the dominant discourse, is clearly demonstrated by the problem of domestic violence. As we have seen, the dramatic changes that have occurred during the past three decades in the United States around the perception of domestic violence as a private family matter have largely been the result of the activities of the battered women's movement. This movement came into being when feminists who were active in the second wave of the women's movement became aware of the pervasiveness and the gendered patterns of the violence that so many of them had experienced within intimate relationships. As shelters sprang up across the country, the volunteers who staffed and the women who sought refuge in them began to develop a new framework for understanding this type of violence. These new understandings soon began making their way into the

larger public sphere through the enactment of legislation and criminal justice reforms. But beyond simply bringing this issue into the radar of political concern, these early activists sought to challenge the moralistic interpretation of domestic violence as the product of the bad habits of poor
and minority populations, which had been adopted by progressive reformers, and replace it with an analysis that linked this violence to structural inequalities and gendered patterns of domination within the patriarchal family. This process of education and contestation that was begun in
the 1970s is far from complete, and as the interview themes demonstrate,
the battered women's movement continues to evolve as it expands its
boundaries to include other publics in its agenda.

Conclusion

Notably absent from the above discussion of reconceptualizing
boundaries is an articulation of a specific formula for determining when
domestic violence should become public and when it should remain private. The absence is not an oversight but a product of the nature of the interviewees' approach to the subject. The two major strategies driving the
approach—education and the stimulation of participation—come out of a
commitment to, and immersion in, the democratic process. In some ways,
the approach to these questions is described more easily by what it does
not do than by what it *does*.

The approach does not attempt to fix the meaning of public and private. What it does very well, however, is to destabilize assumptions about
domestic violence. An important consequence is the opportunity to
reevaluate patterns of thinking as to whether the violence should be
treated as a private or a public problem. The reevaluation is ongoing and
occurs in a variety of settings, including the legislature, the media, schools
and universities, neighborhoods, the workplace, and social service institutions. Legal institutions play an important role in the process by providing
a framework for thinking about the issues and by institutionalizing decisions and then enforcing them. But it is important to recognize that laws
are only one component of the reevaluation. Interviewees repeatedly
made an effort to expand the meaning of public interventions to include
those that do not depend directly on the enactment of state power and
sanctions.

Enlarging the relationship between public and private to include
three distinct sets of boundaries, differing in terms of flexibility and
manner of determination, carries with it several benefits that relate to

the treatment of domestic violence and to the way that we approach the difficult questions revolving around privacy more generally. First, many of the models that have traditionally been employed for understanding the distinction between public and private in a liberal society are premised on unrealistically abstract and essentialized interpretations of the individual, the family, or both (see chapters 1–3). Consequently, these models are frequently inadequate in accounting for the diverse needs of battered women or for the many paradoxes and contradictions so often present in instances of domestic violence. When particular individuals do not fit into the expectations that accompany these constrained interpretations, they are likely to find themselves with few or no public avenues for assistance. This fortifies the private isolation so often experienced by the victims.

The distinct advantage of the multifaceted, triangular model of public and private is a significant increase in the opportunities for establishing meaningful links between private violence and public resources for assistance. For example, in a situation where the victim is unable to turn to legal channels for help or uncomfortable about doing so, if there has been an effort to develop awareness and resources within the community, she will not be forced to face the terrifying absence of alternatives that so many have encountered in the past.

Another attribute of the model developed here is that even as increased flexibility is cultivated in the boundary between family and community, it is still possible to maintain a sharply defined boundary in areas deemed more potentially threatening to values protected by the private sphere. In particular, whenever state-sanctioned legal interventions are involved, it is likely that such clear lines will remain preferable. In the 1980s and 1990s, the U.S. Supreme Court handed down a series of decisions that have seriously undermined Fourth Amendment protections against illegal search and seizure.[57] The decisions are highly relevant to questions of privacy (*Roe v. Wade* notwithstanding), for the Fourth Amendment is the strongest constitutional articulation of the boundary between state power and individual privacy. In his famous dissent in *Olmstead v. United States,* Justice Louis Brandeis eloquently interprets the framers' intent:

They sought to protect Americans in their beliefs, their thoughts, their emotions and their sensations. They conferred, as against the Government, the right to be let alone— the most comprehensive of rights and the right most valued by civilized men. To protect that right, every unjustifiable intrusion by the Government upon the privacy of the individual, whatever the means employed, must be deemed a violation of the Fourth Amendment.[58]

As the Supreme Court backs away from a strong interpretation of the amendment, the right to privacy that Brandeis describes becomes increasingly uncertain.

The Court's relaxation of privacy protections might seem to be a welcome development from the perspective of those who are striving for an aggressive response to domestic violence. After all, as we saw in chapter 4, the widespread deference shown by police and judges to the notion that a "man's home is his castle" has historically supported a stance of noninterference when it comes to spousal abuse. But despite the apparent logic of this position, the erosion of Fourth Amendment protections is detrimental to the effort to stop domestic violence for two major reasons.

First, a commitment to making arrests in cases of serious assaults in the home in no way depends on compromising the procedures that have been established to ensure proper police behavior. When a violent incident is under way or when one member of a household has requested a police presence, the police are not required to get a warrant before entering the premises.[59] The Fourth Amendment was never intended as permission for one person to brutalize another, as long as the violence was kept under wraps. The problems of nonintervention *do not* occur because of the privacy protections embodied in the Fourth Amendment. Instead, the problems are created by the long-standing assumption that assaults in the home are not criminal if they take place within the context of intimate relationships. Furthermore, as I argue in chapter 7, if Brandeis is right, the Fourth Amendment protects Americans "in their beliefs, their thoughts, their emotions and their sensations." When a woman can be beaten with impunity by her domestic partner, her right to this protection, and thus to privacy, has been violated.

Second, since Fourth Amendment protections are important in preventing the abuse of police power, their erosion is detrimental to efforts to stop domestic violence. As Brandeis concludes in his dissent in *Olmstead v. United States*, "Decency, security and liberty alike demand that government officials shall be subjected to the same rules of conduct that are commands to the citizen. . . . If the Government becomes a lawbreaker, it breeds contempt for law; it invites every man to become a law unto himself."[60]

One of the points repeatedly made in the literature on domestic violence and in my interviews concerns the failure of victims to report abuse because they fear the police specifically or state power more generally. Given the sensitive and personal nature of the crime, and the documented reluctance of many to call on the police or other officials, it is absolutely essential that the relationship between citizens and the authorities be characterized by trust and integrity. Maintaining a clear boundary around state power, through upholding Fourth Amendment protections, can only contribute to this important goal.

The importance of preserving clear boundaries between public and private in cases of direct regulation by the state highlights a point that is often misunderstood by those who are uncomfortable with arguments that emphasize the political nature of personal problems. They say that such an emphasis will lead us down a path toward a disutopia, where the privacy and intimacy that defines the family is sacrificed in favor of total regulation and conformity within familial relations. The concerns are understandable and legitimate but often generated when there is an inadequate appreciation of the observation, made by Nicola Lacey, that "to say that what has been thought of as private is within the scope of political critique is not to say that it must necessarily be regulated."[61] I want to underscore that the arguments being made here about the importance of subjecting familial relations to political analysis and about the need to begin to include the health of those relationships within the boundaries of community concern are *not* equivalent to an argument that the family should become a political institution. What will count as a matter of common concern will be decided precisely through discursive contestation. Further, as Ferdinand Schoeman observes, even if the state intervenes in an intimate relationship, we can still characterize and treat that relationship as presumptively private.[62]

Ultimately, one of the primary reasons that a consideration of domestic violence provides so many rich insights into the meaning and value of privacy is that our efforts to address the problem require us to confront—and in many cases to reevaluate—the boundaries that we have drawn around public and private in our lives. As a result of that process, the points where these spheres intersect are brought into sharp focus. These points of intersection represent both opportunities and dangers. The challenge is to develop a model for negotiating these boundaries that simultaneously creates opportunities to cross between public and private and protects the fundamental integrity of each.[63] By providing a way to think through what might be at stake with different types of boundaries, my model does just that.

A final advantage of the triangular, more flexible model is all too easy to take for granted: the way in which its central emphasis on community participation serves to reinforce the process of democratic deliberation. The distinction drawn between public and private by Locke and others was grounded in their desire to create a system of governance that would maximize the liberty and freedom of all individuals. Even with its many limitations, the dichotomous liberal model that resulted has functioned to support these democratic ideals. Still, without the active engagement of citizens, even the most carefully constructed mechanisms of democracy will fail. In their emphasis on boundaries as *products* of the democratic process, the interviews help to remind us of this crucial point.

Seven

Conclusion:Privacy, Principles, and Process

D URING THE PAST TWO CENTURIES, THE AMERICAN family has undergone dramatic changes. Liberal theories of society as well as common-law doctrines of the family have evolved within a paradigm of the family as a unified, apolitical, and hierarchical entity. For many years, the paradigm remained undisturbed. In recent decades, however, largely at the urging of the women's movement, Americans have begun to look more closely at the actual conditions of family life. One of the most troubling patterns to emerge is the startling amount of violence and subordination that routinely exists within the domestic sphere. This information and a growing commitment to ensuring that *all* individuals in the family are safe and cared for have translated into a greater willingness to intervene in family matters in cases of abuse. Still, despite the many advances in our understanding of (and our response to) domestic violence, it is a problem that has yet to show any significant signs of abating.[1]

The increased visibility of domestic violence has not only changed our perception of this particular social problem; it has contributed to awareness of the inherent tensions between the popular notion of the family as a unified and private entity and the importance of protecting the individual's rights. It is clear that Americans are still very concerned about maintaining the family as a primarily private association in which government involvement is kept to a minimum. At the same time, it is also obvious that allowing violence to occur in the context of the family is no longer acceptable. These commitments to both privacy and protection, along with changes in the family structure, have generated many new challenges in the policy and legal arenas. As Americans have begun to confront these challenges, the adequacy of the assumptions that we have traditionally held about the family and its proper relationship to the state has become more and more uncertain.

As explained in chapter 2, embedded within the liberal separation of public and private is a conflation of two models of the private family that treat the domestic realm as the place where persons can realize simultaneously their potential for individualism and autonomy, on the one hand, and their capacity for connection and altruism, on the other. The tensions between the models were for the most part avoided by the designation within liberal theory of the family as a nonpolitical realm and by the assumption that when a conflict between the individual and the collective interests of the family did occur, natural hierarchies and assigned gender roles could be counted on to settle the matter. As the rights and privileges of citizenship have been demanded by and gradually extended to women, the ability to sidestep serious conflicts within the familial realm by relying on such assumptions has decreased proportionately.

Since the tension between the dual imperatives of individualism and connection within the family can no longer be avoided, it is time to fashion strategies for working with it. Toward this end, one of the first things that we must give up is the belief that it is possible to make simple assertions about the private or public nature of a particular issue or of a general area of activities. Instead, we need a model capable of incorporating the possibility that the meaning of public and private will evolve over time in accordance with specific claims and more general commitments to principles such as freedom and privacy. In chapter 6, through analysis of interviews conducted with individuals who have been directly engaged with domestic violence, I took the first step toward developing such a model. The current chapter provides an elaboration of some of the theoretical implications of the alternative model that I have proposed. In particular, I address the importance of a more affirmative conception of privacy, the potential role that principles might play in guiding interventions into domestic violence, and the significance of the democratic process to the challenge of determining where the boundaries between public and private in our society should be drawn.

An Affirmative Conception of Privacy

Throughout this book, I have in the main presented privacy as a highly problematic concept. As the primary physical site for the enactment of liberal privacy rights, the American family has traditionally been sheltered from public scrutiny and intervention. As we saw in chapter 3, the resulting isolation and depoliticization of family life has been portrayed by a wide range of feminists as producing an unacceptable level of vulnerability for many women and children—and a potentially lethal situation in cases where physical violence is present. These are important critiques and should be treated with gravity, but as Ruth Gavison asks: "Does it follow . . . that women have no interest in the values of privacy and intimacy, or that there are no contexts in which women would want to keep the state out of their lives?" Along with Gavison, my answer to this question is "absolutely not." Both women and men desire protection from the scrutiny of the state, the community, and even other family members. It is reasonable to assume that women want privacy, along with the intimacy, freedom, and solitude that it can provide. In light of the tremendous positive potential of privacy, the challenge, as Gavison puts it, is to "differentiate between good arguments, derived from the values associated with privacy, and bad arguments, in which reference to the same values is used to mask exploitation and abuse."[2]

In the following pages, I argue that the difficulties that privacy has historically produced for women do not derive from privacy per se but, rather, from its articulation in American legal discourse as primarily about "the right to be left alone."[3] Two major problems with this negative conception of privacy can be identified. First, and most obvious, is that it fails to provide an affirmative justification for the importance of privacy. The absence is notable because it adds another element of ambiguity to the already challenging task of evaluating whether privacy is contributing to the well-being of *all* citizens. The second problem is that limiting privacy to "the right to be left alone" interferes significantly with our ability to appreciate and understand the role that privacy plays in our relationships.

Articulating a positive conception of privacy is a daunting enterprise. As Judith Thomson notes, "Perhaps the most striking thing about the right to privacy is that nobody seems to have a very clear idea of what it is."[4] The notorious lack of clarity can be attributed at least partially to the fact that we tend to appreciate the value of privacy only after we sense that privacy has been violated in some way. For this reason, most discussions about the meaning of privacy have to do with what it makes possible rather than what it is. Thus, in my effort to devise a more affirmative concept of privacy, I begin by asking why it is important in the first place. Three activities are persistently identified in the literature as requiring privacy: the pursuit of intimacy, the enjoyment of relaxation, and the development of individuality.

In Western cultures, the act of being intimate normally takes place in private settings. The strong association between intimacy and privacy principally reflects cultural and moral attitudes about appropriate behavior. But it would be a mistake to reduce to simply a matter of decorum the importance of privacy to intimacy. Privacy not only shields our relationships from view but also contributes positively to the possibility of developing relationships in the first place. Charles Fried articulates this notion in arguing that privacy is a *prerequisite* for the development of intimate relationships. He declares that friendship and love are not even possible absent the ability to decide to whom we wish to disclose personal information.[5] Fried's point is important: privacy is not just about keeping people out, it is also about letting people in.[6] Privacy is one of the factors that enables us to open ourselves to intimacy and to risk the vulnerability that so often accompanies it.

Another central function of privacy is its contribution to providing people with the space to relax. In this sense, privacy is about excluding the things or people that make us feel as though we must put on a "public face." Privacy allows us leeway to act in ways that might be deemed irresponsible, lazy, or just plain deviant if we were in the presence of others (or at least others whom we did not know very well).[7] Psychological studies have repeatedly determined that to thrive, human beings require periods of private relaxation.[8] The freedom to do as we wish without the pressure to yield to societal expectations about what we *should* be doing can also create the necessary space for creative and artistic activities. Furthermore, relaxation, because of its power to restore and maintain our enthusiasm for public interaction and debate, is arguably a very important prerequisite of political engagement.[9]

A third activity supported by privacy is the pursuit of individual development and personal autonomy. In the field of philosophy, Jeffrey Reiman discusses privacy in terms of its contribution to the cultivation of individuality. According to Reiman, without privacy we would not be capable of distinguishing our thoughts and ideas from those of others, and thus individual autonomy would become unattainable.[10] This function of privacy is particularly relevant for democratic polities, which are premised on the capacity of citizens to develop and express independent perspectives on matters of public significance. Iris Marion Young develops the connection between democratic citizenship and privacy in a discussion of feminists who reject the home as a potential site of empowerment for women due to its history as the site of oppression. Young explains that, although she agrees fully with many aspects of these feminist critiques, it nevertheless remains the case that the home also "carries a core positive meaning as the material anchor for a sense of agency and a shifting and fluid identity." Making the connection to politics explicit, she argues that "this concept of home does not oppose the personal and the political, but instead describes conditions that make the political possible."[11]

In addition to providing a "material anchor" for the development of individual identity that Young speaks of, privacy, or at a minimum the ability to talk confidentially to people whom we trust, can help us to formulate our own opinions and ideas. It is often the case that we test and practice articulating our views in private before we risk asserting them in public. Once we have developed our views, privacy in the form of "decisional privacy" can help to ensure that we have the freedom to realize those views in practice.[12]

Access to Privacy

Are the functions of privacy being realized within familial relationships? To answer this question accurately requires careful attention to the fact that individuals are differently situated in families. In keeping with my emphasis on scrutinizing the meaning of privacy within the context of familial relationships, I will consider these three elements of privacy—the pursuit of intimacy, the enjoyment of relaxation, and the development of individuality and autonomy—in terms of how they might (or might not) be satisfied for a person who lives in a family where domestic violence has occurred.

Regarding intimacy, as Fried correctly tells us, one defining aspect of love and friendship is that they occur in relationships where we have chosen to reveal aspects about ourselves to which others are not privy. The capacity to make such choices implicitly depends on the presence of trust and the absence of domination. It hardly needs noting that the acts of physical assault that define domestic violence violate these two conditions. Once you add the psychological abuse that so often accompanies battering, the picture of the home as a private haven where citizens can lower their guard in order to forge intimate ties is shattered.[13] But the damage that domestic violence does to intimacy extends even further. One of the most commonly identified characteristics of batterers is an obsession with knowing everything that the victim is thinking or doing throughout the entire day.[14] Many a battered woman withdraws from friendships and familial relationships because she fears such interactions will anger her batterer or serve to expose what has been happening.[15] In such scenarios, the ability to develop close connections with others through a process of voluntary disclosures is severely circumscribed.

Second, when domestic violence occurs, the positive role of privacy in providing individuals with a space to relax and develop creatively is also undermined. Yet another pattern in battering behavior is the relative unpredictability of violent outbursts. Many victims report that because they never know when and why the abuse might erupt, they feel as though they are living with a time bomb.[16] One common coping mechanism described by survivors is vigilant prevention: averting any and all situations that might precipitate violence. For example, they take great pains to have dinner ready on time, keep the children quiet, and avoid topics of conversation that might arouse anger. Obviously, when such nerve-racking tactics become an inescapable part of daily life, little time or room is left for relaxation, reflection, or creative pursuits. Providing an important backdrop to such scenarios is the feminist observation that even women who do not live with domestic violence are frequently not afforded adequate opportunities for leisure that privacy can provide. Women's roles as mothers, wives, housekeepers, and often members of the workforce as well mean that their private lives can very easily be consumed by the activities of serving others.[17] The novelist Virginia Woolf made exactly this point when she argued in the essay "A Room of One's Own" that a woman's creativity would forever be stifled if she did not have a place to which she could retreat for at least part of the day.[18]

Finally, the systematic pattern of domination and control that defines so many battering relationships can wreak havoc on the ability victims to develop the sense of autonomy and individuality that many consider to be the most important justification for preserving a private realm. As I explain below, autonomy is a multifaceted and contested ideal. However, most would agree that, at a minimum, personal autonomy includes the ability to make decisions about one's life. Domestic violence has the potential to undermine the autonomy of its victims in a number of different ways. A common characteristic of batterers is the need to maintain absolute control over all matters in the relationship.[19] When one individual in a relationship has an obsessive need for control, the exercise of decisional autonomy, even when it comes to mundane choices such as how long to stay at the supermarket or what to make for dinner, is accompanied by the possibility of severe punishment. But beyond discouraging the free exercise of choice through the threat of violence, the repeated violations of bodily integrity that characterize battering can undermine the capacity of victims to act autonomously. In a discussion of privacy and abortion, Jean L. Cohen explains why this might be the case: "Without recognition by others of one's autonomous control over one's body, of one's bodily integrity, without at least this most basic acknowledgment of one's dignity, the individual's self-image is crippled (loss of self-confidence), as is the security she needs in order to interact successfully with others and to express her own needs and feelings."[20]

On yet a more subtle level, domestic violence can damage the ability of victims to function autonomously even after the direct threat of punishment and bodily violation is removed. The high frequency of post-traumatic stress syndrome among domestic violence victims and survivors helps to clarify why (for at least some individuals) the ability to make decisions can atrophy in such an environment. Through a consideration of some of the most common symptoms of post-traumatic stress disorder, Susan Brison makes an important connection between the ability to exercise autonomy and the experience of trauma. As she explains: "A trauma survivor suffers a loss of control not only over herself but also over her environment—a loss that, in turn, can lead to a constriction of the boundaries of her will. . . . Some reactions that once were under the will's command become involuntary; and some desires that once were motivating can no longer be felt, let alone acted upon."[21] Although controversial, the "battered woman syndrome" and Lenore Walker's theory of "learned helplessness" examined in chapter 4 provide additional insight into the impact that the repeated trauma of being abused can have on the capacity of domestic violence victims to exercise autonomy.

One possible reaction to these points about the value of privacy in facilitating the pursuit of intimacy, relaxation, and autonomy is that they are premised on presumptions about what women should want or need in their private lives. This is a legitimate reaction and, in fact, mirrors some of the critiques developed in chapter 3 of certain feminist approaches. However, in observing that many women (and domestic violence victims in particular) are not afforded the level of privacy that they might desire, I do not intend therefore to prescribe arrangements that would permit all family members to enjoy what I assert is the minimum amount and type of privacy. The attempt would be doomed for several reasons. First, the function of privacy varies according to the objectives that are being sought through the enactment of the privacy right. This variation makes it extremely difficult to specify the ideal amount and type of privacy that individuals need or want.

Second, because privacy is only one right among many, its value is contingent upon continuous choices about how much privacy we can afford to grant the individual. As Gerald Dworkin writes, "The right to privacy cannot be absolute; it must yield on many occasions to other interests which society considers to be of greater importance."[22] Dworkin's observation is brought into greater focus if we simply acknowledge that trade-offs are inescapable as we attempt to maximize our enjoyment and pursuit of the intimacy, relaxation, and autonomy that are supported by privacy. For example, consider the common scenario in which a person decides to sacrifice a certain amount of autonomy and solitude in order to pursue a greater level of intimacy in his or her private relations with others. In light of the inevitability of such choices, our ability to make them wisely can only be improved by engaging in a conscious effort to clarify continuously what is at stake. A restricted understanding of privacy as "the right to be left alone" deprives us of the opportunity to consider a great deal of information that might otherwise positively inform the decisions that we constantly make regarding where the boundaries of public and private should be drawn.[23]

Protecting Privacy within Relationships

The preceding paragraphs highlight the importance of accounting for the social conditions under which differently situated people seek to realize their privacy needs. Once we take the social conditions of privacy more seriously, the fact that most people pursue privacy within the context of intimate relationships becomes much more apparent. It seems, then, that the way in which we conceptualize privacy should include close attention to its relational aspects. Unfortunately, privacy has typically been approached in a manner that serves to drain it of its relational qualities. As I have argued throughout this book, liberal conceptions of privacy have historically been built around a functional interpretation of privacy as a mechanism to ensure that citizens will be granted the freedom to develop as individuals without undue interference from the state. To the extent that the domestic realm is even considered within liberal discussions of public and private, it is largely in terms of providing a private space where individuals can retreat from the pressures of public life.

Two related assumptions underlie this relative lack of attention to the domestic realm. First, serious conflict in the family will be rare relative to the level of conflict that is expected to occur in the public sphere. Second, when conflict does occur in the family, it will be of such a nature that it will be possible to resolve it internally without requiring outside intervention.

As we have seen, domestic violence presents a serious challenge to the liberal framework and the assumptions upon which it rests. Domestic violence forces us to consider the options when a commitment to privacy creates an area wherein one person can assault another person with impunity. The dilemmas associated with domestic violence and privacy serve to call attention to the fact that within a liberal political framework, the right to privacy has two overlapping—and sometimes conflicting—purposes: first, to protect citizens from the government, and second, to protect citizens from other citizens.[24] Matters become even more complicated when the citizen from whom a victim seeks state protection is someone with whom she is in a relationship—and one that she may or may not wish to continue. Designed to protect individuals, legal solutions are mostly confined to the goal of separation. This emphasis leaves the victim with few options for assistance when separation is not desired, not practical, or both.

When we confine our thinking about privacy only to what is required for personal independence, we constrain our ability to address problems such as domestic violence which occur within complex familial relationships that are characterized by autonomy and dependence simultaneously. Both the victim and the perpetrator are individuals and therefore need and desire the elements of autonomy that accompany our understanding of privacy. But they are also deeply involved in familial relationships that require, and are characterized by, dependence, vulnerability, and intimacy. Thus, a critical aspect of the effort to protect individual privacy rights is the importance of supporting people in their efforts to forge intimate links with others.

Recent feminist efforts to reformulate the concept of autonomy provide a helpful starting point for considering how we might successfully meet the complex challenge of empowering and protecting citizens as they simultaneously seek to pursue the ends of connection and individuation within the private sphere.[25] Feminist reformulations typically begin with a critical engagement with liberal conceptualizations of autonomy. Although the content of these critiques is wide-ranging, there are two common elements that are especially pertinent to the problem of domestic violence.

The first is the contention that liberal constructions of autonomy fail to recognize the degree to which individual choices, desires, and interests are themselves socially constituted.[26] According to many feminist theorists, the result is definitions of autonomy that emphasize the ability of individuals to pursue their own ends without any interference from others. These definitions obscure the role that structural conditions and social connections play in supporting or hindering the capacity of the individual to act autonomously.[27] The wide array of conditions, noted throughout this book, include: loyalties to family, religion, and ethnic communities that may discourage a victim from revealing her situation to outsiders; financial, housing, and language barriers; and of course the fear that action might lead to more severe violence directed at herself or those close to her.

Even after a victim takes action to stop the abuse, her ability to act autonomously continues to be constrained. Research on the criminal justice response to battering has revealed the many ways that a victim's opportunities for self-determination are circumscribed.[28] For starters, the very structure of the criminal process is such that once a case goes to court, the domestic violence victim is in the same situation as all other crime victims. Nancy Rourke explains: "The victim is not a party to the action and therefore has no control over its prosecution. The victim is only a witness for the prosecution. By definition, a crime is an offense not against the victim but against the state."[29] Once we take this basic fact of the criminal justice system into account, the tension between the need to treat domestic violence as other crimes are treated (where the state takes over the task of prosecuting offenders) and the importance of working to empower women to make their own choices becomes apparent.[30] The decision (or burden, depending on how one views it) about whether to press charges does not need to be returned entirely to the victim. However, I do think it is important to continuously attend to the consequences of taking state action on behalf of individuals, who may experience this intervention as one more in a long line of autonomy violations.

Another manifestation of this lack of attention to the relational elements of autonomy is a persistent bias in favor of separation as the best way to resolve domestic violence cases. Although separation may in fact be the best outcome for many victims, overemphasizing the importance of independence can easily result in neglecting the crucial importance of connections to others in restoring the autonomy of battered women. In her above-mentioned discussion of the connections between trauma and autonomy, Susan Brison explains that "in order to recover, a trauma survivor needs to be a able to control herself, to control her environment (within reasonable limits), and to be reconnected with humanity. Whether the latter two achievements occur depends, to a large extent, on other people."[31] Part of this dependency on others derives from a trauma survivor's need for "empathic others who are willing to listen to their narrative. Given that the language in which such narratives are conveyed and are understood is itself a social phenomenon, this aspect of recovery from trauma also underscores the extent to which autonomy is a fundamentally relational notion."[32] Brison's points serve to highlight that although domestic violence may in fact undermine a victim's ability to act independently of her batterer, when we seek to restore her independence and self-trust, it is necessary to appreciate that in many respects, the ability to exercise autonomy, especially when trauma is present, is "a function of dependency on others."[33]

Reconceptualizing autonomy to account for the fact that its exercise is impacted by the action (or the failure to act) of others has extremely important implications for the development of a public response to domestic violence, because it provides a conceptual mechanism for understanding the role that institutions and their staffs play in enhancing or diminishing the capacity of battered women to address the abuse in their lives. From their pioneering research on the medical response to domestic violence, Evan Stark and Anne Flitcraft have developed a theory of "institutional victimization" which effectively conveys the impact that failures to respond can have on battered women. Countering a clinical interpretation of passive or hostile behavior on the part of abused women as symptomatic of "inner deterioration," Stark and Flitcraft argue that the sense of entrapment that gives rise to such behavior should be understood instead as "a reality-based response to a history of denial, minimization, and victim blaming by those from whom they have sought support and protection, including police, doctors, social workers, and therapists."[34] When we shift our attention away from victim behavior and toward an analysis of the institutional response to battering, the connection between autonomy and community is brought into focus. As Stark and Flitcraft explain:

Though some women have impaired esteem to start, for most, entrapment and despair only follow a history of frustrating—even punitive—help seeking. Neglect, inappropriate medication, labeling women who persistently seek help, and stigmatizing abused women with secondary problems (such as alcoholism) so that their access to care is effectively blocked—all undermine women's credibility, isolate them, and reinforce behaviors, such as submissiveness and compliance, which increase vulnerability to abuse.[35]

Although Stark and Flitcraft primarily refer to the nature of the medical response, similar observations have been made about the legal response to domestic violence. The presence of long-standing and pervasive patterns of "institutional neglect" within the criminal justice system have led some to argue that instead of the victims lacking autonomy, "it is those with the authority to control and penalize batterers (the police, prosecutors, and judges) who exhibit 'learned helplessness.' "[36]

In addition to highlighting the descriptive flaws produced by approaches to autonomy that emphasize independence above all else, feminist critiques also point to the multiple ways that such approaches favor men in their pursuit of autonomy and discount the capacity of women to act autonomously due to their typically heavier involvement in caregiving.[37] Evidence of this bias can be seen in the pervasive presumption that when a victim of abuse fails to leave her batterer she is, by definition, failing to exercise autonomy.

Countering this presumption is research documenting the variety of ways that women who are being battered utilize the legal and social service systems to challenge the terms of their relationships even though they may ultimately drop the charges or return to their batterers.[38] Sometimes invoking the power of the law is just one step in what is often the long process of leaving,[39] although in other cases calling the police, pressing charges, or obtaining restraining orders is effective in achieving the goal of ending, or at least moderating, the abuse so that the relationship can be sustained.[40] But regardless of the particular outcome, this research highlights the fact that autonomy can be exercised in a variety of ways. In a discussion of women's autonomy and female genital cutting, Diana Meyers makes a similar point, noting that "One striking finding is that autonomy is to be found among accommodators as well as resisters, and that neither group can be presumed to enjoy greater autonomy than the other." She goes on to argue: "If this is so, one cannot identify autonomy or lack of it simply by looking at what people choose or refuse. Autonomy must dwell in the process of deciding, not in the nature of the action decided upon."[41] When considered in the context of domestic violence, Meyer's observations serve to redirect our attention away from a preoccupation with making judgements about the decisions of victims and toward an evaluation of the conditions that limit or support those decisions.[42]

Again, this shift in perspective has important implications for how we go about trying to assist domestic violence victims. When we are unable to recognize the autonomy that is already present in the survival strategies of battered women, we are much more likely to equate "help" with "telling victims what to do."[43] In addition to mirroring the controlling pattern of the battering, such an approach can place victims in serious jeopardy. It is now widely acknowledged that because domestic violence is first and foremost about a struggle for control, one of the most dangerous times in a battering relationship is when a victim tries to leave.[44] Because victims of domestic violence have an intimate knowledge of their situation and of their batterer, they are in the best position to judge the best course of action. For this reason, it is important to affirm the survival skills that have already been demonstrated and to respect a victim's instincts about what needs to happen next. However, even as we acknowledge that women may already be exercising their autonomy both in leaving and in staying, it is also necessary to continuously ask whether these women have as much autonomy as they are entitled to in light of our collective commitment to privacy as a right that is designed to enhance and protect autonomy in all adult citizens.[45] An essential element of this questioning must be an honest recognition that, especially for women, the pursuit of relationship exposes an individual to serious risks.

Combining recognition of the risks with appreciation of the critical importance of families to the social and political health of our society helps to bolster arguments that favor an explicit commitment to do more to assist people in negotiating the risks rather than blaming them when things do not work out, yet they fail to walk away. Christine Littleton succinctly states the challenge to law that such a commitment would entail:

We must have a safe place if we are to survive our desire [to stay], even if only to test whether it *is* our desire rather than a habit of compliance. If law is to help, rather than hinder, this project, it must not only overcome its presumption in favor of separation, but also and simultaneously stop men from battering us and foster alternative means of achieving connection. To fuse the desire for connection with the ability to resist or remove its abuses is the challenge of feminism in the law.[46]

Because legal approaches to privacy are significantly constrained by standards of interpretation and judicial attitudes, reforming them to include a greater appreciation for the relational aspects of privacy, and the autonomy that privacy is designed to protect, is an extremely slow and potentially risky process. Perhaps more immediately promising are efforts, such as those discussed in the interviews, that seek to involve more—and more diverse—community members in positive responses to domestic violence.[47] The triangular model that I have developed builds on feminist accounts of autonomy by helping to facilitate an appreciation of the trade-offs inherent in the pursuit of privacy and by requiring us to recognize that privacy is not simply a matter of leaving people alone. The model provides a framework for analyzing the many ways that the pursuit of both intimacy and autonomy within the private family can be actively supported or hindered by the presence or absence of community resources.[48] Furthermore, as I pointed out previously, the model makes room for an understanding of the ways in which the boundaries that make privacy possible are themselves produced by ongoing relationships between the family, the community, and the state.

The Importance of Principles

An affirmative conception of privacy, by serving as a reminder that *all* individuals in the family need to have the opportunity for the kind of intimacy, relaxation, and autonomy that privacy makes possible, can enrich community involvement in the problem of domestic violence. The articulation of the potential raises a question: What practical steps can be taken to ensure that efforts to address domestic violence will be informed by enhanced notions of privacy? In this section, I argue that the key to bringing our ideals about privacy to bear on prevention and intervention strategies is to attend more carefully to the potential role of principles in cultivating a sense of community concern with domestic violence.

Because its meaning is broad, the term *principle* needs some clarification. The dictionary definition that most closely matches my usage is "a comprehensive and fundamental law, doctrine or assumption on which others are based or from which others are devised."[49] In what way, then, do fundamental democratic principles, such as equality, justice, and liberty, inform our approach to the relationship between domestic violence and privacy? My interest in exploring this question stems from an observation that I made while conducting the interviews. When making their arguments about the importance of committing more public resources to stopping domestic violence, the interviewees very rarely invoked principles such as fairness, equality, or justice.

Several themes in the interview responses seem to explain this lack of use of the language of rights or the principles that tend to be embodied in them. One is the belief that, although clearly relevant to domestic violence, arguments about the rights of victims have little practical application. The prevalence of this view among interviewees accorded with what I had learned through my research on the history of efforts to create a social movement around the issue of domestic violence. One of the defining characteristics of the battered women's movement is its origin in initiatives to provide victims with desperately needed shelter and services.[50] Reflective of an emphasis on direct service provision, many interviewees believed that putting resources into convincing people of the unjustness of domestic abuse was an unaffordable luxury. As on activist, Kathy, described it: "Rights don't address the real needs of victims—they need services not rights."

A related theme was the widespread feeling among the interviewees that talking about rights is an ineffective strategy for getting people to care about the problem of domestic violence. Two explanations for the ineffectiveness were commonly advanced. One was the sense that an emphasis on domestic violence as a rights violation can very easily lead to a situation where people are subtly made to feel guilty for having allowed the violence to continue without having somehow helped. A representative comment from Mary, a lobbyist: "Although I do point out how widespread the problem is and then suggest that given this prevalence the legislature should be doing something about it, I am careful not to introduce an element of blame into my arguments. Once this happens, people tend to get defensive and dialogue stops." Thus, instead of focusing on the victim and therefore our complicity in her pain, those being interviewed spoke overwhelmingly of emphasizing that the violence was a tragedy not only for the victim but also for the community at large.[51]

Rights-based arguments were also thought to be ineffective because of the belief among interviewees that in order to successfully generate widespread public concern about rights violations, there needs to be a preexisting sense of concern for the specific individuals whose rights are being violated. According to the interviewees, many people are not particularly anxious to fight for the rights of domestic violence victims, a reluctance that was attributed to the observation that people who are being battered often "don't make good victims." A "good victim" in this respect is someone who naturally evokes our compassion and our desire to assist. It was pointed out repeatedly in the interviews that rather than inspiring sympathy, victims of domestic violence are commonly the objects of criticism and blame. A variety of factors were given for this response, including: "She slept with the enemy and thus can't be portrayed as clearly innocent"; "the victim's tendency to return to the violent relationship up to nine times before finally leaving"; and the desire of many people to distance themselves from victims so as to "avoid feeling vulnerable to such violence." Numerous interviewees made the point that as long as people continue to hold the victims at least partially responsible for their abuse, arguments that rely on the need to protect the victim's right to be free from abuse are unlikely to prevail.[52] As Aaron, an activist, put it:

I do not tend to use rights arguments because in my experience, they just don't work. People generally don't care about the victim. The tendency is to blame the victim with comments like "She must have deserved it." With this as a prevalent attitude, talking about a victim's right to be free from violence is going to have little effect.

Instead of focusing on fundamental principles of justice and equality, respondents used practical arguments that outlined the devastating effects of domestic violence on the community as a whole. Beyond simply *over-looking* questions of principle, such arguments could be critiqued as fundamentally undermining our ability to uphold shared norms by shifting our focus to issues of self-interest. The dictionary definition cited earlier provides support for such a critique, because it goes on to contrast the meaning of "principled" with "unprincipled expediency and pragmatism."

The apparent contradiction between these two images can be resolved by looking more closely at the nature of principles themselves. As the dictionary definition indicates, a defining element is independence from considerations of "expediency and pragmatism." Although contrasting principles with practical concerns is useful for definitional clarification, it can result in seriously flawed conceptual conclusions about the nature of principles. One of the most common has to do with the assumption that principles and practical concerns are necessarily incompatible. According to this interpretation, principles should remain completely independent from the embodied concerns that typically drive self-interest.[53] Underlying this position is the assumption that it is possible to discern an absolute and unchanging truth that can then be used to guide social action. Without going too deeply into the complex epistemological debates that surround such positions, I want to mention a number of practical reasons for why it might be best to resist an uncritical adoption of this approach to the relationship between principles and social action.

First is the observation repeatedly made by the interviewees that references to abstract principles such as justice usually fail to connect to people's sentiments: a gap that drains principles of their ability to affect or guide actions taken. This problem indicates the importance of striking a balance between aspirations and current realities. If there is too much idealism, people are likely to get defensive or lost. On the other hand, if principles give way to raw self-interest, they are no longer guiding ideals.[54] From this perspective, the interviewees' use of practical concerns—such as increases in crime and cost—to heighten awareness of the public significance of domestic violence represents a creative first step toward developing the linkages between commitments that are already meaningful to individuals (such as safe streets and fiscal responsibility) and the problems that are created by battering. The next step is to move from a concern about how domestic violence impacts one's own priorities to a recognition that those priorities can also include a commitment to defending the rights of victims. In fact, many made it very clear that their strategy was get to people's attention by first explaining how domestic violence affected them personally and then providing them with information about the cycle of violence in order to generate a sense of concern for the victims.[55]

Still, it seems quite clear that making connections between self-interest or practicality and issues deriving from principles, such as matters of justice and liberty, is an aspect of the current response to domestic violence that is in need of development and experimentation. For example, one advocate remarked that the messages of the "there's-no-excuse-for-domestic-violence" public awareness campaign, although extremely useful, still do not adequately address such pressing questions as: *Why* is there no excuse for this behavior? and *Why* is this an issue that should make us all angry? The best way to begin generating answers to these important questions is to start drawing the boundaries between public and private in a way that more explicitly invokes commonly held principles and standards.

Domestic Violence and Citizenship

As a means of illustrating the role that principles might play in the effort to reframe domestic violence as a public problem, I would like to provide a brief description of how the concept of citizenship could be used to clarify why domestic violence should be viewed as a common concern. Although the meaning of citizenship has been the subject of contestation, several fundamental elements can be relied on to make the connection between it and domestic violence. At its most basic level, citizenship expresses the relationship between the democratic state and the individual members of the polity. In the liberal tradition, this relationship is most clearly elaborated through the idea of the social contract. Stated in the bluntest of terms, the social contract describes the state's agreement to protect individuals from foreign invaders and from violations committed by other citizens. In exchange for this protection, citizens agree to transfer to the state their right to exert violent force against their enemies.

As we saw in chapter 2, John Locke extends the protections of the social contract to include family relationships through his stipulation that although the power to make final decisions "naturally falls to the Man's share, as the abler and stronger," husbands do *not* retain the right to determine life and death.[56] Tragically, all too often domestic violence represents a clear example of men improperly taking that right to be their own. Although I do not in any way wish to suggest that Locke ever condoned domestic violence, the structure of Locke's theorization of the family as a private entity functions to decrease the likelihood that women would ac-tually receive the state protection that Locke wants to insist is theirs by right. In chapter 4, through an examination of the history of state inter-ventions (or lack thereof) into domestic violence situations in the United States, we saw evidence of such a failure to uphold women's right to state protection against violations of bodily integrity in the home. With this his-tory in mind, the linkages between the rights conferred to citizens through the terms of the social contract and the need to develop a more adequate public response to domestic violence are clear to see. Consider-ing domestic violence in terms of the rights and responsibilities of citizen-ship provides a useful starting point for thinking about the connections between this problem and other rights that we claim to cherish in our so-ciety.[57] In this regard, Brande Stellings has noted that citizenship "has acted as a constant reminder of the interconnectedness of the material bodies of citizens and the body politic of the republic."[58] Invoking the concept of citizenship provides a mechanism for shifting our attention away from whether individual victims of domestic violence are deserving of our sympathy and toward the ways in which the absence of an effective public response serves to erode the social contract—the very foundation of democratic government.[59] Because the moral legitimacy of government is something that impacts all citizens, connecting battering to citizenship contributes to arguments for greater public concern that are potentially persuasive to individuals, irrespective of their personal experiences with or feelings about the particulars of this problem.

But the potential value of the concept of citizenship extends beyond its capacity to highlight the implications of a failure to honor the right of victims to protection from the state. In order to see this potential, it is necessary to include in our understanding of citizenship the recognition that it implies not only rights but also responsibilities. In addition to re-linquishing the right to exercise force, the social contract also entails an agreement that citizens will contribute to the process of representative de-mocracy. Mainstream accounts of citizen participation have emphasized activities such as running for office, voting, and military service. Although these are certainly central components of political participation, feminists have persuasively argued that, in light of women's relative absence from such activities (first through laws forbidding their participation and later as a result of constraints connected to familial responsibilities), such ac-counts function to position women as second-class citizens relative to men.[60] At a more subtle level, Kathleen Jones and other feminists have also argued that the heavy emphasis on these components serves to reinforce assumptions about "the necessity of annihilating all other particular loyal-ties to locality, family, sex, class, and race in order to become a relationship among equals." Jones also concludes that one of the problematic conse-quences of such assumptions is that "the rights and obligations of citizen-ship appear to depend on the suspension of the primacy of these other di-mensions of human identity and to place the citizen's loyalty at odds, at least theoretically, with these other allegiances."[61] Because of the degree to which women's lives are centered around the bonds and allegiances of home life, such a standard for evaluating citizenship serves to place them at a distinct disadvantage when it comes to successfully meeting the obli-gations of citizenship.

Although they vary in important ways, feminist reformulations of citi-zenship generally emphasize a conception of citizenship that is capable of accounting for the contributions that women make as citizens through ac-tivities that occur in the home and in the community. In addition to en-hancing women's status as contributing citizens, this approach would also help to facilitate an appreciation of the political dimensions of the activi-ties that occur in the private sphere.

Both mainstream and feminist discussions of the parameters of demo-cratic participation are potentially helpful in making the connection be-tween our shared investment in citizenship and the importance of ad-dressing domestic violence. Beginning with the mainstream account, it is not difficult to see how domestic violence might impinge on the abilities of battered women to meet their obligations as citizens. The overwhelm-ing nature of battering means that victims are unlikely to have the time, the freedom, the resources, or the self-confidence to vote, run for office, or participate in political activities of any kind outside the home. Further-more, as we saw in the earlier discussion of autonomy, battering can erode the very capacities that are required for participation in politics. In an ar-ticle comparing battering to tyrannical regimes, Jane Maslow Cohen writes: "It appears to be in the nature of private tyranny to push the vote or any semblance of the vote even further out of the picture. Private tyrants seem to find it either necessary or desirable to maintain the sub-stance of their control through a totalistic process that obliterates the pos-sibility of any alternative form of authority."[62] The private family has been described here and elsewhere as serving an important function in democ-racy by providing citizens with a safe place to develop and practice the de-cision-making skills that are so essential to their responsibilities as citizens. When battered women are deprived of authority in their own lives, these skills are likely to become eroded. Thus, we can see that one of the costs to the community is the loss of the contributions that could have been made by victims through the exercise of their citizenship responsibilities.

Feminist conceptions of citizenship also allow us to link citizenship and battering in new ways. As mentioned, feminists have argued for the need to extend our understanding of participation to include activities that occur in the private sphere but nevertheless represent important contributions to the polity. For example, Jean Elshtain has emphasized the important contribution of women as mothers who are in charge of raising the citizens of tomorrow (see chapter 3). Susan Moller Okin's work (also discussed in chapter 3) provides further insight into the crucial importance of this task through her observation that it is in the family that children learn the meaning of concepts such as equality and fairness.[63] Thus, a household characterized by unequal workloads or physical and mental acts of domination is unlikely to produce citizens with the capacity to make decisions about justice in the public sphere. Again, connecting the negative impacts of domestic violence to the all-important cultivation of future citizens serves to emphasize the ways in which this violence damages all members of a democratic society.

Although extremely diverse, the approaches to citizenship discussed in the preceding pages are united by their primary focus on the relationship between the state and individual members of the polity. This emphasis on the nation-state can be contrasted to interpretations of citizenship that conceptualize it as arising from membership in a community that may not be defined by national boundaries.[64] In an age of accelerating globalization, there are more and more instances where it has become important to consider the implications of belonging to the "human community." Once this step is taken, it becomes possible to utilize a human rights framework in the development of our understanding of the rights and responsibilities associated with citizenship. And in fact, in the case of domestic violence, many commentators have effectively drawn on international human rights discourse in their development of moral arguments in favor of doing more to assist victims of intimate violence.[65]

Approaches to citizenship that define the community in a way that is not so closely tied to the boundaries of particular nation-states have the additional advantage of enhancing our ability to examine the meaning of citizenship for immigrant and refugee populations. The importance of being able to incorporate these populations into discussions of citizenship arises from the fact that, legal or not, these individuals contribute to and influence the communities within which they reside. In the United States, although residents who are not citizens are barred from political

activities such as voting or running for elected office, the Supreme
Court has repeatedly determined that they are still entitled to many of
the social and political rights that are connected to citizenship.[66] However, because these rights are not absolute, their extension is continuously subject to political debate and judicial interpretation, and in recent
years there have been a number of very visible efforts to restrict the access of noncitizens to taxpayer-funded social services.[67] Since the terror-
ist attacks of September 11, 2001, the extension of civil liberty protections to noncitizens has also been subjected to increasing restrictions.
Still, despite these trends, it remains true that regardless of the legal status of the individuals involved, the state retains the responsibility to intervene when criminal statutes forbidding assault are violated within its
borders. For this reason alone, the argument that all individuals who reside in the United States should be afforded state protection when they
are being hurt remains compelling.

Debates about the extent of the rights and social supports that should
be extended to resident noncitizens serve to highlight the role that conceptions of citizenship play in the construction of community boundaries.[68] Stated simply, when individuals are accorded the rights and responsibilities that are associated with citizenship, they are effectively
included as members of the political community. Alternatively, when the
protections that are provided to citizens are denied, the message is clearly
one of exclusion. As the feminist critiques of citizenship discussed earlier
reveal, principles of citizenship have frequently functioned to exclude not
only immigrants but also nonimmigrant women as full members of the
political community. Despite such limitations, it is also clear that the
meanings ascribed to citizenship can be expanded in a way that transforms
this principle into a powerful tool that can be productively invoked by
those who are working to counteract long-standing patterns of neglect
and exclusion.

In a discussion of the application of civil rights remedies to instances
of gender-motivated violence, Brande Stellings articulates the potential of
citizenship in this regard:

Citizenship provides a place from which to launch the project of recognizing
rights, the "process by which hurts that once were whispered or unheard have become claims, and claims that once were unsuccessful have persuaded others and
transformed social life." The process of invoking rights not only manifests a person's membership within a community by demanding that a wrong be righted,
but also strengthens that tie to the community by expressing the person's faith in
placing her fate within the hands of the community.[69]

Stellings's argument brings us back to the discussion in chapter 6 about the democratic potential inherent in the process of translating private problems into public concerns. When we begin with ideals such as citizenship, we are able to construct theories of public and private that allow the precise determination of *where* those boundaries should be drawn to remain a dynamic and democratically determined issue. This is also a characteristic of the approach to these boundaries taken by the interviewees and of the triangular model that I constructed using insights gleaned from the interviews. One of the major advantages of these models is that they do not require us to define any particular issue, behavior, activity, or phenomenon as public or private in advance. However, what a consideration of citizenship contributes to both of these approaches to the public/private split is a reminder of the importance of explicitly and continually asking whether the boundaries that result cohere with the principles that we profess as a democratic polity.[70]

Applications of the Triangular Approach to Other Social Problems

Throughout this book, I have centered my investigation on the significance that the boundaries of and meanings associated with the public/private dualism have for domestic violence. I selected domestic violence as a focus because it is a social problem that poses a direct challenge to a number of deeply held assumptions about the functions of privacy and the prerequisites for its preservation. As we have seen, many of the recurring dilemmas associated with intervening in cases of domestic violence expose a number of key tensions within liberal models of public and private. These tensions raise questions such as: How do we provide assistance to victims in a manner that honors our commitment to maintaining the family as a presumptively private association? How do we work with individuals who are frequently caught between a dual commitment to protecting both individual and familial interests? What are the appropriate roles for the state versus nongovernmental associations in addressing this social problem? Although these questions are associated with the specific challenges and problems connected to efforts to address domestic violence, they are most definitely not limited to one social problem alone.

There are a number of contemporary policy debates that, like those concerning domestic violence, operate to destabilize many of the assumptions that support existing divisions between public and private. The issues involved include, among others, abortion, family poverty, divorce, child abuse and exploitation, juvenile crime, drug and alcohol addiction, same-sex marriage, and gender equality in the home. All of these issues have two elements in common: they originate or are manifested primarily within the family, and their resolution has significant implications for the three spheres that figure in my triangular model: the family, the state, and the community.

Take, for example, the issue of family poverty. Although poverty affects a wide variety of individuals in this society, it is a distinctive problem for "the family" because women and their dependent children make up a disproportionately high percentage of the poor and because a growing number of families live either below or very near the poverty level despite both parents working. As a public policy issue, family poverty inspires efforts to reform state-sponsored welfare programs and proposals to assist families in the lowest income brackets by means of tax credits and similar mechanisms. Questions about state-sponsored welfare provision elicit strong opinions about individual responsibility versus societal and political commitments to assist those in need. During the 1990s these questions were furiously debated, and in 1996 Congress passed the Welfare Reform Act amidst promises that this sweeping legislation would "change welfare as we know it." Among the provisions were strong incentives for states to decrease their welfare roles by requiring recipients to find work within two years.[71] As a result, many states have begun to experiment with developing partnerships with the private sector in an attempt to implement welfare-to-work programs. Although it is still too early to fully evaluate the impact that this legislation has had on the families that rely on these programs, it is clear that the Welfare Reform Act, along with the debates and controversies generated by it, have resulted in a nation-wide reevaluation of the appropriate roles of the state, the marketplace, and the individual in addressing poverty.

Thus, like domestic violence, family poverty is an issue that requires us to confront difficult questions about whether it is fundamentally a private or public problem. Also, as in the case of domestic violence, the significance of the designation is multifaceted, affecting not only the degree to which we accept responsibility for providing assistance but also the strategies and mechanisms that are employed to deliver the assistance. In the case of poverty, over the course of the past two centuries in the United States, various approaches have ranged from an almost exclusive reliance on private charity and churches to large, complex, bureaucratically based programs of public assistance. A look at the historical record indicates that many of the most persistent debates in this policy area have centered around disagreements about which sector of society should be held primarily responsible for addressing the needs of its poorest and most vulnerable members.

One of the advantages of a model that encourages us to view public/private boundaries as the product of a triangular relationship between the family, the community, and the state is that it enables us not only to maintain awareness of the three domains simultaneously but also to think systematically about their interrelation. For example, a common criticism of publicly funded welfare is that the programs have the undesirable effect of weakening the institutions of civil society. Critics argue that as people become reliant on the state to address social problems, the likelihood that those in need will turn to community-based groups diminishes, which in turn saps the motivation for people to organize around the shared goal of offering assistance. Because my model enables us to consider a range of responses to a particular social problem, it enhances our ability to consider such criticisms and to determine, on an ongoing basis, whether the balance between state and nonstate responses is a productive one. Further, the triangular model, by highlighting the ways in which various interventions interact, encourages us to ask questions about whether state interventions are functioning to crowd out a community response (as in the scenario described above) or whether community responses are undermining state-based efforts to maintain certain standards and rights in the provision of social services (as in the examples of faith-based initiatives discussed in the previous chapter).

The approach to public policy that comes out of this model also provides a mechanism for considering the value of recent calls in the United States for reviving the institutions of civil society more generally. One such effort is that of the Council on Civil Society, whose goal is to "assess the condition of civil society at the close of this century and to make recommendations for the future."[72] One of the strategies that this group recommends is adoption of a "new 'civil society model' for evaluating public policies and solving social problems." According to this approach, the first question that we should ask about any policy proposal is: Will this policy strengthen or weaken the institutions of civil society? The next question is: Can this goal be achieved by utilizing and empowering the institutions of civil society?[73] By contributing to the development of recognition of the vital importance of community associations in addressing social problems and the need to consider how government interventions might affect the activities of community associations, my model is consistent with efforts to reevaluate the role of civil society in the United States.

However, unlike these other efforts, my model is *not* designed to achieve a particular agenda—such as the enhancement of civil society—but, rather, to facilitate an understanding of the political stakes, institutional mechanisms, and symbolic status of particular interventions. In this respect, the model has the additional advantage of helping us to maintain a productive balance among the different domains of society by providing us with a framework for critically evaluating our reliance on some more than others to resolve social problems.

In the 1990s, following the fall of communism in Eastern Europe, there was a rediscovery of the concept of civil society and, with it, a tendency to celebrate civil society as the premier realm of political and social freedom. According to Robert Fine, although an understandable response to the decline of totalitarian governments, the trend is problematic in the sense that "when it takes one moment of the complexity of modern ethical life, civil society, and grants it primacy over all other moments—property, family, state, and so on—it unwittingly mirrors its enemy's conceptual armory."[74]

One of the central functions attributed to civil society is its role in balancing state power. But a recognition of the importance of civil society in this area requires an appreciation also for the role that the state plays in tempering and balancing the activities of civil society. As Michael Walzer points out:

Society's "civilians" need the state (and the bureaucracy) to defend them against their own divisiveness, to protect them when they are alone and helpless, to enforce universal standards of care and safety. But every state preys on the society it protects. . . . The problem is to hold the two in some rough balance: central planning and workers' control, state regulation and entrepreneurial initiative, a welfare minimum and local self-help.[75]

Because my model does not depend on the primacy of the state, the family, or the community (the latter being equivalent in this case to civil society), it functions to support and inform the efforts of those who must face the challenge of maintaining the healthy balance to which Walzer refers.

Boundaries as Process

I want to close with an argument in favor of adopting an approach to boundaries that treats them as the changing products of an ongoing process. The first reason for such an approach concerns the challenge of representation. One of the major themes of the critiques of the models of public and private examined in this book has to do with their failure to represent adequately and account for the problems of a broad range of individuals. As I noted in chapter 2, John Locke's model of public and private worked particularly well for the patriarch of the family but not for the rest of the members. In chapter 3, I concluded that although the feminist reconstructions of the public/private relationship attempted to correct for this problem, feminist alternatives furthered the interests of some women at the expense of other women. What all of these models share is an aspiration to devise an ideal relationship between public and private that is capable of maximizing the achievement of principles such as justice, equality, freedom, and liberty.

However, the complexities and paradoxes that arise in cases of domestic violence illustrate the impossibility of ever developing a model of public and private that would adequately protect all individuals under all circumstances. My objective in demonstrating these complexities, however, has not been to make an argument about the need to dispense with the effort to draw boundaries according to the principles that we hold dear. The problem, as I see it, is not with either boundaries or principles but, rather, with the mistaken belief that we will be able to "get them right" once and for all. Furthermore, I want to emphasize that the desire for finality is emblematic of much more than naivete. Believing that ideal boundaries are achievable can operate to undermine the democratic process itself. As Benjamin Barber tells us in *The Conquest of Politics,* "Politics is what men do when metaphysics fails. . . . It is the forging of common actuality in the absence of abstract independent standards. It entails dynamic, ongoing, common deliberation and action and it is feasible only when individuals are transformed by social interaction into citizens."[76]

We would be wise to reflect on why boundaries matter so much to us in the first place. The danger that boundaries are fundamentally designed to prevent is a totalitarian state, where privacy—and the freedom and autonomy it preserves—are extinguished. But totalitarianism can take root only in a society in which people have relinquished their power. Accepting boundaries automatically or habitually, without thinking carefully about whether they achieve our goals, constitutes such a relinquishment. The acceleration of technological change and the social changes that characterize the contemporary age mean that it is simply not possible to take boundaries for granted. The best course is to bring our principles and common sense to bear on where these lines should be drawn. History and tradition can inform how we respond to questions about boundaries and the meanings of public and private but cannot provide us with the answers. The Constitution affirms our capacity to create, and re-create, our society and government. It is important to live up to that challenge, not by unconsciously living out the past patterns or appealing to constants but by engaging the present moment—informed by history and guided by the principles of equality, justice, and freedom. The danger is not in giving up a commitment to stable, transhistorical boundaries but in failing to meet the responsibility to make those boundaries our own.[77]

Thus, the real challenge is *not* to come up with models or generalizations about the public/private split so that we can determine whether it is good or bad, or whether it should be protected or destroyed. Instead, the challenge is to attend vigilantly to the consequences that this dichotomy has for particular individuals in particular situations. We must not forget that, by their very nature, boundaries shut things out. That potentially silencing impact means that we must constantly ask critical questions about boundaries that we seek to erect and protect. What purpose does a particular boundary serve? What do we get from maintaining it? Who gets what? Is the outcome just and democratic? Engaging in this brand of inquiry will enable us to judge the consequences of the boundaries that structure our society against the stated commitments of our political order. From this informed place, we can then seek to adjust boundaries in a manner that will more effectively honor these commitments. But this does not complete our task. The great challenge of the alternative model of public and private developed throughout these pages lies in the fact that because it is grounded in an analysis of particular situations that change over time, delineation of the boundaries between public and private is ongoing. In the end, this means we have no choice but to accept the challenge of every moment—learning from the past, working to realize new ideals in the future, but never sacrificing the present for either.

Notes

Chapter 1. Privacy and Domestic Violence

1. At various points in this book, the reader is likely to notice use of the feminine pronoun to refer to victims and the masculine to designate perpetrators. The decision to use pronouns in this manner is based on two factors. First, although it is true that women are sometimes the perpetrators of violence in the home, in both heterosexual and homosexual relationships, it remains the case that the vast majority of individuals who are seriously injured or killed by domestic violence are female. Second, the perpetration of domestic violence by men against women involves patterns of domination that are directly tied to the victim's gendered status. In this respect, M.P. Johnson's distinction between "common couple violence" and what she terms "patriarchal terrorism" is instructive. Common couple violence involves a temporary loss of control resulting in hitting or pushing between partners. Such violence rarely escalates into life-threatening acts. Patriarchal terrorism, on the other hand, can be traced to "patriarchal traditions of men's right to control 'their' women" and involves not only patterned physical abuse but also economic and psychological subordination designed to isolate and control the victim. According to Johnson, this type of violence is perpetrated almost exclusively by men against women. Clearly, all violence directed at another human being, no matter the gender of the perpetrator, is problematic and deserves careful attention. However, in this study, it is on the latter pattern of violence that I have chosen to direct my attention, and thus domestic violence is characterized throughout as an act that is committed primarily by men against women. M.P. Johnson, "Patriarchal Terrorism and Common Couple Violence: Two Forms of Violence against Women," *Journal of Marriage and the Family* 57 (1995): 283–94.

2. The 1.8 million figure comes from Gerald Hotaling et al., eds., *Family Abuse and Its Consequences* (Newbury Park, Calif.: Sage, 1988). The latter figure is from Michelle Bryger, "Domestic Violence: The Dark Side of Divorce," *Family Advocate* (summer 1990): 48.

3. U.S. Department of Justice [FBI], *Bureau of Justice Statistics, Fiscal Year 1998* (Washington, D.C.: Government Printing Office, 1998).

4. There is currently a lively debate over the terms used to describe the male battering of women. *Domestic violence* is the term most frequently used in both the literature and in the public discourse on this topic. Yet it is important to acknowledge that the term has been rightly criticized as inappropriately gender neutral and also as suggestive that the problem is one with the entire domestic unit rather than with the person who is initiating the violence.

It is possible to include children in the discussion of domestic violence (and in that case the proper term would be *family violence*). However, the problems and power dynamics of the parent-child relationship are different enough to merit treating these topics separately. For the gendered aspects of the term *domestic violence*, see note 1.

5. Lee Anne Hoff, "Collaborative Feminist Research and the Myth of Objectivity," in *Feminist Perspectives on Wife Abuse*, ed. Kersti Yllo and Michelle Bograd (Newbury Park, Calif.: Sage, 1988), 18.

6. As with estimating the rates of domestic violence, the development of hard numbers about the cost of domestic violence has proven to be something of a challenge. One 1992 study put the estimate at between $5 to $10 billion annually, although another has calculated it to be $67 billion. The wide variation in these estimates is largely attributable to differences in how to calculate costs and also what to include as a cost. For a very useful discussion of these studies and the issues that surround the development of such estimates, see Louise Laurence and Roberta Spalter-Roth, "Measuring the Costs of Domestic Violence against Women and the Cost-Effectiveness of Interventions: An Initial Assessment and Proposals for Further Research" (Washington, D.C.: Institute for Women's Policy Research, 1996), 2.

7. The cyclical potential of domestic violence is well established. See Cathy Spatz, *The Cycle of Violence* (Washington, D.C.: Department of Justice, Office of Justice Programs, National Institute of Justice, 1992); and Jana Jasinski and Linda Williams, eds., *Partner Violence: A Comprehensive Review of 20 Years of Research* (Thousand Oaks, Calif.: Sage, 1998). Research also suggests that exposure to violence in the home during childhood can contribute to a range of antisocial behaviors that are exhibited outside the home. See, for example, Joanne Cummings, Debra Pepler, and Timothy Moore, "Behavior Problems in Children Exposed to Wife Abuse: Gender Differences," *Journal of Family Violence* 14 (June 1999): 133–156; and Jeffrey Fagan and Susan Wexler, "Crime at Home and in the Streets: The Relationship between Family and Stranger Violence," *Violence and Victims* 2 (1989).

8. Ethel Klein, Jacquelyn Campbell, Esta Soler, and Marissa Ghez, *Ending Domestic Violence: Changing Public Perceptions, Halting the Epidemic* (Thousand Oaks, Calif.: Sage, 1997), 7–16.

9. Until the nineteenth century, it was legal to beat one's wife if it was undertaken as part of a man's duty to engage in "lawful correction." Blackstone's *Commentaries* includes the following statement: "The husband also might give his wife moderate correction. For as he is to answer to her misbehavior the law thought it reasonable to entrust him with this power of restraining her." Blackstone, *Commentaries,* vol. 1 ([1771] 1966), 432, quoted in *Private Violence and Public Policy: The Needs of Battered Women and the Response of Public Services*, ed. Jan Pahl (London: Routledge, 1985), 11.

10. Pleck, Elizabeth, "Criminal Approaches to Family Violence, 1640–1980," in *Family Violence: A Review of Research,* ed. Lloyd Ohlin and Michael Tonrey (Chicago: University of Chicago Press, 1989), 19.

11. Ibid., 20. Linda Gordon has argued that until the 1970s, the widespread view of domestic violence as a "private or personal problem meant that it was left unaddressed except indirectly through social purity campaigns such as the temperance movement and the progressive era efforts to prevent the abuse of children." Gordon, *Heroes of Their Own Lives: The Politics and History of Family Violence: Boston, 1880–1960* (New York: Viking, 1988), 252–53.

12. Throughout this book, I periodically use the term *victim* to refer to women who are being battered. The designation of battered women as victims is controversial. On the one hand, it expresses a recognition that as victims of violence, battered women should not be blamed for what has happened to them. However, the use of this terminology has been criticized as serving to construct women who are being battered as lacking agency. Although I am sympathetic to this critique, for the purposes of linguistic clarity, I have chosen to use "victim" when necessary. For a nuanced discussion of the issues underlying the victimization/agency debate see, Elizabeth Schneider, *Battered Women and Feminist Lawmaking* (New Haven: Yale University Press, 2000), chap. 5.

13. Nancy Fraser, "Struggle over Needs: Outline of a Socialist-Feminist Critical Theory of Late-Capitalist Political Culture," in *Women, the State, and Welfare*, ed. Linda Gordon (Madison: University of Wisconsin Press, 1990), 210.

14. It should be noted that many victims of domestic violence firmly believe that family problems should *stay* family problems, and hence would not want to challenge this assumption even if they could. However, whether a victim believes in such norms or is simply incapable of challenging them matters little in terms of the effect of the norms in contributing to the extreme social isolation that so many victims of abuse experience.

15. Donald Dutton, "The Criminal Justice Response to Wife Assault," *Law and Human Behavior* 11, no.3 (1987): 189–206.

16. Cited in Donald Dutton, *The Domestic Assault of Women: Psychological and Criminal Justice Perspectives* (Vancouver: University of British Columbia Press, 1995).

17. L. Crites, "Wife Abuse: The Judicial Record," in *Women, the Courts, and Equality*, ed. Laura Crites and Winifred Hepperle (Newbury Park, Calif.: Sage, 1992), 42; A. Binder and J. Meeker "The Development of Social Attitudes towards Spousal Abuse," in *Domestic Violence: The Changing Criminal Justice Response*, ed. E.S. Buzawa and C.G. Buzawa (Westport, Conn.: Auburn House, 1992); and Del Martin, *Battered Wives* (San Francisco: Glide, 1976).

18. Lisa Lerman, "Criminal Prosecution of Wife Beaters," *Response* 4 (1981): 1–18.

19. Anne Jones, *Next Time She'll Be Dead: Battering and How to Stop It* (Boston: Beacon, 1994), 148.

20. In a discussion of how information about domestic violence is transmitted between public officials and service providers and victims, Margaret Borkowski, Mervyn Murch, and Val Walker suggest an approach that recognizes the existence of "two potential contradictory forces at work . . . one seeking to keep it private, the other trying to make it public. In studying the response of community services to marital violence, one is to some extent studying the dynamic interaction between these forces, often operating simultaneously and creating ambiguities and dilemmas for the people concerned, clientele and practitioners alike." Borkowski, Murch, and Walker, *Marital Violence: The Community Response* (London: Tavistock, 1983), 112.

21. Pleck, "Criminal Approaches to Family Violence," 19.

22. Even in the absence of suspicions about the applicability of theory to efforts to put an end to domestic violence, the severe lack of resources available to address this widespread problem dictates that the lion's share of energy will necessarily be spent on meeting the immediate needs of the victims.

23. Supporting this point is an argument made by Stanley Benn and Gerald Gaus: "The distinction between publicness and privateness is a practical one, part of a conceptual framework that organizes action in a social environment. . . . Because human beings are agents

and not simply behaving subjects, any description of their actions . . . must include that agent's own understanding of what he is doing, and that requires reference to the conceptual universe within which he acts." Benn and Gaus, eds., *Public and Private in Social Life* (London: Croom Helm, 1983), 5–6.

24. Locke characterized both the family and civil society as private. The subsequent absence of sustained discussions within political theory of the relationship between the domestic sphere and politics may in fact be attributable to Locke's success in framing the family as a thoroughly nonpolitical institution.

25. Karl Marx effectively challenged the liberal assumption that economic relationships were not political. As a result of his critiques, many theorists now include economic activities as part of the public realm. However, as Martha Ackelsberg and Mary Lyndon Shanley point out, these reconfigurations never seriously question the liberal assumption that the sphere of familial relations "was not an important locus of constructed power relationships and was, therefore, largely irrelevant to 'politics.'" Ackelsberg and Shanley, "Privacy, Publicity, and Power: A Feminist Rethinking of the Public-Private Distinction," in *Revisioning the Political: Feminist Reconstructions of Traditional Concepts in Western Political Theory*, ed. Nancy Hirschmann and Christine Di Stefano (Boulder: Westview, 1996), 215.

26. Carole Pateman, *The Disorder of Women: Democracy, Feminism, and Political Theory* (Oxford: Basil Blackwell, 1989), 122.

27. These critiques are explored in chapter 3.

Chapter 2. The Family as a Private Entity

1. John Locke, *Two Treatises of Government* [1690], ed. Peter Laslett (Cambridge: Cambridge University Press, 1988), *Second Treatise*, section 77. Subsequent citations to this work are to this edition and are given in parentheses as follows: II, 77.

2. In *Uneasy Access: Privacy for Women in a Free Society* (Totowa, N.J.: Rowman and Littlefield, 1988), Anita Allen provides an excellent analysis of the tension between attachment and individuation within the context of liberal privacy rights. Notably, although she argues that a serious tension exists, she is clear that they are *not* contradictory goals (p. 72).

3. This is not to suggest that these are all worthless enterprises. However, I do *not* think that Locke can be shown to have accepted the occurrence of domestic violence in the family, and a number of the arguments in this chapter make this point clear. At the same time, many of the points I make regarding the implications of Locke's theory for domestic violence are indebted to those who have critiqued Locke for his patriarchal bias and sexist views. See, for example, Carole Pateman, *The Sexual Contract* (Stanford: Stanford University Press, 1988); and Lorenne Clark, "Women and Locke: Who Owns the Apples in the Garden of Eden?" in *The Sexism of Social and Political Theory*, ed. Lorenne Clark and Lynda Lange (Toronto: University of Toronto Press, 1979), 16–40.

4. Linda Nicholson, *Gender and History: The Limits of Social Theory in the Age of the Family* (New York: Colombia University Press, 1986), 165.

5. Robert Filmer, *Patriarcha and Other Political Works*, ed. Peter Laslett (Oxford: Basil Blackwell, 1949).

6. Gordon Schochet, *Patriarchalism in Political Thought: The Authoritarian Family and Political Speculation and Attitudes Especially in Seventeenth-Century England* (Oxford: Basil Blackwell, 1975), 193.

7. Thomas Hobbes, *Leviathan* [1651], ed. Richard Tuck (Cambridge: Cambridge University Press, 1991), 100.

8. Daniela Gobbetti, *Private and Public: Individuals, Households, and Body Politic in Locke and Hutcheson* (New York: Routledge, 1992), 66–67.

9. In a discussion of the *Second Treatise* and *Some Thoughts concerning Education* (where Locke details his specific recommendations for the proper education of children in the family), Uday Singh Mehta argues that rather than supporting the goal of individuality, Locke's proposals for facilitating children's reasoning abilities through moral education function to stifle it. Mehta, *The Anxiety of Freedom: Imagination and Individuality in Locke's Political Thought* (Ithaca: Cornell University Press, 1992), 124.

10. Ibid., 120.

11. John Locke, *A Third Letter for Toleration*, quoted in Geraint Parry, "Individuality, Politics, and the Critique of Paternalism in John Locke," *Political Studies* 5 (1964): 175.

12. Teresa Brennan and Carole Pateman, "'Mere Auxiliaries to the Commonwealth': Women and the Origins of Liberalism," *Political Studies* 27 (June 1979): 185.

13. Pateman, *The Sexual Contract*, 22.

14. Nicholson, *Gender and History*, 140.

15. Zillah Eisenstein, *The Radical Future of Liberal Feminism* (New York: Longman, 1981), 33–49.

16. Ibid.

17. Ibid., 42.

18. In seventeenth-century England, the law of coverture specified that when a woman married, her legal status as an individual was suspended: the husband was assigned the responsibility to ensure that she behaved both publicly and privately in a manner befitting a good wife. It was this responsibility that formed the basis for granting husbands legal authority to chastise their wives. Blackstone's *Commentaries* provide insight into the common-law stance on this issue: "The husband also, by the old law might give his wife moderate correction. For, as he is to answer for her misbehavior, the law thought it reasonable to entrust him with his power of restraining her, by domestic chastisement." Quoted in Emerson Dobash and Russell Dobash, *Violence against Wives: A Case against Patriarchy* (New York: Free Press, 1979), 60.

19. Violence against wives has a very long history: laws authorizing husbands to chastise their wives date back to 753 B.C., when Romulus ruled in Rome. Lewis Okun, *Woman Abuse: Replacing Facts with Myths* (Albany: State University of New York Press, 1983), 2. Evidence that wife abuse was common can be found not only in legal codes but also in religious documents, personal testimonies from victims, court records, newspaper accounts, and published discussions by authors such as Francis Power Cobbe, "Wife Torture in England," *Contemporary Review* 32 (1878); and John Stuart Mill, *The Subjection of Women* [1858], ed. Wendell Robert Carr (Cambridge, Mass.: MIT Press, 1989).

20. It is important to remember that for Locke, providing such intervention in cases of potential conflict *outside the family* is the essential function of government.

21. Julie Matthaei, *An Economic History of Women in America: Women's Work, the Sexual Division of Labor, and the Development of Capitalism* (New York: Schocken, 1982), 108–14.

22. Lorenne Clark makes this point, with a special emphasis on how it relates to women's relationship to property in seventeenth-century marriage contracts, in "Women and Locke: Who Owns the Apples in the Garden of Eden?"

23. John Stuart Mill, in *The Subjection of Women*, makes this same point when he describes a women's decision to marry in seventeenth-century England as the equivalent of a "Hobson's choice: 'that or none'" (29).

24. Mary Lyndon Shanley, *Feminism, Marriage, and the Law in Victorian England* (Princeton: Princeton University Press, 1989), 176.

25. Mary Walsh, "Locke and Feminism on Private and Public Realms of Activities," *Review of Politics* (March 1996): 251–77.

26. Ibid., 276.

27. In light of my focus on domestic violence between intimate partners, I am limiting the discussion to adults within the family. This is not to suggest that there are not many related and equally important questions regarding the status of children in this sphere.

28. See Nicholson, *Gender and History*, 158–59, for an excellent discussion of the theoretical implications of disrupting this boundary within Locke's theory.

29. Ibid., 165.

30. In a discussion that I see as particularly relevant to the dilemmas that battered women face, Jean Elshtain argues that traditional liberal models such as Locke's fail to provide women with a vocabulary to articulate their position in the family. According to Elshtain, women were left with only two choices: to identify themselves with the rationalistic self-interest of the public sphere or the sentimentality of the private sphere. Elshtain, *Public Man, Private Woman: Women in Social and Political Thought* (Princeton: Princeton University Press, 1981). This observation helps to explain the double bind that is created for so many victims of domestic violence. If a woman's role in the family is identified with the rational sphere, then failure to leave an abusive husband is likely to be portrayed as irrational. Furthermore, it becomes much easier to blame women for getting into the situation in the first place—because they "should have known better." If, on the other hand, a woman's role in the family is viewed through the sentimental lens, we are likely to assume that as the moral beacon of the domestic sphere she should put family above all else. According to this paradigm, if she leaves she is a failed wife and if she stays she can be blamed for endangering her children.

Chapter 3. Feminist Re-Visions of the Public/Private Dichotomy

1. Carole Pateman, *The Disorder of Women: Democracy, Feminism, and Political Theory* (Stanford: Stanford University Press, 1989), 11.

2. My evaluation of these theories in terms of how well they address the dilemmas raised by a particular social problem mirrors the approach of Nancy Fraser to the process of evaluating critical theory. Using feminist theory as her example, Fraser suggests that when assessing the power of a particular theory, certain questions should be primary, including: "How well does it theorize the situation and prospects of the feminist movement? [and] To what extent does it serve the self-clarification of the struggles and wishes of contemporary women?" Fraser, "What's Critical about Critical Theory? The Case of Habermas and Gender," in *Feminism as Critique: On the Politics of Gender*, ed. Seyla Benhabib and Drucilla Cornell (Minneapolis: University of Minnesota Press, 1987), 32.

3. When domestic violence incidents are categorized by injurious effect, women are victims 94 percent of the time. David Finkelhor et al., *The Dark Side of Families: Current Family Violence Research* (Beverly Hills: Sage, 1983).

4. Anne Jones, *Next Time She'll Be Dead: Battering and How to Stop It* (Boston: Beacon, 1995), 154.

5. Jean Bethke Elshtain, *Public Man, Private Woman: Women in Social and Political Thought* (Princeton: Princeton University Press, 1981); Susan Moller Okin, "Gender, the Public and the Private," in *Political Theory Today*, ed. David Held (Stanford: Stanford University Press, 1991); and Pateman, *The Disorder of Women*.

6. Michelle Zimbalist Rosaldo and Louise Lamphere, eds. *Woman, Culture, and Society* (Stanford: Stanford University Press, 1972).

7. Zillah Eisenstein, *The Radical Future of Liberal Feminism* (New York: Longman, 1981), 15.

8. Susan Moller Okin, *Justice, Gender, and the Family* (New York: Basic, 1989), 179.

9. Judith Baer, *Women in American Law: The Struggle toward Equality from the New Deal to the Present* (New York: Holmes and Meier, 1996), 118.

10. Antonio Novello, "A Medical Response to Domestic Violence," *Journal of the American Medical Association* 267 (1992): 3132.

11. Naomi Cahn and Lisa Lerman, "Prosecuting Woman Abuse," in *Woman Battering,* ed. Michael Steinman (Cincinnati: Anderson, 1991), 95–96.

12. Anne Bottomley, "What's Happening in Family Law," in *Women-in-Law: Explorations in Law, Family, and Sexuality,* ed. Julia Brophy and Carol Smart (London: Routledge, 1985).

13. Heidi Hartmann, "The Family as the Focus of Gender, Class, and Political Struggle: The Example of Housework," *Signs* (spring 1981): 275.

14. Baer, *Women in American Law,* 11.

15. M. P. Johnson, "Patriarchal Terrorism and Common Couple Violence: Two Forms of Violence against Women," *Journal of Marriage and the Family* 57 (1994): 283–94.

16. Eisenstein, *The Radical Future of Liberal Feminism,* x.

17. Pateman, *The Disorder of Women,* 120.

18. Zillah Eisenstein, *The Female Body and the Law* (Berkeley: University of California Press, 1988), 15.

19. Frances Olsen, "The Family and the Market: A Study of Ideology and Legal Reform," *Harvard Law Review* 96, no. 7 (1983): 837.

20. Linda Gordon, *Heroes of Their Own Lives: The Politics and History of Family Violence* (New York: Viking, 1988).

21. Richard Gabel and Paul Harris, "Building Power and Breaking Images: Critical Legal Theory and the Practice of Law," *New York University Review of Law and Social Change* 11 (1982–83): 369.

22. Iris Marion Young, *Justice and the Politics of Difference* (Princeton: Princeton University Press, 1990), 110.

23. Pateman, *The Disorder of Women,* 3.

24. Shulamith Firestone, *The Dialectic of Sex: The Case for a Feminist Revolution* (New York: Bantam Books, 1970).

25. MacKinnon has critiqued Firestone's suggestion that the answer to women's oppression lies in freeing women from childbirth through technological advances because of its implicit acceptance of the patriarchal contention that women's inferiority to men can be traced to the natural order. Catharine MacKinnon, "Feminism, Marxism, Method, and the State: Towards a Feminist Jurisprudence," *Signs* 8 (1983): 639.

26. Catharine MacKinnon, *Feminism Unmodified: Discourses on Life and Law* (Cambridge, Mass.: Harvard University Press, 1984).

27. MacKinnon takes the radical stance that because it is occurring in the context of a society characterized by gender oppression, virtually all heterosexual sex subordinates women. Even consensual sex is problematic in her view, because women's desires are themselves the products of oppressive social relations and therefore cannot be trusted.

28. MacKinnon, "Feminism, Marxism, Method, and the State," 657.

29. I have settled on the term *conservative feminism* to describe Elshtain's views because I believe that although her arguments are properly designated as feminist, because of their explicit concern with the needs and interests of women, they are also conservative in the sense that they include a strong focus on traditional conception of womanhood, the family, and the importance of respecting the "moral imperatives" of human existence. For a more extended discussion of this issue, see Judith Stacey, "The New Conservative Feminism," *Feminist Studies* 9, no. 3 (fall 1985).

30. Elshtain does not limit her concerns about the overpersonalization of politics to radical feminist agendas. See her "Homosexual Politics: The Paradox of Gay Liberation," *Salamagundi* (fall 1982), 252–80.

31. Elshtain, *Public Man, Private Women,* 222.

32. Ibid., 328.

33. Ibid., 331.

34. Ibid., 336.

35. Sara Ruddick, "Maternal Thinking," *Feminist Studies* 6 (1980): 342–67.

36. Elshtain, *Public Man, Private Women,* 337.

37. Ibid., 329–30.

38. It is worth noting that Mill assumed that actual physical violence was much more likely to occur within the lower classes, who lacked the "moral education" that prevented upper class men from taking advantage of their wives legal subordination. John Stuart Mill, *The Subjection of Women* [1869] (Cambridge, Mass.: MIT Press, 1970), 46.

39. Ibid., 16.

40. Ibid., 48–49. As Andrea Nye points out, this assumption limits the relevance of Mill's arguments for the liberation of women to members of the educated middle class who had the option of staying at home. Nye, *Feminist Theory and the Philosophies of Man* (London: Croom Helm, 1988), 20.

41. Mary Wollstonecraft, *A Vindication of the Rights of Women* [1792] (Buffalo: Prometheus Books, 1989), 98–99.

42. During the seventy-plus year struggle for suffrage, there were recurring divisions within the movement over the question of whether arguments for the vote should challenge traditional conceptions of feminine responsibilities. For a discussion of this history, see Carl Degler, *At Odds: Women and the Family in America from the Revolution to the Present* (Oxford: Oxford University Press, 1980); and Eleanor Flexnor, *Century of Struggle: The Woman's Rights Movement in the United States* (Cambridge, Mass.: Harvard University Press, 1975). For a critical argument about the wisdom of relying on appeals to women's moralizing potential, see Jean Bethke Elshtain, "Moral Woman and Immoral Man: A Consideration of the Public-Private Split and its Political Ramifications," *Politics and Society* 4 (1974): 453–73.

43. Elizabeth Janeway, *Man's World, Woman's Place* (New York: Delta Books, 1971).

44. Betty Friedan, *The Feminine Mystique* (New York: Dell, 1974), 371.

45. Susan Moller Okin, *Justice, Gender, and the Family* (New York: Basic, 1989).

46. Ibid., 31.

47. Ibid., 126.

48. Ibid., 181.

49. The Commonwealth Fund Commission on Women's Health, *Domestic Violence Fact Sheet* (New York, 1996).

50. Gail Goolkasian, "The Judicial System and Domestic Violence: An Expanding Role," *Response* 9 (1986): 2.

51. Susan Schechter, *Women and Male Violence: The Visions and Struggles of the Battered Women's Movement* (Boston: South End, 1982).

52. M. P. Koss et al., *No Safe Haven: Male Violence against Women at Home, at Work, and in the Community* (Washington, D.C.: American Psychological Association, 1994).

53. MacKinnon, "Feminism, Marxism, Method, and the State," 148.

54. Jane Flax, "Postmodernism and Gender Relations in Feminist Theory," in *Feminism/Postmodernism*, ed. Linda Nicholson (London: Routledge, 1990). Many feminists have been skeptical about the wisdom of adapting postmodernism to feminism. Of particular concern is the challenge that postmodernism poses to the ability to make political claims around the unitary concept of gender. In the edited collection *Feminism/Postmodernism*, both sides of this debate are well represented.

55. Elizabeth Spelman, *Inessential Women: Problems of Exclusion in Feminist Thought* (Boston: Beacon, 1988).

56. In recent years, a number of liberal feminists have sought to develop theories that account for the limitations of rights-based solutions. For example, Susan Moller Okin insists that a liberal theory of justice should include a consideration of what occurs in the home, which points to the importance of considering why women do not exercise their right to exit an abusive relationship. The positive potential of this particular approach to reconceptualizing public and private boundaries in cases of domestic violence is explored further in chapter 7.

57. Elshtain, *Public Man, Private Women*, 336.

58. One possible response to this critique is that maternal values do not necessarily need to be embodied by the mother, thus taking the pressure off women. However, throughout her writings Elshtain expresses a strong preference for a traditional family structure and has objected to progressive efforts by both feminists and gay rights activists to support unconventional family groupings as long as they are loving and mutually supportive. Elshtain, "On Feminism, Family, and Community," *Dissent* 29 (winter 1983).

59. Maternal feminist theories have been critiqued as lacking an adequately developed account of how maternal ethics will transform the values and priorities of the public sphere. Mary Dietz, "Citizenship with a Feminist Face: The Problem with Maternal Thinking," *Political Theory* 13 (February 1985): 25. This gap in maternal theories is particularly serious in terms of the points being made here, for it suggests that this ideal society may never in fact be realized. Thus, the importance of considering the implication of the theory for women prior to the actualization of an ethical polity guided by maternal ethics is even greater.

60. Lenore Walker, "Psychology and Violence against Women," *American Psychologist* 44 (1989): 695.

61. Joan Tronto, "Beyond Gender Difference to a Theory of Care," *Signs* 12 (summer 1987): 649.

62. Elshtain, *Public Man, Private Women*, 229–39.

63. Ibid., 336.

64. Judith Stacey argues that despite their many differences, what unites conservative feminists is their rejection of the liberal and radical arguments that contribute to politicizing intimate relationships due to a shared desire to avoid the need to engage in direct struggles against male domination. Judith Stacey, "The New Conservative Feminism," 210.

65. MacKinnon, *Feminism Unmodified*, 100.

66. Carol Brown, "Mothers, Fathers, and Children: From Private to Public Patriarchy," in *The Unhappy Marriage of Marxism and Feminism*, ed. Lydia Sargent (London: Pluto, 1981), 244.

67. Angela Harris, "Race and Essentialism in Feminist Legal Theory," *Stanford Law Review* 42 (1990): 581.

68. As Kimberle Crenshaw explains, "Women of color are often reluctant to call the police, a hesitancy likely due to a general unwillingness among people of color to subject their private lives to the scrutiny and control of a police force that is frequently hostile. There is also a more generalized community ethic against public intervention, the product of a desire to create a private world free from the diverse assaults on the public lives of racially subordinated people. The home is not simply a man's castle in the patriarchal sense, but may also function as a safe haven from the indignities of life in a racist society." Crenshaw, "Mapping the Margins: Intersectionality, Identity Politics, and Violence against Women of Color," *Stanford Law Review* 43 (1991): 1241.

Chapter 4. The Legal Regulation of Domestic Violence

1. Paul Kahn, *The Cultural Study of Law: Reconstructing Legal Scholarship* (Chicago: University of Chicago Press, 1999).

2. The constitutive function of law has been explored by a wide range of scholars. See especially Karl Klare, "Law Making as Praxis," *Telos* 40 (1979): 122; Douglas Hay et al., *Albion's Fatal Tree: Crime and Society in Eighteenth-Century England* (New York: Free Press, 1975); and more recently, John Brigham, *The Constitution of Interests: Beyond the Politics of Rights* (New York: New York University Press, 1996).

3. Joseph Gusfield, "Moral Passage: The Symbolic Process in Public Designations of Deviance," *Social Problems* 15 (1967): 175.

4. In recent years, sociolegal scholars have begun to directly address the issue of whether the law should be viewed as an effective tool by those who seek to enact social change. See Michael McCann, *Rights at Work: Law and the Politics of Pay Equity* (Chicago: University of Chicago Press, 1993); Gerald Rosenberg, *The Hollow Hope: Can Courts Bring About Social Change?* (Chicago: University of Chicago Press, 1991); Stuart Scheingold, "Constitutional Rights and Social Change: Civil Rights in Perspective," in *Judging the Constitution: Critical Essays in Judicial Lawmaking*, ed. Michael McCann and Gerald Houseman (Glenview, Ill.: Scott, Foresman, 1989); Kristin Bumiller, *The Civil Rights Society: The Social Construction of Victims* (Baltimore: Johns Hopkins University Press, 1988).

5. Blackstone's *Commentaries*, quoted in Emerson R. Dobash and Russell Dobash, *Violence against Wives: A Case against Patriarchy* (New York: Free Press, 1979), 60.

6. For a discussion of the law of marital unity, see Norma Basch, "Invisible Women: The Legal Fiction of Marital Unity in Nineteenth-Century America," *Feminist Studies* 5 (summer 1979): 346–66.

7. Dobash and Dobash, *Violence against Wives,* 62.

8. Ibid., 61.

9. Lawrence Friedman, *A History of American Law* (New York: Simon and Schuster, 1985); cf. Dennis R. Nolan, "Sir William Blackstone and the New American Republic," *New York University Law Review* 51 (1976): 731–32.

10. According to Elizabeth Pleck, the Massachusetts Bay Colony enacted the first law in the Western world expressly forbidding wife abuse. According to the *Body of Laws and Liberties of Massachusetts,* "Everies Marryed woeman shall be free from bodilie correction or stripes by her husband, unlesse it be in his owne defence upon her assault." Cited in Elizabeth Pleck, "Criminal Approaches to Family Violence, 1640–1980," in *Family Violence,* ed. L. Ohlin and M. Tonry (Chicago: University of Chicago Press, 1989).

11. State supreme court decisions that featured an explicit recognition of the legal right of chastisement include: *Bradley v. State*, 1 Miss. (1 Walker) 156, 158 (1824); *State v. Black*, 60 N.C. (Win.) 262 (1864); *State v. Hussey*, 44 N.C. (Busb) 123 (1852); *Richards v. Richards*, 1 Grant's Cas. 389, 392–93 (Pa. 1856); *State v. Rhodes*, 61 N.C. 44 (1865): all cited in Nan Oppenlander, "The Evolution of Law and Wife Abuse," *Law and Policy Quarterly* 3 (October 1981): 387–88. Yet as Oppenlander points out, "Husbands who murdered their spouses were prosecuted. But the courts held that nonpermanent injury from which the wife could recover did not constitute assault" (388).

12. Pleck, "Criminal Approaches to Family Violence," 82.

13. *Richardson v. Lawhon*, 4 KY L. Rptr 998, 999 (1883); cf. Reva Siegal, " 'The Rule of Love': Wife Beating as Prerogative and Privacy," *Yale Law Journal* 105 (1996): 2117–87. Other cases cited by Siegal as repudiating the law of chastisement include: *Fulgham v. State*, 46 Ala. 143, 147 (1871); *Commonwealth v. McAfee*, 108 Mass. 458, 461 (1871); *Harris v. State*, 14 So 266 (Miss 1894); *Gorman v. State*, 42 Tex. 221, 223 (1875).

14. Barbara Epstein, *The Politics of Domesticity: Women, Evangelism, and Temperance in Nineteenth-Century America* (Middletown, Conn.: Wesleyan University Press, 1981), cited in Siegal, " 'The Rule of Love.' "

15. Margaret May, "Violence in the Family: An Historical Perspective," in *Violence in the Family*, ed. J. P. Martin (New York: Wiley and Sons, 1978). It is important to note that these arguments were not directed at providing women with rights so that they could leave their husbands.

16. Barbara Laslett, "The Family as a Public and Private Institution: An Historical Perspective," *Journal of Marriage and the Family* 35 (1973): 480

17. John Demos, *Past, Present, and Personal: The Family and the Life Course in American History* (New York: Oxford University Press, 1986), 36. This vision of the family was adhered to most strongly by the middle and upper classes, who could afford to maintain a separation between the household and the marketplace. According to Milton C. Regan, Jr., although they represented a small minority of the population, the strength of their influence was built on a fervent belief in the correctness of their ways, economic status, the "emergence in the United States of a national culture that drew sustenance from dissemination of the printed word," and other factors. Regan, *Family Law and the Pursuit of Intimacy* (New York: New York University Press, 1993).

18. Elizabeth Pleck, *Domestic Tyranny: The Making of Social Policy against Family Violence from Colonial Times to the Present* (New York: Oxford University Press, 1987).

19. See Richard Posner, "The Right to Privacy," *Georgia Law Review* 12 (1978): 396–97, for an argument about the positive relationship between increased wealth and privacy.

20. Within the field of family law, this historical transition is frequently described as a movement from status to contract. Under the common law, marriage was approached as a status relationship, that is, one entered marriage as a means of securing some type of status in society. Accordingly, the role of the state was to ensure the stability of those status relationships by making divorces very difficult to obtain, except in cases where one partner violated the status of the other through an act such as adultery. Richard Chused, *Private Acts in Public Places: A Social History of Divorce in the Formative Era of American Family Law* (Philadelphia: University of Pennsylvania Press, 1994). The emergence of the contract as the governing framework for regulating marriage came out of a growing emphasis on marriage as a relationship driven by the needs and desires of individuals rather than as a continuation of traditional social roles. For a discussion of status versus contract in family law, see Martha

Albertson Fineman, *The Illusion of Equality: The Rhetoric and Reality of Divorce Reform* (Chicago: University of Chicago Press, 1991), 18–19; and Regan, *Family Law and the Pursuit of Intimacy*, 35–42.

21. *State v. Rhodes,* 61 N.C. (Phil. Law) at 45, cited in Siegal, " 'The Rule of Love,' " 2155.

22. Siegal, " 'The Rule of Love,' " 2153.

23. *Drake v. Drake,* 177 N.W. 624, 625 (Minn. 1920) cited in Siegal, " 'The Rule of Love,' " 2166.

24. Chused, *Private Acts in Public Places,* 122–23.

25. Siegal, " 'The Rule of Love,' " 2169–70. This particular argument provides a very good example of the complex position of law within American culture as simultaneously constitutive of and reflective of that culture. Although judicial pronouncements about the altruistic family clearly mirrored popular sentiments, the invocation of these sentiments within a legal framework also served to add something new: institutional authority to a set of assumptions and norms about relationships that were previously treated as privately negotiated matters.

26. Linda Gordon, *Heroes of Their Own Lives: The Politics and History of Family Violence* (New York: Viking, 1988), 252–53.

27. Pleck, *Domestic Tyranny,* 136–37.

28. Susan Edwards, *Policing Domestic Violence: Women, the Law, and the State* (London: Sage, 1989).

29. Susan Schechter, *Women and Male Violence: The Visions and Struggles of the Battered Women's Movement* (Boston: South End, 1982), 29.

30. Pleck, *Domestic Tyranny,* 190.

31. See chapter 3 for a more detailed elaboration of these feminist arguments.

32. Nadine Taub and Elizabeth Schneider, "Women's Subordination and the Role of Law," in *The Politics of Law: A Progressive Critique,* ed. David Kairys (New York: Pantheon, 1990), 122–23.

33. Richard Gabel and Paul Harris, "Building Power and Breaking Images: Critical Legal Theory and the Practice of Law," *New York University Review of Law and Social Change* 11 (1982–83): 370.

34. Elizabeth Schneider, "The Violence of Privacy," *Connecticut Law Review* 23 (1991): 985.

35. Molly Chaudhuri and Kathleen Daly, "Do Restraining Orders Help Battered Women's Experience with Male Violence and Legal Process?" in *Domestic Violence: The Changing Criminal Justice Response,* vol. 1 of *Studies in Crime, Law, and Justice,* ed. Eva S. Buzawa and Carl G. Buzawa (Westport, Conn.: Auburn House, 1992).

36. Donileen Loseke, "Lived Realities and the Construction of Social Problems: The Case of Wife Abuse," *Symbolic Interaction* 10 (1987): 231.

37. Ronet Bachman and L. Saltzman, "Violence against Women: Estimates from the Redesigned Survey" (Washington, D.C.: U.S. Department of Justice, Bureau of Justice Statistics, 1995).

38. Schneider, "The Violence of Privacy," 981.

39. M. Douglas, "The Battered Woman Syndrome," in *Domestic Violence on Trial: Psychological and Legal Dimensions of Family Violence,* ed. Daniel Sonkin (New York: Springer, 1987), 40.

40. Lenore Walker, *The Battered Woman* (New York: Harper and Row, 1979), 364–67.

41. Ibid., 46.

42. Some of the crimes that battered woman syndrome has been used as a defense for in-clude fraud, assault, and failure to protect charges in cases where children are injured or killed. As Stark points out, battered woman syndrome (BWS) is now frequently classified as a form of post-traumatic stress disorder (PTSD). BWS and PTSD are also used in prosecu-tions of batterers (e.g., to explain why victims fail to report abuse, or even lie about it when asked) and in civil matters to establish liability in cases involving divorce, custody, and per-sonal injury restitution. See Evan Stark, "Re-Presenting Woman Battering: From Battered Woman Syndrome to Coercive Control," *Albany Law Review* 58 (1995): 974.

43. Ibid., 999.

44. The utilization of battered woman syndrome as part of a defense strategy may be more effective for some women than for others. For example, Linda Ammons argues that the effectiveness of testimony about battered woman syndrome in cases involving African Amer-ican women is likely to be compromised by racial stereotypes about them which "include that a black woman is either very strong or somehow inherently bad, but never weak or pas-sive." Ammons, "Mules, Madonnas, Babies, Bathwater, Racial Imagery, and Stereotypes: The African-American Woman and the Battered Woman Syndrome," *Wisconsin Law Review* (1995): 1007. Sharon Angella Allard goes even further in her critique of battered woman syndrome, arguing that in addition to being limited by existing racial stereotypes, its applica-tion functions to reinforce traditional gender role stereotypes. Although damaging to all women, these stereotypes are especially problematic for black women. Allard, "Rethinking Battered Woman Syndrome: A Black Feminist Perspective," *UCLA Women's Law Journal* 1 (1991): 206.

45. Christine Littleton, "Women's Experience and the Problem of Transition: Perspec-tives on Male Battering of Women," *University of Chicago Legal Forum* (1989): 38.

46. In an interesting discussion of the consequences of such portrayals, Donald Downs argues that battered woman syndrome—by portraying victims of domestic abuse as lacking self-control and individual responsibility—functions to portray women as second-class citi-zens, for as he points out, these are "the very attributes that make citizenship possible." See, for example, Downs, *More Than Victims: Battered Women, the Syndrome Society, and the Law* (Chicago: University of Chicago Press, 1996), 219.

47. For a discussion of the ways in which the reliance of the battered woman syndrome on explanations of diminished capacity can lead to problems for women who are seeking cus-tody, see Myra Sun and Elizabeth Thomas, "Custody Litigation on Behalf of Battered Women," *Clearinghouse Review* 21 (1987): 563.

48. Martha Mahoney, "Legal Images of Battered Women: Redefining the Issue of Sepa-ration," *Michigan Law Review* 90 (1991): 25.

49. Schechter, *Woman and Male Violence*, 252.

50. This movie starring Farah Fawcett received a great deal of publicity and has been widely discussed. It was based on a book about the case of Francine Hughes, who after years of incredibly brutal and humiliating abuse, set fire to her husband's bed while he was asleep. Hughes was tried for first degree murder but after a dramatic trial was acquitted of murder by reason of temporary insanity.

51. Martha Minow, "Needs and the Door to the Land of Change: Law, Language, and Family Violence," *Vanderbilt Law Review* 43 (1990): 1665.

52. Bachman and Saltzman, "Violence against Women."

53. Mahoney, "Legal Images of Battered Women," 5.

54. Joyce Gelb, "The Politics of Wife Abuse," in *Families Politics and Public Policy*, ed. Irene Diamond (New York: Longman, 1983), 253.

55. Laura Crites, "Wife Abuse: The Judicial Record," in *Women, the Courts, and Equality*, ed. Laura Crites and Winifred Hepperle (Newbury Park, Calif.: Sage, 1987), 47.

56. Lloyd Ohlin and Michael Tonry, "Family Violence in Perspective," in *Family Violence: Crime and Justice, a Review of Research*, ed. Lloyd Ohlin and Michael Tonry (Chicago: University of Chicago Press, 1989), 6.

57. Michelle Fine, "Contradictions: An Essay Inspired by Women and Male Violence," *Feminist Studies* 11 (summer 1985): 399. One of the most serious drawbacks of going public with abuse is that in order to bring the force of law to bear against her abuser, a woman must portray herself to the world as a victim. For an excellent elaboration of how the structure of the law requires women to assume victim status, see Bumiller's *Civil Rights Society*.

58. This question is also problematic in that the focus on the response of the victim replaces the focus on the violence of the batterer. See Janet Fagan and Susan Wexler, "Crime at Home and in the Streets: The Relationship between Family and Stranger Violence," *Violence and Victims* 2 (1987): 5.

59. It also obscures the ways in which battering and alternatives to battering might be radically different for poor or minority women than for women who have financial and emotional support.

60. Walker, *The Battered Woman*, 163.

61. Michelle Fine points out that even feminist reformers frequently fail to appreciate the tension that exists between the goals of autonomy and self-sufficiency and the need for community. Fine, "Contradictions," 402.

62. Richard Gelles and Murray Strauss, *Intimate Violence* (New York: Simon and Schuster, 1988).

63. Littleton, "Women's Experience and the Problem of Transition," 41.

64. A recent focus group study of immigrant women's perceptions of the criminal justice response to battering in Canada found a very common fear among study participants that "invoking police intervention could bring dishonor and shame to an immigrant woman's husband, family and ethnic community, and thus could sever their relationships with those who could assist and support them." Sandra Wahholz and Baukje Miedema, "Risk, Fear, Harm: Immigrant Women's Perceptions of the 'Policing Solution' to Woman Abuse," *Crime, Law, and Social Change* 34 (2000): 308.

65. Gelles and Strauss, *Intimate Violence*, 39.

66. Anne Jones, *Next Time She'll Be Dead: Battering and How to Stop It* (Boston: Beacon, 1994), 211.

67. Although my focus is on the issue of domestic violence, this is clearly not the only area where a problem that was previously treated as private is now being framed as a social issue requiring a public response. Other examples include child abuse, sexual harassment, and employment discrimination.

Chapter 5. The Power of Participation

1. I located potential interviewees through a "snowballing technique," beginning with several contacts that I had made through conferences and colleagues and then asking them to put me in touch with others working in the field. This sampling technique would not work well if the goal were to produce statistical generalizations, but it worked quite well for my purpose of generating analytical conclusions.

2. In light of the importance of community size to privacy issues, the region of northern California within which I conducted my interviews was ideal, because within two hours' driving time, I could reach a very large city (San Francisco), a small city (Sacramento), several suburban communities (Vacaville, Davis, Woodland, and Dixon), and a small agricultural community (Winters). Additionally, the region is characterized by a great deal of racial, ethnic, class, and religious diversity. Finally, interviewing individuals in the capital, Sacramento, had the considerable advantage of providing access to elected officials and bureaucrats. I do not want to make the claim that this region of northern California is representative of the United States as a whole, but the analytical insights and recommendations for future research that resulted from this project seem to be applicable across state boundaries.

3. Robert Dingwall, "Accounts, Interviews, and Observations," in *Context and Method in Qualitative Research*, ed. Gale Miller and Robert Dingwall (London: Sage, 1997), 56.

4. Ibid., 58.

5. An important theme within feminist discussion of epistemology is the insight that all knowledge is constructed from a particular standpoint. Accordingly, it is very important when making knowledge claims to be clear about the standpoint(s) that influenced the constitution of that knowledge. Remaining attentive to the presence and operation of standpoints helps us to recognize the limitations of particular claims while serving as a constant reminder of the partiality of all knowledge. Critics of this approach warn that it represents a dangerous slide into a relativist stance that undermines our ability to act decisively in the world. I believe, to the contrary, that relinquishing our search for absolute truth is much more likely to improve the effectiveness of the actions that we take because it enhances our ability to recognize the gaps and biases in our understanding of the problem that we seek to address. For a prominent treatment of these issues see Dorothy Smith, *The Everyday World as Problematic: A Feminist Sociology* (Boston: Northeastern University Press, 1987), chaps. 2 and 3.

6. My belief that such a project might be helpful is based on Elizabeth Grosz's assertion that "it is no longer a matter of maintaining a theoretical purity at the cost of political principles; nor is it simply a matter of the *ad hoc* adoption of theoretical principles according to momentary needs or whims: it is a question of negotiating a path between always impure positions, seeing that politics is always already bound up with what it contests (including theories), and theories are always implicated in various political struggles (whether this is acknowledged or not)." Grosz, "A Note on Essentialism and Difference," in *Feminist Knowledge: Critique and Construct*, ed. Sneja Gunew (London: Routledge, 1990), 332.

7. All of the individuals who were interviewed for this study were involved with legal institutions at some level. Some were most active in the regulatory side of the law, and some were deeply involved in legislation; many worked within the criminal justice system, and others saw themselves as working outside of legal institutions but were nevertheless clear that their work on behalf of victims of domestic violence was profoundly affected by law.

8. Throughout this chapter, the phrase "the law" should not be interpreted literally as a description of the law as a hegemonic institution. In fact, "the law" can be broken apart into distinct categories such as civil, criminal, public, and regulatory law. Furthermore, although logical coherence and consistency is certainly a major component of legal doctrine, I agree with Carol Smart's assertion that law should be understood not "as a homogenous entity but as a collection of practices and discourses which do not all operate together with one purpose." Smart, *The Ties That Bind* (London: Routledge, 1984), 22.

9. The theme of the limitations of legal intervention is also significant for its potential

contribution to the debate about the efficacy of the law as a tool of social change. See, for example, Michael McCann, *Rights at Work: Law and the Politics of Pay Equity* (Chicago: University of Chicago Press, 1993); Gerald Rosenberg, *The Hollow Hope: Can Courts Bring About Social Change?* (Chicago: University of Chicago Press, 1991); and Stuart Scheingold, "Constitutional Rights and Social Change: Civil Rights in Perspective," in *Judging the Constitution: Critical Essays on Judicial Lawmaking,* ed. Michael McCann and Gerald Houseman (Glenview, Ill.: Scott, Foresman, 1989).

10. Joel Handler, *Social Movements and the Legal System: A Theory of Law Reform and Social Change* (New York: Academic Press, 1978); Marc Galanter, "Why the 'Haves' Come Out Ahead: Speculations on the Limits of Legal Change," *Law and Society Review* 9 (1974): 95.

11. A number of interviewees talked about the growth of the Russian community and the troubling combination within that community of both high incidents of domestic violence and a deeply ingrained distrust of the police.

12. After making this statement, this interviewee went on to note that although the conflation is not actually correct, it is still possible to capitalize on the common misconception that there is a necessary connection between something being illegal and wrong.

13. Joel Garner, Jeffrey Fagan, and Christopher Maxwell, "Published Findings from the Spousal Assault Replication Program: A Critical Review," *Journal of Quantitative Criminology* 118 (1995): 3; and Lawrence Sherman, *Policing Domestic Violence: Experiments and Dilemmas* (New York: Free Press, 1992).

14. In fact, a number of interviewees talked about instances in which they had sought to intervene and had either been frustrated by a lack of response from the victim or had received a violent reaction from the perpetrator.

15. Susan Schechter, a longtime activist in the battered women's movement and author of several books on the subject, talks about the importance of community watchdog groups to the success of the strategy of suing police departments for failures to protect victims of domestic violence. She argues that without such groups, such litigation accomplishes very little. Schechter, *Women and Male Violence: The Visions and Struggles of the Battered Women's Movement* (Boston: South End, 1982), 160.

16. An example of what it might mean to consider the special needs presented in custody cases where domestic violence has occurred would be arranging for a third party to deliver the children in order to minimize contact between the parents.

17. In mentioning these costs, the interviewees were not implying that the current police or judicial response is adequate or that taxpayers' money should not be used to help meet these expenses. Their point was simply that the problem costs us an enormous amount of money, which suggests that alleviating the problem could also save a great deal of money.

Chapter 6. Reconstructing the Boundaries of Community Concern

1. For a consideration of both the regulative and the symbolic impacts of legal intervention on the degree to which domestic violence is treated as a public or a private problem, see chapter 4. The larger question of whether the operation of law on society is primarily instrumental or constitutive is the focal point of a long-standing and fascinating debate within sociolegal studies. For a good introduction to this debate, see Austin Sarat and Thomas Kearns, "Beyond the Great Divide: Forms of Legal Scholarship and Everyday Life," in *Law in Everyday Life*, ed. Austin Sarat and Thomas Kearns (Ann Arbor: University of Michigan Press, 1993).

2. For this reason, it is important to differentiate my descriptive usage of the term *the community* from the way in which it is normatively employed by communitarian theorists. The latter use *the community* to describe groups of individuals who have a collective sense of identity that is developed through a belief in and adherence to a set of shared beliefs and practices. See, for example, Alasdair MacIntyre, *After Virtue* (Notre Dame: University of Notre Dame Press, 1984); and Charles Taylor, *Sources of Self* (Cambridge, Mass.: Harvard University Press, 1989).

3. To the contrary, I agree with critics who argue that celebrations of community as a normative ideal are highly problematic due to the exclusion of difference that they necessarily entail. I also want to distance myself from approaches that reinforce an oppositional relationship between community and individualism. Iris Marion Young explains why this opposition is so problematic: "As is the case with many dichotomies, in this one the possibilities for social ontology and social relations appear to be exhausted in the two categories. For many writers, the rejection of the individualism logically entails asserting community, and conversely any rejection of community entails that one necessarily supports individualism." Young, "The Ideal of Community and the Politics of Difference," in *Feminism/Postmodernism*, edited by Linda Nicholson (New York: Routledge, 1990), 307.

4. At the level of material consequences, there is obviously a significant difference between a sanction that can result in arrest and possible imprisonment and one that cannot. Avishai Margalit makes a more subtle but no less important distinction regarding the relationship between gossip, humiliation, and privacy: "Violation of privacy in traditional gossip societies is not meant to exclude people from the society let alone from humanity in general. On the contrary, gossip based partly on violation of privacy creates a sticky sense of belonging." Margalit, *The Decent Society* (Cambridge, Mass.: Harvard University Press, 1996), 206.

5. Interaction between a nonstate actor and a citizen can entail state sanctions, as seen, for example, in laws that mandate professionals to override confidentiality agreements and notify social service or criminal justice agencies if they obtain information that a child is being harmed. In some states this requirement has been extended to include adult victims of abuse. A 1994 California law requires medical personnel to make a report to the police if they provide medical services to a person that they suspect has an injury inflicted "by means of a firearm" or if "the injury is the result of assaultive or abusive conduct." California Penal Code 11160–11163.2. Every interviewee who mentioned this law indicated some level of uneasiness with the mandatory aspect of the requirement. A representative comment came from one activist, who explained, "A lot of women do not want the police to be called and may accurately believe that doing so will place them in greater danger. The fear among a lot of us is that women will be afraid to seek medical care if they think that it will result in the involvement of law enforcement in their lives." For more on this law, see Areilla Hyman, "Mandatory Reporting of Domestic Violence by Health Care Providers: A Misguided Approach" (San Francisco: Family Violence Prevention Fund, 1994).

6. As Richard Hixson points out, because we are interdependent beings, privacy cannot exist in a vacuum. See Hixson, *Privacy in Public Society: Human Rights in Conflict* (New York: Oxford University Press, 1987), 22. And in the words of Alida Brill: "Privacy is granted to an individual only when others agree to honor that privacy, be it by compliance with the law or by community custom." Brill, *Nobody's Business: Paradoxes of Privacy* (Reading, Mass.: Addison-Wesley, 1990), xv.

7. The literature on civil society is voluminous and extends across many different fields. Several works that are especially relevant to the questions raised in this book are: Jean

Cohen, *Civil Society and Social Theory* (Cambridge, Mass.: MIT Press, 1982); John Keane, *Democracy and Civil Society* (London: Verso, 1988); Adam Seligman, *The Idea of Civil Society* (New York: Free Press, 1992); and Thomas Janoski, *Citizenship and Civil Society* (Cambridge: Cambridge University Press, 1998).

8. See also Carole Pateman, *The Disorder of Women: Democracy, Feminism, and Political Theory* (Oxford: Basil Blackwell, 1989), 122; and chapter 1, above.

9. For an excellent overview of this issue in the international context, see Charles Maier, ed., *Changing Boundaries of the Political: Essays on the Evolving Balance between the State and Society, Public and Private in Europe* (Cambridge: Cambridge University Press, 1987).

10. As Stanley Benn and Gerald Gaus point out, many philosophers (most notably J.S. Mill and J. Hayek) make this as a normative point and argue that "a large part of public activity 'ought' to take place in nonpolitical voluntary association." Benn and Gaus, *Public and Private in Social Life* (London: Croom Helm, 1983), 53.

11. Michael Walzer provides further insight into the relationship between the state and the community and the influence of this relationship on the public character of activities that take place within a community context. See Walzer, "The Civil Society Argument," in *The Citizenship Debates,* ed. Gershon Shafir (Minneapolis: University of Minnesota Press, 1998), 304.

12. *Dodge v. Salvation Army,* 1989 U.S. Dist. LEXIS 4797; 4 Empl. Prac. Dec. (CCH) ¶3, 619.

13. However, the need to enforce standards of nondiscrimination when it comes to the *recipients* of the social services that are provided with public monies has not been seriously challenged. Jeffrey Rosen, "Religious Rights: Why the Catholic Church Shouldn't Have To Hire Gays," *New Republic,* February 26, 2001, 16.

14. One possible response to this emphasis on multiple points of exchange is to argue that rather than expanding the meaning of our conception of "public," we should just reject the dichotomy between private and public altogether. However, although it is clear that the dichotomization of these two spheres is problematic, many compelling reasons still exist for maintaining a clear boundary between the state and the family.

15. Because this focus on community intervention can be clearly connected to assessments about where the movement was at the time of the interviews, it is important to recognize the views expressed at that time may have changed.

16. In making this argument, I am relying on a distinction between *direct* state interventions (such as the imposition of criminal sanctions) and *indirect* interventions (such as the provision of shelters, counseling, and public assistance). In many cases, indirect interventions are funded either partially or entirely by public money.

17. Margaret Borkowski, Mervyn Murch, and Val Walker, *Marital Violence: The Community Response* (London: Tavistock, 1983), 112.

18. Some studies have concluded that the effectiveness of legal interventions can be correlated to the health of the social milieu in which they occur. Lawrence Sherman underscores the irony imbedded in this conclusion: "The weaker the social fabric becomes, the stronger the argument to use criminal sanction in its place: if the family can't control the problem, the attitude is to let the police and prisons do it. But the weaker the social fabric becomes, the more danger there may be that criminal sanctions will fail or backfire by provoking anger rather than reintegration." Sherman, *Policing Domestic Violence: Experiments and Dilemmas* (New York: Free Press, 1992), 248.

19. Peter Stevens, *Community Policing in Action: A Practitioner's Guide* (Kenwyn: Juta

and Co., 1995); and Roberta Cronin, *Innovative Community Partnerships: Working To-gether for Change* (Washington, D.C.: U.S. Dept. of Justice, Office of Juvenile Justice and Delinquency Prevention, 1994).

20. Sherman, *Policing Domestic Violence*, 213.

21. For example, one study of African American women who had utilized shelter services found that the level of violence suffered by these women was more severe than that of white women, suggesting a greater resistance to utilizing shelter services in cases of moderate violence. This study also identified the presence of additional barriers associated with patterns of institutional racism faced by African American women in their efforts to escape violence. Cris Sullivan and Maureen Rumptz, "Adjustment and Needs of African American Women Who Utilized a Domestic Violence Shelter," *Violence and Victims* 9 (1994): 283–84.

22. See, for example, Jenny Rivera, "Domestic Violence against Latinas by Latino Males: An Analysis of Race, National Origin, and Gender Differentials," *Boston College Third World Law Journal* 14 (1994): 231–57; and Karin Wang, "Battered Asian American Women: Community Responses from the Battered Women's Movement and the Asian American Community," *Asian Law Journal* 3 (May 1996): 151–84. These authors also emphasize the critical need to develop alternate programs in close collaboration with community-based organizations and advocates who represent the populations being served. For the importance of cultural sensitivity to the development of successful domestic violence prevention programs and an interesting discussion of utilizing popular culture to this end, see William Oliver, "Preventing Domestic Violence in the African American Community," *Violence against Women* 6 (May 2000): 533.

23. See, for example, Ola Barnett and Alyce LaViolette, *It Could Happen to Anyone: Why Battered Women Stay* (Newbury Park, Calif.: Sage, 1993). One review of this book praises the authors for their thoroughness and sensitive analysis, although regretting the authors' choice to center the book around the question of why battered women stay: a choice that prevents them from addressing "the better question, 'Why don't men just stop battering women?'" *Journal of Family Violence* 12 (1997): 235–36.

24. For a sustained argument about why these questions interfere with our ability to address domestic violence productively, see Anne Jones, *Next Time She'll Be Dead: Battering and How to Stop It* (Boston: Beacon, 1994), 152. Jones traces our preoccupation with why battered women stay to the 1920s, when the most widely accepted answer was that it was a consequence of "low intelligence." During the 1940s and 1950s, this explanation was replaced with "masochism," only to be supplanted by "isolation" in the 1960s and 1970s. Today, as discussed in chapter 4, one of the most popular (and controversial) explanations centers on Lenore Walker's theory of "learned helplessness."

25. For more on these contradictions, see chapter 2.

26. One of the primary factors that contributes to a pattern of victim-blaming is frustration with battered women who report the abuse but then fail to follow through with stated intentions to leave. This cycle of inaction by victims, resulting in service providers and public officials giving up on them, is especially unfortunate when we consider that at least one very good study shows victims will follow through if we help them. Cited in Jones, *Next Time She'll Be Dead*, 140–45.

27. For more on the individualistic basis of the U.S. legal system, see chapter 4. I am not suggesting that such an orientation is inappropriate. The critical undertone of this observation is centered instead on the limits of relying exclusively on legal mechanisms to respond to domestic violence.

28. One obvious objection to this approach is that the advantages of taking the pressure off victims to generate a public response are outweighed by the risk that this shift will deny them the power to determine when, where, and under what circumstances they wish to be assisted. However, as a number of the interviewees pointed out, although attention to victim empowerment is essential, when serious assaults take place outside the home, the state does not request permission from the victim before pressing charges. For an excellent discussion of the issue of victim empowerment as it relates to the policy of mandatory prosecution in domestic violence cases see, Linda Mills, "Killing Her Softly: Intimate Abuse and the Violence of State Intervention," *Harvard Law Review* 113 (December 1999): 550–613.

29. Christine Littleton, "Women's Experience and the Problem of Transition: Perspectives on Male Battering of Women," *University of Chicago Legal Forum* 23 (1989): 27.

30. The definition of *public* being used here defines an issue as public when it becomes an object of collective concern and action. As discussed in chapter 4, this understanding of the term can be contrasted with definitions that treat *public* and *state intervention* as equivalent.

31. In this respect, using education programs about domestic violence as a strategy is very similar to the practice of consciousness-raising as a political tactic within the women's movement during the 1970s and 1980s.

32. Patricia Boling, *Privacy and the Politics of Intimate Life* (Ithaca: Cornell University Press, 1996), 112.

33. Ibid., 120.

34. For some prominent examples of participatory-democratic theories see, Carole Pateman, *Participation and Democratic Theory* (Cambridge: Cambridge University Press, 1970); Benjamin Barber, *Strong Democracy: Participatory Politics for a New Age* (Berkeley: University of California Press, 1984); Jane Mansbridge, *Beyond Adversary Democracy* (Chicago: University of Chicago Press, 1980).

35. Hanna Pitkin, "Justice: On Relating Private and Public," *Political Theory* 9 (August 1981): 345.

36. Boling, *Privacy and the Politics of Intimate Life*, 153.

37. Evan Stark, "Re-Presenting Woman Battering: From Battered Woman Syndrome to Coercive Control," *Albany Law Review* 58 (1995): 986.

38. Evan Stark and Anne Flitcraft, *Women at Risk: Domestic Violence and Women's Health* (Thousand Oaks, Calif.: Sage Publications, 1996), 79.

39. Ibid.

40. Linda Gordon, *Heroes of Their Own Lives: The Politics and History of Family Violence* (New York: Penguin, 1988), 27–58.

41. Ibid., 20.

42. Ibid., 29.

43. Ibid., 21.

44. The failure of emergency room physicians to identify domestic violence as the cause of injuries has been well documented. Evan Stark, Anne Flitcraft, and William Frazier, "Medicine and Patriarchal Violence: The Social Construction of a 'Private' Event," *International Journal of Health Services* 9 (1979). Studies conducted to explain this failure have found that among the most common reasons given by medical personnel is the belief that their ability to help was limited to treating injuries. Meghan McGrath et al., "Violence against Women: Provider Barriers to Intervention in Emergency Departments," *Academic Emergency Medicine* 4 (April 1997); Nancy Sugg et al., "Domestic Violence and Primary Care: Attitudes, Practices, and Beliefs," *Archives of Family Medicine* 8 (July–August 1999).

45. For example, within the battered women's movement, there has been a great deal of discussion about the implications of requiring academic credentials when hiring shelter workers. Although it was not a dominant theme in the interviews, several interviewees presented this as a major tension point in their work. According to critics of this trend, the move toward professionalization has served to blunt the political content of the domestic violence movement, as individuals who came to the movement as a result of their own experiences with violence or because of their commitment to grassroots efforts to assist women are replaced by those who see the field as a career. For a clear description of the ways that professionalization requirements can serve to depoliticize shelter work, see Nancy Fraser, "Struggle over Needs: Outline of a Socialist-Feminist Critical Theory of Late-Capitalist Political Culture," in *Women, the State, and Welfare*, ed. Linda Gordon (Madison: University of Wisconsin Press, 1990), 213–15. For an examination of the link between professionalization and depoliticization at a specific shelter, see Karen Kendrick, "Producing the Battered Woman: Shelter Politics and the Feminist Voice," in *Community Activism and Feminist Politics: Organizing across Race, Class, and Gender*, ed. Nancy Naples (New York: Routledge, 1998).

46. Patricia Gagne, *Battered Women's Justice: The Movement for Clemency and the Politics of Self-Defense* (New York: Twayne, 1998), 157.

47. See, for example, Gillian Walker, *Family Violence and the Women's Movement: The Conceptual Politics of Struggle* (Toronto: University of Toronto Press, 1990); and Elizabeth Schneider, "The Violence of Privacy," *Connecticut Law Review* 23 (1991): 981.

48. Susan Schechter, *Women and Male Violence: The Visions and Struggles of the Battered Women's Movement* (Boston: South End, 1982), 201.

49. Nancy Fraser, "Rethinking the Public Sphere: A Contribution to the Critique of Actually Existing Democracy," in *Habermas and the Public Sphere*, ed. Craig Calhoun (Cambridge, Mass.: MIT Press, 1992), 2.

50. Ibid., 18. Fraser defines egalitarian multicultural societies as heterogeneous "societies whose basic framework does not generate unequal social groups in structural relations of dominance and subordination" (ibid., 16). Accordingly, stratified societies are "societies whose basic institutional framework generates unequal social groups in structural relations of dominance and subordination" (ibid., 13). I think it is reasonable to assume that the United States belongs in the latter classification.

51. Ibid., 17.

52. Ibid., 14.

53. Ibid., 15.

54. Domestic violence coalitions also provide a nice example of Fraser's observation that it is likely that individuals will be part of multiple publics at the same time and that these memberships may partially overlap. Ibid., 18.

55. The diversity inherent in coalitions has a number of interesting implications for the meaning of coalition activity as either public or private. To the extent that they provide a protected space where individuals can come together around a matter of common concern, coalitions include features that are associated with the private home. However, treating coalitions as surrogate homes can be hazardous. Bernice Johnson Reagon explains the problem in very direct terms: "Some people will come to a coalition and they rate the success of the coalition on whether or not they feel good when they get there. They're not looking for a coalition; they're looking for a home!" Reagon, "Coalition Politics: Turning the Century," in *Feminism and Politics*, ed. Anne Phillips (Oxford: Oxford University Press, 1998), 245.

One consequence of confusing coalition with home is that it creates an incentive to silence or shut out voices that generate discomfort among the dominant members.

56. Enthusiasm for a coalition approach is not confined to those I interviewed. When Congress passed the Violence against Women Act in 1996, included in the terms for the receipt of federal funding was the mandate to work collaboratively on this problem. This approach has also been embraced by major federal funding agencies such as the National Institute of Justice. See Martha Witwer and Cheryl Crawford, "NIJ Research Report: A Coordinated Approach to Reducing Family Violence," National Institute of Justice and the American Medical Association, NCJ 155184, October 1995.

57. See especially *Oliver v. United States,* 466 U.S. 170, 104 S. Ct. 1735, 80 (1984); and *California v. Greenwood,* 486 U.S. 35, 108 S. Ct. 1625, 100 (1988).

58. *Olmstead v. United States,* 277 U.S. 438, S. Ct. 564, 72 L. Ed. 944 (1928).

59. See, for example, *Arizona v. Hicks,* 480 U.S. 321, 107 S. Ct. 1149, for a delineation of the exigent-circumstances exception to the warrant requirement.

60. *Olmstead v. United States,* 277 U.S. 438, S. Ct. 564, 72 L. Ed. 944 (1928).

61. Nicola Lacey, "Theory into Practice? Pornography and the Public/Private Dichotomy," *Journal of Law and Society* 20 (spring 1993): 98. See also Elizabeth Frazer and Nicola Lacey, *The Politics of Community: A Feminist Critique of the Liberal–Communitarian Debate* (Toronto: University of Toronto Press, 1993), 75–76.

62. Ferdinand Schoeman, "Privacy: Philosophical Dimensions," *American Philosophical Quarterly* 21 (1984): 199.

63. Craig Coleman makes a similar point in his discussion of the importance of recognizing the positive contribution of privacy to public life and democratic politics. Coleman, "Democracy and Private Space: An Alternative Justification of the Right to Private Property" (paper presented at the Midwest Political Science Association meeting, April 19, 1998), 19.

Chapter 7. Conclusion

1. Although there is no evidence suggesting that there has been a sizable drop in the numbers of actual incidents of domestic violence, it is nevertheless appropriate to characterize the "claims defining this as a social issue" as "successful," for as Donileen Loseke points out, as recently as the 1960's, "the phenomenon was not named and the act and actors of wife abuse were socially invisible." Loseke, "Lived Realities and the Construction of Social Problems: The Case of Wife Abuse," *Symbolic Interaction* 10 (1987): 233.

2. Ruth Gavison, "Feminism and the Public/Private Distinction," *Stanford Law Review* 45 (1992).

3. The depiction of privacy as "a right to be left alone" was first delineated by Samuel Warren and Louis Brandeis in their pivotal law review article "The Right to Privacy," *Harvard Law Review* 4 (1890): 193–220. This conception of privacy has been adopted by various justices in the Supreme Court in a long line of important cases, e.g., *Time v. Hill,* 385 U.S. 374 (1967); *Gertz v. Robert Welch, Inc.,* 418 U.S. 323 (1974); *Katz v. United States,* 389 U.S. 347 (1967); *Whalen v. Roe,* 429 U.S. 589 (1977).

4. Judith Jarvis Thomson, "Privacy," *Philosophy and Public Affairs* 1 (1971): 47.

5. Charles Fried, "Privacy," *Yale Law Journal* 77 (1968): 484–85.

6. Patricia Boling, *Privacy and the Politics of Intimate Life* (Ithaca: Cornell University Press, 1996), 22.

7. For a discussion of the psychological significance of this aspect of privacy, see Sigmund Freud, *Totem and Taboo: Resemblances between the Psychic Lives of Savages and Neurotics,*

trans. A.A. Brill (New York: Vintage, 1946), cited in Alan Westin, *Privacy and Freedom* (New York: Atheneum, 1967), 404.

8. Sydney Jourard, "Some Psychological Aspects of Privacy," *Law and Contemporary Problems* 31 (1966): 307, cited in Gavison, "Feminism and the Public/Private Distinction," 448.

9. Westin, *Privacy and Freedom*, 35.

10. Jeffrey Reiman, "Intimacy, Privacy and Personhood," *Philosophy and Public Affairs* 26 (1977): 30–36.

11. Iris Marion Young, *Intersecting Voices: Dilemmas of Gender, Political Philosophy, and Policy* (Princeton: Princeton University Press, 1997), 159.

12. For a useful discussion of the unique characteristics of "decisional privacy," see Anita Allen, *Uneasy Access: Privacy for Women in a Free Society* (Totowa, N.J.: Rowman and Littlefield, 1987).

13. It is important not to conflate intimacy and love. Many victims of domestic violence report that despite the abuse, they continue to love their husbands or boyfriends. In arguing that domestic violence undermines the prerequisites for intimacy, I am not suggesting that women who claim to love their abusers are lying or suffering from a delusion.

14. Jan Stets, *Domestic Violence and Control* (New York: Springer, 1989).

15. Kathleen Ferraro, "An Existential Approach to Battering," in *Family Abuse and Its Consequences,* ed. Gerald Hotaling et al. (Newbury Park, Calif.: Sage, 1988).

16. Norman Denzen, "Toward a Phenomenology of Domestic, Family Violence," *American Journal of Sociology* 90 (1984): 438–513.

17. According to Charlotte Perkins Gilman, the location of privacy rights within the family operates to ensure that women, because of their many responsibilities within the domestic sphere, are effectively denied the opportunity to enjoy these rights. Gilman, *Women and Economics* (New York: Small, Maynard, and Company, 1898), cited in Allen, *Uneasy Access*, 190.

18. Virginia Woolf, *A Room of One's Own* (London: Hogarth, 1929).

19. Karla Fischer, Neil Vidmar, and Rene Ellis, "The Culture of Battering and the Role of Mediation in Domestic Violence Cases," *Southern Methodist University Law Review* 46 (1993): 2117–73.

20. Jean L. Cohen, "Democracy, Difference, and the Right to Privacy," in *Democracy and Difference: Contesting the Boundaries of the Political*, ed. Seyla Benhabib (Princeton: Princeton University Press, 1996), 206.

21. Susan Brison, "Outliving Oneself: Trauma, Memory, and Personal Identity," in *Feminists Rethink the Self,* ed. Diana Tietjens Meyers (Boulder: Westview, 1997), 27–28.

22. Gerald Dworkin, "Privacy and the Law," in *Privacy*, ed. John Young (New York: Wiley and Sons, 1978), 115.

23. In some cases, the "choices" we make about boundaries will be collective, such as when we pass laws that criminalize particular acts even when they occur in private. Despite the obvious visibility of the boundaries that are established through law, most choices about privacy take place informally and on an individual basis.

24. Anita Allen, "The Jurispolitics of Privacy," in *Reconstructing Political Theory: Feminist Perspectives*, ed. Mary Lyndon Shanley and Uma Narayan (University Park: Pennsylvania State University Press, 1997), 69.

25. Although I will be focusing here on feminist reformulations of autonomy, it should be noted that there are a number of contemporary philosophers whose approach to autonomy

is sensitive to its relational elements. See, for example, Ferdinand Schoeman, *Privacy and Social Freedom* (Cambridge: Cambridge University Press, 1992); Stanley Benn, "Individuality, Autonomy and Community," in *Community as a Social Ideal*, ed. Eugene Kamenka (New York: St. Martin's, 1982); and Joel Feinberg, *Harm to Self* (Oxford: Oxford University Press, 1986). For a useful discussion of the areas of convergence between feminist and mainstream philosophical accounts of autonomy, see Marilyn Friedman, "Autonomy and Social Relationship: Rethinking the Feminist Critique," in *Feminists Rethink the Self*, ed. Meyers.

26. Alison Jaggar, *Feminist Politics and Human Nature* (Totowa, N.J.: Rowman and Allanheld, 1985): 44; Lorraine Code, *What Can She Know? Feminist Theory and the Construction of Knowledge* (Ithaca: Cornell University Press, 1991), 77–85.

27. Jennifer Nedelsky, "Reconceiving Autonomy: Sources, Thoughts, and Possibilities," *Yale Journal of Law and Feminism* 1 (1989): 7–11.

28. For an insightful discussion of the meaning of agency in the context of a domestic violence court, see Judith Wittner, "Reconceptualizing Agency in Domestic Violence Court," in *Community Activism and Feminist Politics: Organizing across Race, Class, and Gender*, ed. Nancy Naples (New York: Routledge, 1998).

29. Nancy Rourke, "Domestic Violence: The Challenge to Law's Theory of the Self," in *Kindred Matters: Rethinking the Philosophy of the Family*, ed. Diana Tietjens Meyers, Kenneth Kipnis, and Cornelius F. Murphy, Jr. (Ithaca: Cornell University Press, 1993), 262.

30. For a discussion of how these tensions play out in the controversy over laws that mandate victim participation in prosecutions of domestic violence, see Cheryl Hanna, "No Right to Choose: Mandated Victim Participation in Domestic Violence Prosecutions," *Harvard Law Review* 109 (June 1996): 1849. Hanna argues that in light of the real costs to women who are forced to testify against their batterers, steps should be taken by prosecutors to reduce their reliance on victim testimony. For an insightful review of this issue in the context of debates regarding mandatory arrest and prosecution policies, see Linda Mills, "Mandatory Arrest and Prosecution Policies for Domestic Violence: A Critical Literature Review and the Case for More Research to Test Victim Empowerment Approaches," *Criminal Justice and Behavior* 25 (September 1998): 306. For further development of the argument that state interventions often replicate the violence of battering, see Linda Mills, "Killing Her Softly: Intimate Abuse and the Violence of State Intervention," *Harvard Law Review* 113 (1999): 550.

31. Brison, "Outliving Oneself," 28.

32. Ibid., 29.

33. Ibid., 28. For an insightful discussion of the relationship between autonomy and "self-trust," see Trudy Govier, "Self-Trust, Autonomy, and Self-Esteem," *Hypatia* 8 (winter 1993), especially 111–12.

34. Evan Stark and Anne Flitcraft, "Personal Power and Institutional Victimization: Treating the Dual Trauma of Woman Battering," in *Post-Traumatic Therapy and Victims of Violence*, ed. Frank Ochberg (New York: Brunner/Mazel, 1988), 116–17. Despite significant improvements since Stark and Flitcraft made these arguments, their critiques of the institutional response to domestic violence still stand. For example, in a recent article on battered women's assessments of the responses of the criminal processing system, Edna Erez and Joanne Belknap conclude that "despite a quarter of a century of feminist scholars' and activists' campaigning to change the systemic responses to woman battering, there has not been a significant change in the sexist and victim-blaming attitudes of legal agents who serve domestic violence victims." Erez and Belknap, "In Their Own Words: Battered Women's As-

sessment of the Criminal Processing System's Responses," *Violence and Victims* 13 (1998): 252.

35. Stark and Flitcraft, "Personal Power and Institutional Victimization," 125.

36. Erez and Belknap, "In Their Own Words," 251, citing E. W. Gondolf and E. R. Fisher, *Battered Women as Survivors: An Alternative to Treating Learned Helplessness* (New York: Lexington Books, 1988).

37. Seyla Benhabib, *Situating the Self: Gender, Community, and Postmodernism in Contemporary Ethics* (New York: Routledge, 1992), 155–57.

38. Linda Gordon, *Heroes of Their Own Lives: The Politics and History of Family Violence: Boston, 1880–1960* (New York: Viking, 1988); and Karla Fischer and Mary Rose, "'When Enough Is Enough': Battered Women's Decision Making around Court Orders of Protection," *Crime and Delinquency* 41 (October 1995).

39. Fischer and Rose, "When Enough is Enough," 427.

40. Wittner, "Reconceptualizing Agency in Domestic Violence Court."

41. Diana Meyers, "Feminism and Women's Autonomy: The Challenge of Female Genital Cutting," *Metaphilosophy* 31 (October 2000): 470.

42. In this respect, Martha Minow has emphasized the importance of enriching "rights-based theories with strong attention to relationships and their pre-conditions." Minow, *Making All the Difference: Inclusion, Exclusion, and American Law* (Ithaca: Cornell University Press, 1990). Or, as Donna Coker argues, "Liberation does not necessarily mean the woman will chose to leave the batterer. Rather, interventions are more or less liberating depending on whether they put material, spiritual, and social resources in women's hands." Coker, "Enhancing Autonomy for Battered Women: Lessons from Navaho Peacemaking," *UCLA Law Review* 47 (1999): 10, n. 36.

43. From the very earliest days of the battered women's movement, activists have grappled with the challenge of respecting the authority of victims' perceptions about their situation while simultaneously countering destructive self-perceptions. As the movement has become more professionalized, the tension between the expert voice and the victim's voice has only increased. See, for example, Karen Kendrick, "Producing the Battered Woman: Shelter Politics and the Power of the Feminist Voice," in *Community Activism and Feminist Politics*, ed. Naples, 155; and Donileen Loseke, *The Battered Woman and Shelters: The Social Construction of Wife Abuse* (Albany: State University of New York Press, 1992).

44. Martha Mahoney, "Legal Images of Battered Women: Redefining the Issue of Separation," *Michigan Law Review* 90 (1991): 1–94.

45. Meyers, "Feminism and Women's Autonomy," 475.

46. Christine Littleton, "Women's Experience and the Problem of Transition: Perspectives on Male Battering of Women," *University of Chicago Legal Forum* (1989): 49.

47. In an article on the use of Navaho peacemaking to address battering, Donna Coker argues that one of the weaknesses of traditional criminal adjudication is that because "the 'zone of dispute' is narrowly focused on the offender and the state," there is "no structural way of addressing the culpability of family in supporting the abuse or of recognizing family's interest in stopping it." As a result "formal legal interventions offer little that disrupts familial supports for battering." Coker, "Enhancing Autonomy for Battered Women," 47. Coker's analysis serves to extend the community portion of the triangular model proposed here to include members of the extended family, who have a potentially vital role to play in providing victims with support and in transmitting community disapproval to the batterer.

48. Although my alternative model of public/private has been developed through a con-

sideration of the problem of domestic violence, it can also be applied to a range of other social problems that entail questions of privacy. For example, the recognition of the importance that community and state resources play in facilitating privacy rights is also clearly relevant to an issue such as abortion. My triangular model would allow for a consideration of
the right to an abortion as requiring both noninterference and public resources simultaneously.

49. *Webster's Third International Dictionary, Unabridged* (Springfield, Mass.: G. and C.
Merriam, 1976).

50. According to Anne Jones, the fact that the battered women's movement arose from
immediate need rather than abstract theory has created a situation "in which social action
precedes the premise from which it should follow: namely that all women have an absolute
right to be free from bodily harm." Anne Jones, *Next Time She'll Be Dead: Battering and
How to Stop It* (Boston: Beacon, 1994), 13.

51. This same concern about not alienating people through blame was very apparent
when questions were asked about feminism. Many of the interviewees consciously distanced
themselves from feminist arguments because of their feeling that gender-based arguments
(although frequently true) tend to alienate people, and men in particular.

52. In the interviews, survivors of domestic violence also talked repeatedly about how
their own self-blame prevented them from believing that they had a right to be free from
physical and emotional abuse. The tendency of victims to blame themselves can be understood as part of an attempt to formulate an explanation for why batterers commit acts of violence against persons they proclaim to love. A number of survivors specifically described the
freeing impact that counselors' explanations about the causes of battering had on their eventual ability to apply principles such as justice to their situation.

53. The edited volume *Beyond Self-Interest* provides a wide range of excellent arguments
about why it is a mistake to assume that the pursuit of self-interest and the common good are
necessarily incompatible goals. Jane Mansbridge, ed., *Beyond Self-Interest* (Chicago: University of Chicago Press, 1990).

54. In her influential 1981 article, "Justice: On Relating Public and Private," Hanna
Pitkin counters the claim made by Arendt and others that letting bodily, economic, and
other social concerns into the public sphere will taint public discourse with selfish and short-
sighted issues. From Pitkin's perspective, it is through concepts such as justice that we are
able to transform our particular interests into "a common language of purposes and aspirations." *Political Theory* 9 (August 1981): 347.

55. Jane Mansbridge has argued that such emotional or personally based appeals are actually central to all appeals to "the public good." "We activate commitment to principle in part
by appealing to people's emotional attachments to the aspects of their identity most linked
to that principle." Mansbridge, "Reconstructing Democracy," in *Revisioning the Political:
Feminist Reconstructions of Traditional Concepts in Western Political Theory*, ed. Nancy
Hirschmann and Christine Di Stefano (Boulder: Westview, 1996), 125.

56. John Locke, *Two Treatises of Government* [1690], ed. Peter Laslett (Cambridge: Cambridge University Press, 1988), *Second Treatise*, sections 82 and 83.

57. The 1994 Violence against Women Act included a civil rights remedy that made it
possible for victims to make civil claims utilizing the argument that the violence experienced
was motivated by gender. On May 15, 2000, the Supreme Court ruled that provision un-
constitutional because Congress does not have the authority under either the Commerce
Clause or the Fourteenth Amendment to provide a federal civil remedy for victims of gen-

der-motivated violence. *Brzonkala v. Morrison*, 120 S. Ct. 1740, 146 L.Ed.2d 658 (2000). For a discussion of this provision and its implications, see Victoria Nourse, "Where Violence, Relationship, and Equality Meet: The Violence against Women Act's Civil Rights Remedy," *Wisconsin Women's Law Journal* 11 (1996): 1. For a discussion of additional developments in civil remedies applying to domestic violence, see Catherine Klein and Leslye Orloff, "Protecting Battered Women: Latest Trends in Civil Legal Relief," *Women and Criminal Justice* 10 (winter 1999): 29.

58. Brande Stellings, "The Public Harm of Private Violence: Rape, Sex Discrimination, and Citizenship," *Harvard Civil Rights–Civil Liberties Law Review* 28 (1993): 214.

59. Andrea Brenneke, "Civil Rights Remedies for Battered Women: Axiomatic and Ignored," *Law and Inequality* 11 (1992): 19.

60. Mary Dietz, "Context Is All: Feminism and Theories of Citizenship"; Teresa Brennan and Carole Pateman, "Mere Auxiliaries to the Commonwealth: Women and the Origins of Liberalism"; and Genevieve Lloyd, "Selfhood, War, and Masculinity," all in *Feminist Challenges: Social and Political Theory*, ed. Carole Pateman and Elizabeth Gross (Boston: Northeastern University Press, 1986); and Jean Bethke Elshtain, *Women and War* (New York: Basic, 1987).

61. Kathleen Jones, "Citizenship in a Woman-Friendly Polity," *Signs* 15 (1990): 810–11.

62. Jane Maslow Cohen, "Regimes of Private Tyranny: What Do They Mean to Morality and for the Criminal Law?" *University of Pittsburgh Law Review* 57 (1996): 769.

63. Susan Moller Okin, *Justice, Gender, and the Family* (New York: Basic, 1989).

64. Ruth Rubio-Marin provides an illuminating discussion of the ways in which these competing conceptions of community have contributed to the confusions and contradictions of U.S. immigration policies. Rubio-Marin, *Immigration as a Democratic Challenge: Citizenship and Inclusion in Germany and the United States* (Cambridge: Cambridge University Press, 2000).

65. For a discussion of the value of a human rights framework for those seeking to stop domestic violence see, Michele Beasley and Dorothy Thomas, "Domestic Violence as a Human Rights Issue," in *The Public Nature of Private Violence*, ed. Martha Fineman and Roxanne Mykitiuk (New York: Routledge, 1994).

66. Rubio-Marin, *Immigration as a Democratic Challenge*, 143–73.

67. The most significant event in this regard was the passage in 1994 of Proposition 187 in California. This measure, which was the product of a popular referendum, served to severely limit the ability of illegal immigrants in California to access state-funded social services, including public schools and health care. For a discussion of the referendum and the politics of its passage, see R.A. Boswell "Restrictions on Non-citizens' Access to Public Benefits: Flawed Premise, Unnecessary Response," *University of California at Los Angeles Law Review* 42 (1995).

68. In her book *Moral Responsibility and the Boundaries of Community* (Chicago: University of Chicago Press, 1992), Marion Smiley provides a nuanced elaboration of the ways in which philosophical principles (in this case responsibility) serve to influence the boundaries of community.

69. Stellings, "The Public Harm of Private Violence," 215. Stellings quotes Martha Minow, "Interpreting Rights: An Essay for Robert Cover," *Yale Law Journal* 96 (1987): 1860, 1867.

70. In making the argument for the utility of using principles as a point of shared understanding, I want to be clear that concepts such as citizenship are themselves the product of

deliberation. Kathleen Jones articulates this extremely well when she states: "Neither citizenship nor the experiences of women should be seen as static and fixed by nature. . . . Rather, they are part of an ongoing historical process of the transformation of modern society and modern political communities—a process that continuously renegotiates the boundaries of public space and redefines the characteristics of those who occupy it as full members—as citizens." Jones, "Citizenship," 812.

71. Although I am using the issue of poverty to apply my model to an issue other than domestic violence, it should be noted that these problems very frequently overlap in the lives of women. Even though domestic violence occurs across classes, studies have consistently shown that women receiving welfare are more likely than other women to have experienced abuse at the hands of a male intimate. M. Sable, M. K. Libbus, D. D. Huneke, and K. Anger, "Domestic Violence among AFDC Recipients: Implications for Welfare-to-Work Programs," *Affilia* 14 (1999): 199–216. In response to the high rates of domestic violence among welfare recipients, the Welfare Reform Act includes a provision called the Family Violence Option (FVO). This provision allows states to grant temporary exemptions from work requirements and child support enforcement steps if a woman can demonstrate that she is a victim of domestic violence. J. Raphael, "The Family Violence Option: An Early Assessment," *Violence against Women* 5 (1999): 449–66. The FVO represents an important example of the dilemmas that arise when the state seeks to intervene in order to satisfy competing objectives: promoting independence and "responsibility" among welfare recipients and providing protection, support, and social services to individuals who are being abused within the family.

72. *A Call to Civil Society: Why Democracy Needs Moral Truths* (New York: Institute for American Values, 1998), 3.

73. Ibid., 18.

74. Robert Fine, "Civil Society Theory, Enlightenment and Critique," in *Civil Society: Democratic Perspectives,* ed. Robert Fine and Shirin Rai (London: Frank Cass, 1997), 25.

75. Michael Walzer, "Socializing the Welfare State," in *Democracy and the Welfare State,* ed. Amy Gutmann (Princeton: Princeton University Press, 1988), 18.

76. Benjamin Barber, *The Conquest of Politics: Liberal Philosophy in Democratic Times* (Princeton: Princeton University Press, 1988), 29.

77. Approaching boundaries as constantly subject to change does not necessarily involve a contradiction in terms. In a democratic society, the stability and legitimacy of boundaries are maintained not by their unchanging nature but by a particular procedure for altering them, the features of which include going through established channels, adhering to democratic principles of representation, and providing principled reasons for proposed changes.

Bibliography

Ackelsberg, Martha A., and Mary Lyndon Shanley. "Privacy, Publicity, and Power: A Feminist Rethinking of the Public-Private Distinction." In *Revisioning the Political: Feminist Reconstructions of Traditional Concepts in Western Political Theory*, ed. Nancy Hirschmann and Christine Di Stefano. Boulder: Westview, 1996.

Allard, Sharon Angella. "Rethinking Battered Woman Syndrome: A Black Feminist Perspective." *UCLA Women's Law Journal* 1 (1991).

Allen, Anita. "The Jurispolitics of Privacy." In *Reconstructing Political Theory: Feminist Perspectives,* ed. Mary Lyndon Shanley and Uma Narayan. University Park: Pennsylvania State University Press, 1997.

———. *Uneasy Access: Privacy for Women in a Free Society*. Totowa, N.J.: Rowman and Littlefield, 1988.

Ammons, Linda. "Mules, Madonnas, Babies, Bathwater, Racial Imagery, and Stereotypes: The African-American Woman and the Battered Woman Syndrome." *Wisconsin Law Review* (1995).

Avishai, Margalit. *The Decent Society*. Cambridge, Mass.: Harvard University Press, 1996.

Bachman, Ronet, and L. Saltzman. "Violence against Women: Estimates from the Redesigned Survey." Washington, D.C.: U.S. Department of Justice, Bureau of Justice Statistics, 1995.

Baer, Judith. *Women in American Law: The Struggle toward Equality from the New Deal to the Present*. New York: Holmes and Meier, 1996.

Barber, Benjamin. *The Conquest of Politics: Liberal Philosophy in Democratic Times*. Princeton: Princeton University Press, 1988.

———. *Strong Democracy: Participatory Politics for a New Age*. Berkeley: University of California Press, 1984.

Barnett, Ola, and Alyce LaViolette. *It Could Happen to Anyone: Why Battered Women Stay*. Newbury Park, Calif.: Sage, 1993.

Basch, Norma. "Invisible Women: The Legal Fiction of Marital Unity in Nineteenth-Century America." *Feminist Studies* 5 (summer 1979): 346–66.

Beasley, Michele, and Dorothy Thomas. "Domestic Violence as a Human Rights Issue." In *The Public Nature of Private Violence*, ed. Martha Fineman and Roxanne Mykitiuk. New York: Routledge, 1994.

Benhabib, Seyla. *Situating the Self: Gender, Community, and Postmodernism in Contemporary Ethics.* New York: Routledge, 1992.

Benn, Stanley. "Individuality, Autonomy and Community." In *Community as a Social Ideal,* ed. Eugene Kamenka. New York: St. Martin's, 1982.

Benn, Stanley, and Gerald Gaus. *Public and Private in Social Life.* London: Croom Helm, 1983.

Binder, A., and J. Meeker. "The Development of Social Attitudes towards Spousal Abuse." In *Domestic Violence: The Changing Criminal Justice Response,* ed. E. S. Buzawa and C. G. Buzawa. Westport, Conn.: Auburn House, 1992.

Boling, Patricia. *Privacy and the Politics of Intimate Life.* Ithaca: Cornell University Press, 1996.

Borkowski, Margaret, Mervyn Murch, and Val Walker. *Marital Violence: The Community Response.* London: Tavistock, 1983.

Boswell, R. A. "Restrictions on Non-citizens' Access to Public Benefits: Flawed Premise, Unnecessary Response." *University of California at Los Angeles Law Review* 42 (1995).

Bottomley, Anne. "What's Happening in Family Law." In *Women-in-Law: Explorations in Law, Family, and Sexuality,* ed. Julia Brophy and Carol Smart. London: Routledge, 1985.

Brennan, Teresa, and Carole Pateman. "'Mere Auxiliaries to the Commonwealth': Women and the Origins of Liberalism." *Political Studies* 27 (June 1979).

Brenneke, Andrea. "Civil Rights Remedies for Battered Women: Axiomatic and Ignored." *Law and Inequality* 11 (1992).

Brigham, John. *The Constitution of Interests: Beyond the Politics of Rights.* New York: New York University Press, 1976.

Brill, Alida. *Nobody's Business: Paradoxes of Privacy.* Reading, Mass.: Addison-Wesley, 1990.

Brison, Susan. "Outliving Oneself: Trauma, Memory, and Personal Identity." In *Feminists Rethink the Self,* ed. Diana Tietjens Meyers. Boulder: Westview, 1997.

Brown, Carol. "Mothers, Fathers, and Children: From Private to Public Patriarchy." In *The Unhappy Marriage of Marxism and Feminism,* ed. Lydia Sargent. London: Pluto, 1981.

Bryger, Michelle. "Domestic Violence: The Dark Side of Divorce." *Family Advocate* (summer 1990).

Bumiller, Kristin. *The Civil Rights Society: The Social Construction of Victims.* Baltimore: Johns Hopkins University Press, 1988.

Buzawa, Eva Schlesinger, ed. *Domestic Violence: The Criminal Justice Response.* Thousand Oaks, Calif.: Sage, 1996.

Cahn, Naomi, and Lisa Lerman. "Prosecuting Woman Abuse." In *Woman Battering,* ed. Michael Steinman. Cincinnati: Anderson, 1991.

Chaudhuri, Molly, and Kathleen Daly. "Do Restraining Order Legal Processes Help?" In *Domestic Violence: The Changing Criminal Justice Response,* ed. Eve Buzawa and Carl Buzawa. Thousand Oaks, Calif.: Sage, 1992.

Chused, Richard. *Private Acts in Public Places: A Social History of Divorce in the Formative Era of American Family Law.* Philadelphia: University of Pennsylvania Press, 1994.

Clark, Lorenne. "Women and Locke: Who Owns the Apples in the Garden of Eden?"

In *The Sexism of Social and Political Theory*, ed. Lorenne Clark and Lynda Lange. Toronto: University of Toronto Press, 1979.

Cobbe, Frances Power. "Wife Torture in England." *Contemporary Review* 32 (1878).

Code, Lorraine. *What Can She Know? Feminist Theory and the Construction of Knowledge*. Ithaca: Cornell University Press, 1991.

Cohen, Jane Maslow. "Regimes of Private Tyranny: What Do They Mean to Morality and for the Criminal Law?" *University of Pittsburgh Law Review* 57 (1996).

Cohen, Jean. *Civil Society and Social Theory*. Cambridge, Mass.: MIT Press, 1982.

———. "Democracy, Difference and the Right to Privacy." In *Democracy and Difference: Contesting the Boundaries of the Political*, ed. Seyla Benhabib. Princeton: Princeton University Press, 1996.

Coker, Donna. "Enhancing Autonomy for Battered Women: Lessons from Navaho Peacemaking." *UCLA Law Review* 47 (1999).

Coleman, Craig. "Democracy and Private Space: An Alternative Justification of the Right to Private Property." Paper presented at the Midwest Political Science Association Meeting, April 19, 1998.

Commonwealth Fund Commission on Women's Health. *Domestic Violence Fact Sheet*. 1996.

Crenshaw, Kimberle. "Mapping the Margins: Intersectionality, Identify Politics, and Violence against Women of Color." *Stanford Law Review* 43 (1991).

Crites, Laura. "Wife Abuse: The Judicial Record." In *Women, The Courts, and Equality*. ed. Laura Crites and Winifred Hepperle. Newbury Park, Calif.: Sage, 1987.

Cronin, Roberta. *Innovative Community Partnerships: Working Together for Change*. Washington, D.C.: U.S. Dept. of Justice, Office of Juvenile Justice and Delinquency Prevention, 1995.

Cummings, Joanne, Debra Pepler, and Timothy Moore. "Behavior Problems in Children Exposed to Wife Abuse: Gender Differences." *Journal of Family Violence* 14 (June 1999): 133–56.

Degler, Carl. *At Odds: Women and the Family in America from the Revolution to the Present*. Oxford: Oxford University Press, 1980.

Demos, John. *Past, Present, and Personal: The Family and the Life Course in American History*. New York: Oxford University Press, 1986.

Denzen, Norman. "Toward a Phenomenology of Domestic, Family Violence." *American Journal of Sociology* 90 (1984).

Dietz, Mary. "Citizenship with a Feminist Face: The Problem with Maternal Thinking." *Political Theory* 13 (February 1985).

Dingwall, Robert. "Accounts, Interviews, and Observations." In *Context and Method in Qualitative Research*, ed. Gale Miller and Robert Dingwall. London: Sage, 1997.

Dobash, Emerson, and Russell Dobash. *Violence against Wives: A Case against Patriarchy*. New York: Free Press, 1979.

Douglas, M. "The Battered Woman Syndrome." In *Domestic Violence on Trial: Psychological and Legal Dimensions of Family Violence*, ed. Daniel Sonkin. New York: Springer, 1987.

Downs, Donald. *More Than Victims: Battered Women, the Syndrome Society, and the Law*. Chicago: University of Chicago Press, 1996.

Dutton, Donald. "The Criminal Justice Response to Wife Assault." *Law and Human Behavior* 11 (1987).

——. *The Domestic Assault of Women: Psychological and Criminal Justice Perspectives.* Vancouver: University of British Colombia Press, 1995.

Dworkin, Gerald. "Privacy and the Law." In *Privacy,* ed. John Young. New York: Wiley and Sons, 1978.

Edwards, Susan. *Policing Domestic Violence: Women, the Law and the State.* London: Sage, 1989.

Eisenstein, Zillah. *The Female Body and the Law.* Berkeley: University of California Press, 1988.

——. *The Radical Future of Liberal Feminism.* New York: Longman, 1981.

Elshtain, Jean Bethke. "Homosexual Politics: The Paradox of Gay Liberation." *Salamagundi* (fall 1982): 252–80.

——. "Moral Woman and Immoral Man: A Consideration of the Public-Private Split and Its Political Ramifications." *Politics and Society* 4 (1974).

——. "On Feminism, Family, and Community." *Dissent* 29 (winter 1983).

——. *Public Man, Private Woman: Women in Social and Political Thought.* Princeton: Princeton University Press, 1981.

——. *Women and War.* New York: Basic, 1987.

Epstein, Barbara. *The Politics of Domesticity: Women, Evangelism, and Temperance in Nineteenth-Century America.* Middletown, Conn.: Wesleyan University Press, 1981.

Erez, Edna, and Joanne Belknap. "In Their Own Words: Battered Women's Assessment of the Criminal Processing System's Responses." *Violence and Victims* 13 (1998).

Fagan, G., and S. Wexler. "Crime at Home and in the Streets: The Relationship between Family and Stranger Violence." *Violence and Victims* 2 (1989).

Feinberg, Joel. *Harm to Self.* Oxford: Oxford University Press, 1986.

Ferraro, Kathleen. "An Existential Approach to Battering." In *Family Abuse and Its Consequences,* ed. Gerald Hotaling et al. Newbury Park, Calif.: Sage, 1988.

Filmer, Robert. *Patriarcha and Other Political Works,* ed. Peter Laslett. Oxford: Basil Blackwell, 1949.

Fine, Michelle. "Contradictions: An Essay Inspired by Women and Male Violence." *Feminist Studies* 11 (summer 1985).

Fine, Robert. "Civil Society Theory, Enlightenment and Critique." In *Civil Society: Democratic Perspectives,* ed. Robert Fine and Shirin Rai. London: Frank Cass, 1997.

Fineman, Martha Albertson. *The Illusion of Equality: The Rhetoric and Reality of Divorce Reform.* Chicago: University of Chicago Press, 1991.

Finkelhor, David, et al. *The Dark Side of Families: Current Family Violence Research.* Beverly Hills: Sage, 1983.

Firestone, Shulamith. *The Dialectic of Sex: The Case for a Feminist Revolution.* New York: Bantam Books, 1970.

Fischer, Karla, and Mary Rose. " 'When Enough Is Enough': Battered Women's Decision Making around Court Orders of Protection." *Crime and Delinquency* 41 (October 1995).

Fischer, Karla, Neil Vidmar, and Rene Ellis. "The Culture of Battering and the Role of Mediation in Domestic Violence Cases." *Southern Methodist University Law Review* 46 (1993): 2117–73.

Flax, Jane. "Postmodernism and Gender Relations in Feminist Theory." In *Feminism/Postmodernism,* ed. Linda Nicholson. London: Routledge, 1990.

Flexnor, Eleanor. *Century of Struggle: The Woman's Rights Movement in the United States*. Cambridge, Mass.: Harvard University Press, 1975.

Fraser, Nancy. "Rethinking the Public Sphere: A Contribution to the Critique of Actually Existing Democracy." In *Habermas and the Public Sphere*, ed. Craig Calhoun. Cambridge, Mass.: MIT Press, 1992.

——. "Struggle over Needs: Outline of a Socialist-Feminist Critical Theory of Late-Capitalist Political Culture." In *Women, the State, and Welfare*, ed. Linda Gordon. Madison: University of Wisconsin Press, 1990.

——. "What's Critical about Critical Theory? The Case of Habermas and Gender." In *Feminism as Critique: On the Politics of Gender*, ed. Seyla Benhabib and Drucilla Cornell. Minneapolis: University of Minnesota Press, 1987.

Frazer, Elizabeth, and Nicola Lacey. *The Politics of Community: A Feminist Critique of the Liberal–Communitarian Debate*. Toronto: University of Toronto Press, 1993.

Freud, Sigmund. *Totem and Taboo: Resemblances between the Psychic Lives of Savages and Neurotics*. Trans. A.A. Brill. New York: Vintage, 1946.

Fried, Charles. "Privacy." *Yale Law Journal* 77 (1968).

Friedan, Betty. *The Feminine Mystique*. New York: Dell, 1974.

Friedman, Lawrence. *A History of American Law*. New York: Simon and Schuster, 1985.

Friedman, Marilyn. "Autonomy and Social Relationship: Rethinking the Feminist Critique." In *Feminists Rethink the Self*, ed. Diana T. Meyers. Boulder: Westview, 1997.

Gabel, Richard, and Paul Harris. "Building Power and Breaking Images: Critical Legal Theory and the Practice of Law." *New York University Review of Law and Social Change* 11 (1982–83).

Gagne, Patricia. *Battered Women's Justice: The Movement for Clemency and the Politics of Self-Defense*. New York: Twayne, 1998.

Galanter, Marc. "Why the 'Haves' Come Out Ahead: Speculations on the Limits of Legal Change." *Law and Society Review* 9 (1974).

Garner, Joel, Jeffrey Fagan, and Christopher Maxwell. "Published Findings from the Spousal Assault Replication Program: A Critical Review." *Journal of Quantitative Criminology* 118 (1995).

Gavison, Ruth. "Feminism and the Public/Private Distinction." *Stanford Law Review* 45 (1992).

Gelb, Joyce. "The Politics of Wife Abuse." In *Families, Politics, and Public Policy*, ed. Irene Diamond. New York: Longman, 1983.

Gelles, Richard, and Murray Strauss. *Intimate Violence*. New York: Simon and Schuster, 1988.

Gilman, Charlotte Perkins. *The Home: Its Work and Influence*. New York: McClure Philipps, 1903.

Gobbetti, Daniela. *Private and Public: Individuals, Households, and Body Politic in Locke and Hutcheson*. New York: Routledge, 1992.

Gondolf, E.W., and E.R. Fisher. *Battered Women as Survivors: An Alternative to Treating Learned Helplessness*. New York: Lexington Books, 1988.

Goolkasian, Gail A. "The Judicial System and Domestic Violence: An Expanding Role." *Response* 9 (1986).

Gordon, Linda. *Heroes of Their Own Lives: The Politics and History of Family Violence: Boston, 1880–1960*. New York: Viking, 1988.

Govier, Trudy. "Self-Trust, Autonomy, and Self-Esteem." *Hypatia* 8 (winter 1993).

Grosz, Elizabeth. "A Note on Essentialism and Difference." In *Feminist Knowledge: Critique and Construct*, ed. Sneja Gunew. London: Routledge, 1990.

Gusfield, Joseph. "Moral Passage: The Symbolic Process in Public Designations of Deviance." *Social Problems* 15 (1967).

Handler, Joel. *Social Movements and the Legal System: A Theory of Law Reform and Social Change*. New York: Academic Press, 1978.

Hanna, Cheryl. "No Right to Choose: Mandated Victim Participation in Domestic Violence Prosecutions." *Harvard Law Review* 109 (June 1996).

Harris, Angela. "Race and Essentialism in Feminist Legal Theory." *Stanford Law Review 42* (1990).

Hartmann, Heidi. "The Family as the Focus of Gender, Class, and Political Struggle: The Example of Housework." *Signs* (spring 1981).

Hay, Douglas, et al. *Albion's Fatal Tree: Crime and Society in Eighteenth-Century England*. New York: Free Press, 1975.

Hixson, Richard. *Privacy in Public Society: Human Rights in Conflict*. New York: Oxford University Press, 1987.

Hobbes, Thomas. *Leviathan*. Ed. Richard Tuck. Cambridge: Cambridge University Press, 1991.

Hoff, Lee Ann. "Collaborative Feminist Research and the Myth of Objectivity." In *Feminist Perspectives on Wife Abuse*, ed. Kersti Yllo and Michelle Bograd. Newbury Park, Calif.: Sage, 1988.

Hotaling, Gerald, et al. *Family Abuse and Its Consequences*. Newbury Park, Calif.: Sage, 1988.

Hyman, Areilla. "Mandatory Reporting of Domestic Violence by Health Care Providers: A Misguided Approach." San Francisco: Family Violence Prevention Fund, 1994.

Institute for American Values. *A Call to Civil Society: Why Democracy Needs Moral Truths*. New York: Institute for American Values, 1998.

Jaggar, Allison. *Feminist Politics and Human Nature*. Totowa, N.J.: Rowman and Allanheld, 1985.

Janeway, Elizabeth. *Man's World, Woman's Place*. New York: Delta Books, 1971.

Janoski, Thomas. *Citizenship and Civil Society*. Cambridge: Cambridge University Press, 1998.

Jasinski, Jana, and Linda Williams, eds. *Partner Violence: A Comprehensive Review of 20 Years of Research*. Thousand Oaks, Calif.: Sage, 1998.

Johnson, M. P. "Patriarchal Terrorism and Common Couple Violence: Two Forms of Violence against Women." *Journal of Marriage and the Family* 57 (1994): 283–94.

Jones, Anne. *Next Time She'll Be Dead: Battering and How to Stop It*. Boston: Beacon, 1994.

Jones, Kathleen. "Citizenship in a Woman-Friendly Polity." *Signs* 15 (1990).

Jourard, Sidney. "Some Psychological Aspects of Privacy." *Law and Contemporary Problems* 31 (1966).

Kahn, Paul. *The Cultural Study of Law: Reconstructing Legal Scholarship*. Chicago: University of Chicago Press, 1999.

Keane, John. *Democracy and Civil Society*. London: Verso, 1988.

Kendrick, Karen. "Producing the Battered Woman: Shelter Politics and the Feminist

Voice." In *Community Activism and Feminist Politics: Organizing Across Race, Class, and Gender*, ed. Nancy Naples. New York: Routledge, 1998.

Klare, Karl. "Law Making as Praxis." *Telos* 40 (1979).

Klein, Catherine, and Leslye Orloff. "Protecting Battered Women: Latest Trends in Civil Legal Relief." *Women and Criminal Justice* 10 (winter 1999).

Koss, M. P., et al. *No Safe Haven: Male Violence against Women at Home, at Work, and in the Community*. Washington, D.C.: American Psychological Association, 1994.

Lacey, Nicola. "Theory into Practice? Pornography and the Public/Private Dichotomy." *Journal of Law and Society* 20 (spring 1993).

Laslett, Barbara. "The Family as a Public and Private Institution: An Historical Perspective." *Journal of Marriage and the Family* 35 (1973).

Lerman, Lisa. "Criminal Prosecution of Wife Beaters." *Response* 4 (1981): 1–18.

Littleton, Christine. "Women's Experience and the Problem of Transition: Perspectives on Male Battering of Women." *University of Chicago Legal Forum* (1989).

Lloyd, Genevieve. "Selfhood, War, and Masculinity." In *Feminist Challenges: Social and Political Theory*, ed. Carole Pateman and Elizabeth Gross. Boston: Northeastern University Press, 1986.

Locke, John. *A Third Letter for Toleration: To the Author of the Third Letter concerning Toleration* [1692]. Quoted in Parry, Geraint. "Individuality, Politics, and the Critique of Paternalism in John Locke." *Political Studies* 5 (1964).

——. *Two Treatises of Government* [1690], ed. Peter Laslett. Cambridge: Cambridge University Press, 1988.

Loseke, Donileen. *The Battered Woman and Shelters: The Social Construction of Wife Abuse*. Albany: State University of New York Press, 1992.

——. "Lived Realities and the Construction of Social Problems: The Case of Wife Abuse." *Symbolic Interaction* 10 (1987): 229–43.

MacIntyre, Alasdair. *After Virtue*. Notre Dame: University of Notre Dame Press, 1984.

MacKinnon, Catharine. "Feminism, Marxism, Method, and the State: Towards a Feminist Jurisprudence." *Signs* 8 (1983).

——. *Feminism Unmodified: Discourses on Life and Law*. Cambridge, Mass.: Harvard University Press, 1984.

Mahoney, Martha. "Legal Images of Battered Women: Redefining the Issue of Separation." *Michigan Law Review* 90 (1991).

Maier, Charles. *Changing Boundaries of the Political: Essays on the Evolving Balance between the State and Society, Public and Private in Europe*. Cambridge: Cambridge University Press, 1987.

Mansbridge, Jane. *Beyond Adversary Democracy*. Chicago: University of Chicago Press, 1980.

——. "Reconstructing Democracy." In *Revisioning the Political: Feminist Reconstructions of Traditional Concepts in Western Political Theory*, ed. Nancy Hirschmann and Christine Di Stefano. Boulder: Westview, 1996.

——. ed. *Beyond Self-Interest*. Chicago: University of Chicago Press, 1990.

Margalit, Avishai. *The Decent Society*. Cambridge, Mass.: Harvard University Press, 1996.

Martin, Del. *Battered Wives*. San Francisco: Glide, 1976.

Matthaei, Julie. *An Economic History of Women in America: Women's Work, the Sexual Division of Labor, and the Development of Capitalism*. New York: Schocken, 1982.

May, Margaret. "Violence in the Family: An Historical Perspective." In *Violence in the Family,* ed. J. P. Martin. New York: Wiley and Sons, 1978.

McCann, Michael. *Rights at Work: Law and the Politics of Pay Equity.* Chicago: University of Chicago Press, 1993.

McGrath, Meghan, et al. "Violence against Women: Provider Barriers to Intervention in Emergency Departments." *Academic Emergency Medicine* 4 (April 1997).

Mehta, Uday Singh. *The Anxiety of Freedom: Imagination and Individuality in Locke's Political Thought.* Ithaca: Cornell University Press, 1992.

Meyers, Diane. "Feminism and Women's Autonomy: The Challenge of Female Genital Cutting." *Metaphilosophy* 31 (October 2000).

Mill, John Stuart. *The Subjection of Women.* Ed. Wendell Robert Carr. Cambridge, Mass.: MIT Press, 1989.

Mills, Linda. "Killing Her Softly: Intimate Abuse and the Violence of State Intervention." *Harvard Law Review* 113 (December 1999): 550–613.

——. "Mandatory Arrest and Prosecution Policies for Domestic Violence: A Critical Literature Review and the Case for More Research to Test Victim Empowerment Approaches." *Criminal Justice and Behavior* 25 (September 1998).

Minow, Martha. *Making All the Difference: Inclusion, Exclusion, and American Law.* Ithaca: Cornell University Press, 1990.

——. "Needs and the Door to the Land of Change: Law, Language, and Family Violence." *Vanderbilt Law Review* 43 (1990).

Nedelsky, Jennifer. "Reconceiving Autonomy: Sources, Thoughts, and Possibilities." *Yale Journal of Law and Feminism* 1 (1989).

Nicholson, Linda. *Gender and History: The Limits of Social Theory in the Age of the Family.* New York: Colombia University Press, 1986.

Nolan, Dennis. "Sir William Blackstone and the New American Republic." *New York University Law Review* 51 (1976).

Nourse, Victoria. "Where Violence, Relationship, and Equality Meet: The Violence against Women Act's Civil Rights Remedy." *Wisconsin Women's Law Journal* 11 (1996).

Novello, Antonio. "A Medical Response to Domestic Violence." *Journal of the American Medical Association* 267 (1992).

Nye, Andrea. *Feminist Theory and the Philosophies of Man.* London: Croom Helm, 1988.

Ohlin, L., and M. Tonry. "Family Violence in Perspective." In *Family Violence,* ed. L. Ohlin and M. Tonry. Chicago: University of Chicago Press, 1989.

Okin, Susan Moller. "Gender, the Public and the Private." In *Political Theory Today,* ed. David Held. Stanford: Stanford University Press, 1991.

——. *Justice, Gender, and the Family.* New York: Basic, 1989.

Okun, Lewis. *Woman Abuse: Replacing Facts with Myths.* Albany: State University of New York Press, 1983.

Oliver, William. "Preventing Domestic Violence in the African American Community." *Violence against Women* 6 (May 2000): 533.

Olsen, Frances. "The Family and the Market: A Study of Ideology and Legal Reform." *Harvard Law Review* 96 (1983).

Oppenlander, Nan. "The Evolution of Law and Wife Abuse." *Law and Policy Quarterly* 3 (October 1981).

Pahl, Jan, ed. *Private Violence and Public Policy: The Needs of Battered Women and the Response of Public Services.* London: Routledge, 1985.

Parry, Geraint. "Individuality, Politics, and the Critique of Paternalism in John Locke." *Political Studies* 5 (1964).

Pateman, Carole. *The Disorder of Women: Democracy, Feminism, and Political Theory.* Stanford: Stanford University Press, 1989.

——. *Participation and Democratic Theory.* Cambridge: Cambridge University Press, 1970.

——. *The Sexual Contract.* Stanford: Stanford University Press, 1988.

Pitkin, Hanna. "Justice: On Relating Public and Private." *Political Theory* 9 (August 1981).

Pleck, Elizabeth. "Criminal Approaches to Family Violence, 1640–1980." In *Family Violence: A Review of Research,* ed. L. Ohlin and M. Tonrey. Chicago: University of Chicago Press, 1989.

——. *Domestic Tyranny: The Making of Social Policy against Family Violence from Colonial Times to the Present.* New York: Oxford University Press, 1987.

Posner, Richard. "The Right to Privacy." *Georgia Law Review* 12 (1978).

Raphael, J. "The Family Violence Option: An Early Assessment." *Violence against Women* 5 (1999): 449–66.

Reagon, Bernice Johnson. "Coalition Politics: Turning the Century." In *Feminism and Politics,* ed. Anne Phillips. Oxford: Oxford University Press, 1998.

Regan, Milton. *Family Law and the Pursuit of Intimacy.* New York: New York University Press, 1993.

Reiman, Jeffrey. "Intimacy, Privacy, and Personhood." *Philosophy and Public Affairs* 26 (1977).

Rivera, Jenny. "Domestic Violence against Latinas by Latino Males: An Analysis of Race, National Origin, and Gender Differentials." *Boston College Third World Law Journal* 14 (1994): 231–57.

Rosaldo, Michelle Zimbalist, and Louise Lamphere, eds. *Woman, Culture, and Society.* Stanford: Stanford University Press, 1972.

Rosen, Jeffrey. "Religious Rights: Why the Catholic Church Shouldn't Have to Hire Gays." *New Republic,* February 26, 2001.

Rosenberg, Gerald. *The Hollow Hope: Can Courts Bring About Social Change?* Chicago: University of Chicago Press, 1991.

Rourke, Nancy. "Domestic Violence: The Challenge to Law's Theory of the Self." In *Kindred Matters: Rethinking the Philosophy of the Family,* ed. Diana Tietjens Meyers, Kenneth Kipnis, and Cornelius F. Murphy, Jr. Ithaca: Cornell University Press, 1993.

Rubio-Marin, Ruth. *Immigration as a Democratic Challenge: Citizenship and Inclusion in Germany and the United States.* Cambridge: Cambridge University Press, 2000.

Ruddick, Sara. "Maternal Thinking." *Feminist Studies* 6 (1980).

Sarat, Austin, and Thomas Kearns. "Beyond the Great Divide: Forms of Legal Scholarship and Everyday Life." In *Law in Everyday Life,* ed. Austin Sarat and Thomas Kearns. Anne Arbor: University of Michigan Press, 1993.

Schechter, Susan. *Women and Male Violence: The Visions and Struggles of the Battered Women's Movement.* Boston: South End, 1982.

Scheingold, Stuart. "Constitutional Rights and Social Change: Civil Rights in Perspective." In *Judging the Constitution: Critical Essays on Judicial Lawmaking*, ed. Michael McCann and Gerald Houseman. Glenview, Ill.: Scott, Foresman, 1989.

Schneider, Elizabeth. *Battered Women and Feminist Lawmaking*. New Haven: Yale University Press, 2000.

——. "The Violence of Privacy." *Connecticut Law Review* 23 (1991).

Schochet, Gordon. *Patriarchalism in Political Thought: The Authoritarian Family and Political Speculation and Attitudes Especially in Seventeenth-Century England*. Oxford: Basil Blackwell, 1975.

Schoeman, Ferdinand. *Privacy and Social Freedom*. Cambridge: Cambridge University Press, 1992.

——. "Privacy: Philosophical Dimensions." *American Philosophical Quarterly* 21 (1984).

Seigal, Reva. "'The Rule of Love': Wife Beating as Prerogative and Privacy." *The Yale Law Journal* 105 (1996).

Seligman, Adam. *The Idea of Civil Society*. New York: Free Press, 1992.

Shanley, Mary Lyndon. *Feminism, Marriage, and the Law in Victorian England*. Princeton: Princeton University Press, 1989.

Sherman, Lawrence, et al. *Policing Domestic Violence: Experiments and Dilemmas*. New York: Free Press, 1992.

Smart, Carol. *The Ties That Bind*. London: Routledge, 1984.

Smiley, Marion. *Moral Responsibility and the Boundaries of Community: Power and Accountability from a Pragmatic Point of View*. Chicago: University of Chicago Press, 1992.

Smith, Dorothy. *The Everyday World as Problematic: A Feminist Sociology*. Boston: Northeastern University Press, 1987.

Spalter-Roth, Roberta. "Measuring the Costs of Domestic Violence against Women and the Cost-Effectiveness of Interventions: An Initial Assessment and Proposals for Further Research." Washington, D.C.: Institute for Women's Policy Research, 1996.

Spatz, Cathy. *The Cycle of Violence*. Washington, D.C.: U.S. Department of Justice, Office of Justice Programs, National Institute of Justice, 1992.

Stacey, Judith. "The New Conservative Feminism." *Feminist Studies* 9 (fall 1985).

Stark, Evan. "Re-Presenting Woman Battering: From Battered Woman Syndrome to Coercive Control." *Albany Law Review* 58 (1995).

Stark, Evan, and Anne Flitcraft. "Personal Power and Institutional Victimization: Treating the Dual Trauma of Woman Battering." In *Post-Traumatic Therapy and Victims of Violence*, ed. Frank Ochberg. New York: Brunner/Mazil, 1988.

——. *Women at Risk: Domestic Violence and Women's Health*. Thousand Oaks, Calif.: Sage, 1996.

Stark, Evan, Anne Flitcraft, and William Frazier. "Medicine and Patriarchal Violence: The Social Construction of a 'Private' Event." *International Journal of Health Services* 9 (1979).

Stellings, Brande. "The Public Harm of Private Violence: Rape, Sex Discrimination, and Citizenship." *Harvard Civil Rights-Civil Liberties Law Review* 28 (1993).

Stets, Jan. *Domestic Violence and Control*. New York: Springer, 1989.

Stevens, Peter. *Community Policing in Action: A Practitioners Guide*. Kenwyn: Juta and Co., 1995.

Sugg, Nancy, et al. "Domestic Violence and Primary Care: Attitudes, Practices, and Beliefs." *Archives of Family Medicine* 8 (July–August 1999).

Sullivan, Cris, and Maureen Rumptz. "Adjustment and Needs of African American Women Who Utilized a Domestic Violence Shelter." *Violence and Victims* 9 (1994).

Sun, Myra, and Elizabeth Thomas. "Custody Litigation on Behalf of Battered Women." *Clearinghouse Review* 21 (1987).

Taub, Nadine, and Elizabeth Schneider. "Women's Subordination and the Role of Law." In *The Politics of Law: A Progressive Critique*, ed. D. Kairys. New York: Pantheon, 1990.

Taylor, Charles. *Sources of Self.* Cambridge, Mass.: Harvard University Press, 1989.

Thomson, Judith Jarvis. "Privacy." *Philosophy and Public Affairs* 1 (1971).

Tronto, Joan. "Beyond Gender Difference to a Theory of Care." *Signs* 12 (summer 1987).

U.S. Department of Justice [FBI], *Bureau of Justice Statistics, Fiscal Year 1998.* Washington, D.C.: Government Printing Office, 1998.

Wahholz, Sandra, and Baukje Miedema. "Risk, Fear, Harm: Immigrant Women's Perceptions of the 'Policing Solution' to Woman Abuse." *Crime, Law, and Social Change* 34 (2000).

Walker, Gillian. *Family Violence and the Women's Movement: The Conceptual Politics of Struggle.* Toronto: University of Toronto Press, 1990.

Walker, Lenore. *The Battered Woman.* New York: Harper and Row, 1979.

——. "Psychology and Violence against Women." *American Psychologist* 44 (1989): 695–702.

Walsh, Mary. "Locke and Feminism on Private and Public Realms of Activities." *Review of Politics* (March 1996).

Walzer, Michael. "The Civil Society Argument." In *The Citizenship Debates,* ed. Gershon Shafir. Minneapolis: University of Minnesota Press, 1998.

——. "Socializing the Welfare State." In *Democracy and the Welfare State,* ed. Amy Gutmann. Princeton: Princeton University Press, 1988.

Wang, Karin. "Battered Asian American Women: Community Responses from the Battered Women's Movement and the Asian American Community." *Asian Law Journal* 3 (May 1996): 151–84.

Warren, Samuel, and Louis Brandeis. "The Right to Privacy." *Harvard Law Review* 4 (1890).

Westin, Alan. *Privacy and Freedom.* New York: Atheneum, 1967.

Wittner, Judith. "Reconceptualizing Agency in Domestic Violence Court." In *Community Activism and Feminist Politics: Organizing across Race, Class, and Gender,* ed. Nancy Naples. New York: Routledge, 1998.

Witwer, Martha, and Cheryl Crawford. "NIJ Research Report: A Coordinated Approach to Reducing Family Violence." National Institute of Justice and the American Medical Association, NCJ 155184, October 1995.

Wollstonecraft, Mary. *A Vindication of the Rights of Women* [1792]. Buffalo: Prometheus Books, 1989.

Woolf, Virginia. *A Room of One's Own.* London: Hogarth, 1929.

Young, Iris Marion. "The Ideal of Community and the Politics of Difference." In *Feminism/Postmodernism,* ed. Linda Nicholson. New York: Routledge, 1990.

——. *Intersecting Voices: Dilemmas of Gender, Political Philosophy, and Policy.* Prince-

ton: Princeton University Press, 1997.
——. *Justice and the Politics of Difference*. Princeton: Princeton University Press, 1990.

Cases Cited

Arizona v. Hicks, 480 U.S. 321, 107 S.Ct. 1149 (1987).
Bradley v. State, 1 Miss. (1 Walker) 156, 158 (1824).
California v. Greenwood, 486 U.S. 35, 108 S.Ct. 1625, 100 (1988).
Gertz v. Robert Welch, Inc., 418 U.S. 323 (1974).
Katz v. United States, 389 U.S. 347 (1967).
Oliver v. United States, 466 U.S. 170, 104 S.Ct. 1735, 80 (1984).
Olmstead v. United States, 277 U.S. 438, S.Ct. 564, 72 L.Ed. 944 (1928).
Rhodes, 61 N.C. (Phil. Law) at 453 (1868).
Richards v. Richards, 1 Grant's Cas. 389, 392–93 (1856).
Robbins v. State, 20 Ala. 36, 39 (1852).
State v. Black, 60 N.C. (Win.) 262, (1864).
State v. Buckley, 2 Del. (2 Harr.) 552 (1838).
State v. Hussey, 44, N.C. (Busb) 123 (1852).
Time v. Hill, 385 U.S. 374 (1967).
Whalen v. Roe, 429 U.S. 589 (1977).

Index

Ackelsberg, Martha, 168 n. 25
advocacy, 106–8, 121, 122, 123, 126, 132,
    183 n. 28, 185 nn. 54, 55
Allen, Anita, 168 n. 2
Arendt, Hannah, 126
authority: common-law doctrine of marital
    chastisement, 60–65, 80–81, 174 n. 10;
    of government, 6, 87–88, 134–36, 179
    nn. 8, 9. *See also* paternal authority

Barber, Benjamin, 163
battered women: and child custody
    arrangements, 107–8, 180 n. 16; coping
    strategies of, 34, 45, 53–54, 143; and the
    decision to leave, 50–51, 149–50, 167 n.
    14, 189 nn. 42, 47; financial hardship of,
    75–76; homicide and, 71–73, 110–11,
    130, 177 n. 44; and "learned helpless-
    ness," 71–72, 144; political activism for,
    73–74, 105–7, 130–31, 180 n. 15, 185
    n. 45; and privacy, 2, 36–42, 55–56,
    63–65, 68–72, 135–36, 146; psychologi-
    cal abuse of, 71–73, 142–45, 147–49,
    151–52, 177 nn. 44, 46, 190 n. 52; psy-
    chosocial risk factors, 93, 108, 121; rela-
    tions with batterers, 55–56, 75–76, 187
    n. 13; reporting of domestic violence,
    2–4, 55–56, 123, 135–36, 167 nn.14,
    20, 174 n. 68, 181 n. 5, 183 n. 26; re-
    sources for, 46–47, 68, 91–93, 105, 107,
    116, 119, 121, 151, 183 n. 21; staying in
    relationship, 30–31, 75–76, 122–23, 173
    n. 56, 183 n. 26; syndrome, 71–73, 177
    nn. 44, 46; as victims, 73–74, 78, 147,
    151–52, 178 n. 57, 188 n. 34, 190 n. 52;

withdrawal of battering claims, 75–76,
    178 n. 57, 183 n. 26. *See also* battered
    women's movement; batterers; commu-
    nity; family; legal system; women
battered women's movement, 55, 68–72,
    88, 130–33, 177 n. 44, 185 n. 45
batterers: and child custody arrangements,
    107–8, 180 n. 16; coercion and control
    by, 127–28, 142, 149–50, 165 n. 1; cop-
    ing strategies with, 34, 45, 53–54, 143;
    legal sanctions against, 56, 67–72,
    74–76, 89–92, 97–98, 178 nn. 57, 64;
    psychological abuse by, 71–73, 142–45,
    147–49, 151–52, 177 nn. 44, 46, 190 n.
    52; psychosocial risk factors, 93, 108,
    121; restraining orders and, 74–76, 91.
    See also family; men; women
Benn, Stanley, 167 n. 23, 182 n. 10
Blackstone, William, 60–61, 166 n. 9, 169
    n. 18
Boling, Patricia, 126, 127
Borkowski, Margaret, 121
Bottomley, Anne, 34
Brandeis, Louis, 134–35, 186 n. 3
Brennan, Teresa, 24
Brison, Susan, 144, 147–48
Brown, Carol, 55–56

children: childbirth, 16, 35–36, 38, 171 nn.
    25, 27; custody of, 107–8, 180 n. 16; de-
    velopment of, 21–22, 40–41, 48, 51–54,
    62–63, 157, 169 n. 9, 172 nn. 28, 29;
    domestic violence and, 1, 51–52, 72,
    110, 129–30, 157, 166 n.7; Locke on,
    16, 19, 21, 22, 169 n. 9; women's role in